WILD CHILD

COMING HOME TO NATURE

PATRICK
BARKHAM

GRANTA

Granta Publications, 12 Addison Avenue, London W11 4QR
First published in Great Britain by Granta Books, 2020

A CIP catalogue record is available from the British Library
9 8 7 6 5 4 3 2 1

ISBN 978 1 78378 191 1
eISBN 978 1 78378 192 8

www.granta.com

Typeset in n Road,

Printe ¦YY

This book is dedicated to Emma Harwood and Hayley Room and everyone else who helps children spend time in wild places.

CONTENTS

Author's Note   viii

1 Wild Children   1

2 Beginnings in Nature   9

3 A Dandelion Spring   37

4 Nests, Chicks, Death – and Stuffing   83

5 Dipping into Ponds   113

6 A Dandelion Summer   133

7 The Joy of Caterpillars   155

8 Autumn Dandelions   181

9 Collecting   207

10 Growing Up   237

11 Dandelions in Winter   261

12 The Spinney at the Bottom of the Field   281

Appendix: Sixty-One Things to Do and Ways of Being with Children Outdoors   293

References   319

Select Bibliography   335

Acknowledgements   341

Author's Note

Apart from my own children's, the names of children at the various schools and Forest Schools I visited have been changed, and in some cases other details too, so as to protect their identities.

1

Wild Children

'All of you with little children and who have no need to count expense, or even if you had such need, take them somehow into the country among green grass and yellow wheat – among trees – by hills and streams, if you wish their highest education, that of the heart and the soul, to be completed. Therein shall they find a Secret, a knowledge not to be written, not to be found in books. They shall know the sun and the wind, the running water, and the breast of the broad earth. Under the green spray, among the hazel boughs where the nightingale sings, they shall find a Secret, a feeling, a sense that fills the heart with an emotion never to be forgotten. They will forget their books – they will never forget the grass fields.'

Richard Jefferies

A wild child entered my life on the night I first heard a tawny owl call 'kerr-wick, kerr-wick' in the dark trees behind my home. She has dark eyes, a mane of brown hair and she roams our garden like a little lion. Nothing seems to escape her gaze. She possesses the eyes of a hawk, the ears of a bat and the talons of an eagle. She schemes like a hyena, runs like a cheetah and pounces like a tiger. Her name is Esme and she has had an urgent appointment with the wild since she was very young.

She was stuffing soil into her mouth at six months old and could distinguish between a jay and a magpie as a toddler. She was catching butterflies with her bare hands at three. She is seven now, and loves to run free, poke hands into birds' nests, squeeze frogs, catch crickets, hold chicks. She is also an intuitive freedom fighter who sides with the underdog – usually other animals – and chafes against the strictures of parental surveillance and the school system.

Esme is one of an endangered species. A few of my generation, and more from preceding generations, were once wild children. Today the wild child is functionally extinct in the Western world. The idea that a child of, say, nine would roam without adult company through copses and spinneys close to their home is anathema. The self-directed child, playing freely among an abundance of other animals, plants and peers, belongs to a lost civilisation. And we have lost it in the blink of an eye.

We live in a time of unprecedented gloom about enveloping environmental crises. We must adapt to unimaginably rapid climatic changes. We are increasing in number. Our energy and our thirst for a good life are throttling other life on the planet. But these crises may prove unsolvable unless we fix another problem: our children are growing up without green space and wild things. Our contact with species other than our own is lessening. Our time in nature is curtailed. We have little clue where our food comes from. Most of us live increasingly confined to the structures made by our own species, on a planet ever more ravaged by that species.

It hasn't always been like this. We forget how life has been for 14,990 of 15,000 or so generations of *Homo sapiens*. For by far the greater part of our existence as the 'wise man', we have lived outdoors. It was only in the nineteenth century that most of us moved inside to work, learn and play. By 1861, more of Britain's population were recorded living in towns and cities than in the countryside, and we became the first urban nation. Today, more than eighty-three per cent of British people are 'urban'. Our alienation from the natural world may be older and deeper than many other nations', but there are now thirty-two countries even more urban than us.

Most of us in Britain are fortunate to live in an era of unsurpassed comfort, liberated from the back-breaking outdoor labour that sent our forebears to their premature graves. But we are myopic when it comes to our good health, and seduced by ease and easy stimulation. We forget what we and our children need, and neglect what makes us well. Across the affluent world, outdoor teachers tell the same stories – of children wondering what mud is, or where milk comes from; of children who have never before set foot on grass, never visited the seaside, or think a blue tit can kill them. I visited a permaculture garden in Athens where teachers fielded questions from Greek city kids such as 'Who hung the lemons on the tree?'

I could devote many chapters to assessing the growing body of scientific evidence showing the harmful impact of our dislocation from other species. I could quote the accumulated wisdom of traditional thought and contemporary artists, and seek to prove the damaging impact of a life lived on concrete, in polluted air, and beholden to electronic screens – on us, and on our planet. Although the medical establishment currently suggests that guilt-stricken parents needn't feel too terrible about children's screen time, most of us instinctively understand that excessive electronic time indoors alters our mood, disrupts our sleep and affects our mental and physical health. We need to know more precisely why green space is good for us, why other species make us happy and well. But I don't want to harangue or blame people. No one has ever been terrified or rebuked into embracing nature. I want to tell a more empowering and hopeful story about the pleasure, fascination and joy we may find in the ordinary wildlife we can still encounter in our everyday lives. I want to celebrate the power and importance of neighbourhood nature. (I should mention that in doing so I do not want to imply that we have a solely transactional relationship with nature. We depend upon other species for our existence and they do us many great favours, but every wild thing has as much of a right to live on this planet as we do, regardless of whether we derive pleasure or usefulness from their company.)

Three wild things currently dominate my life. Alongside my daughter Esme is her elder twin, Milly, and their younger brother Ted. What follows includes some small, true tales from their childhoods, and mine, about our relationships with the species around us. Naturalists from another century would scorn the paucity of my family's encounters – the wood pigeons, the common butterflies, the roadkill – but these everyday meetings with fellow animals, plants and fungi still nourish us. I believe we can even today find a niche in nature. Wherever we live, in countryside, city or town, we can form intimate bonds with fellow species in our local area, if we make space and take time to look up, or down, or more closely. We are part of nature. We do not live here, with 'wildlife' over there. There is only us, one animal among many.

As my children learn about the world, they are teaching me what I've forgotten since I was a child, and what it is to be a parent. Thanks to them, I've spent a year volunteering at an outdoor nursery, and I will recall some of those experiences here too.

I'm writing about our personal lives, but I don't want to suggest that I'm a paragon of parental virtue or a model citizen of planet Earth; I've had three children, so I can't give lectures about sustainable population growth. *Wild Child* describes the portion of our lives where I seek to maintain our proximity to nature. There are plenty of times when my family and I are not enjoying rapturous natural experiences. Under the trickle of everyday pressures, I'm as mediocre as most contemporary fathers. Some mornings, our children are glued to the television for an hour while I catch up on sleep. We drive a car that emits diesel particulates. Snowdrifts of plastic toys form inside our home. Our children eat sausages and crave sugary sweets. We're sucked into ways of eating and consuming that cannot continue.

'It's easy to worry about nature when you don't have to fret about putting food on the table,' some people argue. But I reject the idea that access to nature is an indulgence for the privileged. Access to nature is a human right that must be championed more than ever for less privileged members of society. High-quality green public space is more crucial for low-income families than for anyone else. It's a source of free entertainment, free exercise, free good health and even free food. Living fractionally closer to nature saves money and makes parenting easier, wherever we live and whatever our income. I believe that nature can and must become central to all our childhoods once again.

I hope the stories that I tell contribute to the case for institutional change in our schools, cities, hospitals and even our farms, as we belatedly acknowledge our need for nature in everyday life. Wild life is not a luxury, nor a middle-class lifestyle choice; it is part of everyone's existence. We are all enriched by being on nodding terms with the other species with whom we share our miraculously life-giving planet.

Hope, writes the naturalist Mark Cocker, is written into all our encounters with the natural world. To watch a small murmuration of starlings, which I've just spied outside the window of my study overlooking an industrial estate, is a profoundly uplifting experience. To meet the eye of a blackbird is a moment of genuine connection.

Here is fun, here is surprise, here is rapture; here is where we want and need to be; here is home.

2

Beginnings in Nature

*'Every child is born a naturalist. [Their] eyes are, by nature,
open to the glories of the stars, the beauty of the flowers,
and the mystery of life.'*

Ritu Ghatourey

There's long grass, daffodils and the rough bark of an old Bramley apple tree. Poopy, our tortoiseshell cat, is in the high grass with me. Maybe I am not yet walking; I can't remember. Other things that summer: peonies, plump maroon blooms like folded skin and scent of old lady; orange nasturtiums with saucer-shaped leaves that bleed white and smell cabbagey when you snap them; nettles, dangling, stinging and smelling of green dust.

First memories are capricious, wobbly and of dubious chronology. Some are photographs masquerading as memories. Others become favourite family tales that illustrate an indubitable truth about our character, as smooth as pebbles on a beach and glib in their meaning. Memories that disrupt our chosen narrative are pushed aside. But we seek founding myths because we know from science and psychology, from instinct and popular conversation, that our early months and years make us who we are.

I'm reluctant to declare it significant that my first memories are outdoor ones. I was outdoors a lot, but I don't believe I was born to love the natural world and others are not. Show me a child who cannot make a home in nature, given the opportunity. I didn't possess an unusually potent affinity with nature but the circumstances of my childhood gave it to me.

Gradually, the horizon of early memory lifts. Remembered objects – sweet, heavy lilac blooms, a grey rabbit, yellow tendrils of weeping willow – are in a garden. The Arcadia of early childhood was given physical form in our blessed plot. In the early 1970s, Mum and Dad moved to an unlovable 1960s bungalow, won over by its land: one L-shaped acre of old orchard and valley meadow which they sculpted into a wild garden. They followed the Good Life. Mum kept goats, Lady and Isadora; we drank their milk and, with curiosity and no sense of contradiction, cuddled and then ate their kids, Daffodil, and George, who was born on St George's Day. The garden and little meadow beyond were a house of rooms and passageways: behind shrubs, within conifers, beyond hedges, inside ditches; unseen sites for hiding, denning, nesting, dreaming. Children require privacy, places of retreat. I crouched between the prickly gooseberry bushes with their sour fruit; skulked in the raspberry cage when a July thunderstorm came; clambered up the young Scots pine so no grownup could reach my feet.

My earliest memory of actually being indoors? Those pictures are hazier and from later on: Daddy gets on his hands and knees in the living room while my older sister Henny and I rumpus all over him, rolling and tumbling like gleeful fox cubs; I play behind the frosted glass door in the hallway with Maui, my invisible friend; I stand in our dimly lit dining room, looking through to the kitchen where Mummy is cooking, the Archers' theme tune on Radio 4; I have Mum to myself; Henny has gone to primary school but I am yet to go.

That the biggest trauma of my early childhood was, aged nine, moving house shows how lucky I was. I didn't mind changing houses but I did mind changing gardens: I grieved for the outdoor terrain I lost. Being banished from this Eden of orchard, ordered vegetables and unruly meadow marked the end of my innocence; the world opened wider, and I stumbled into some difficult experiences that unravel inside me still. At least leaving behind this childhood paradise preserved it for ever, parcelling up my early years in a warm, safe outdoor place. I've been trying to get back there ever since.

Aged four, or seven, or eleven, I was not a Wild Child. I was a serious small person who was content to play alone. I did not consciously 'love nature'. It was not forced upon me; it was not part of my identity. Like all true luxuries, nature was simply the fabric of my life, and I took it for granted.

I was fortunate to grow up in a rural place in a time when country-dwellers were no longer condemned to arduous work on the land. My dad was a university lecturer who took the slow coach into Norwich thirteen miles away. My mum was a teacher turned full-time mother. We were middle-class, obviously, but it was the era of the Oil Price Shock, the Thatcherite crunch on the public sector and spiralling interest rates, and we didn't have conspicuous cash. My parents shared a rusty ten-year-old MK3 Cortina estate; we were late to videos and never had a computer; Scalextric and Soda Streams were found only at friends' houses – although their absence from mine was probably a cultural choice as much as an economic one.

My major obsession was not the environment but the invention that changed the character of the British countryside, and, eventually, childhood, more than any other. 'I want to be a garage-man,' I told the boiler-suited mechanic peering dubiously at the undersides of our Cortina. 'Ah, they do a very important job protecting the Queen,' he replied. He thought I'd said 'Guardsman'. He didn't realise he was my idol, that I loved cars. My most prized Matchbox car was a lime-green Cortina saloon which I drove along the borders of the living-room rug. I could identify makes of car from the sound of their engines alone: at least, I could recognise the thrum of a Beetle, the whine of a 2CV and the chug of a Peugeot diesel. I hoovered up free sales brochures for the new Sierra ('Man and Machine in Perfect Harmony') and pored over the respective trims of the GL and the Ghia. The first book I wrote was an illustrated reference work entitled 'Barkham Family Cars'.

An electronic screen played a part in my childhood, but not really until I was five, when we sold our small black-and-white telly and rented a colour Triton TV. Mum rationed our screen time, disapproving of my Saturday evening schedule of American shows, beginning at 5.25 p.m. with *The Dukes of Hazzar*d, which was the gateway drug to *The Fall Guy*, *The A-Team* and *Knight Rider*.

Aged seven, eight and nine, my world expanded beyond our garden and I wandered further, in an apparently safe world. Next to the football lawn at the bottom of our garden was a gate straight onto Booton Common, twenty acres of boggy grassland and alder and oak woodland beside a small beck. My best friend Jeremy was a farmer's son, who lived opposite, so we wandered around his farmyard, popped over to his granny's bungalow next door and bustled between gardens like a pair of curious robins. We invented a call sign – 'Oooh-oooh-uh-ah!' It was our walkie-talkie. Each of us used it to check whether the other was available to play, without actually leaving our gardens or knocking on a door. Our homes were separated by a small dead-end lane imaginatively known as The Street. A group of us, seven children aged between seven and fourteen, biked up and down and hung about on the lane. My parents worried about vehicles whizzing around its sharp right-angled bend; an old neighbour, Sonny Long, hand-painted a wooden sign – PLEASE SLOW CHILDREN PLAYING – which was erected at the corner.

The village children walked to school accompanied only by big kids – ten-year-olds. I didn't walk because my primary was three miles away but in summer we sometimes cycled there. Later, I cycled there alone now and again. My route included a stretch of country road where reckless motorists could reach sixty miles an hour, but there were many fewer vehicles than today, of course. On my cycle to school, I'd meet a couple at most. It was the era of the BMX but I had a secondhand purple Tomahawk, a poor boy's Chopper – small front wheel, large back wheel, long banana-style seat. I invented an advertising jingle and sang it to myself as I freewheeled downhill:

> Take away the strain
> On a country lane
> With Tomahawk!

These were years of great sprawling imaginative projects, which were not games but deeply real. One day Jeremy and I decided to be stuntmen, and dress in 'boilersuits' (the overalls worn by every farmer's son) and build a ramp for our bikes.

Another day we launched a chocolate-bar-making company. We formed a pop group, gelled up our hair like punks and corralled the grownups for an outdoor performance. I penned a staccato-sounding number that was informed by Adam Ant:

> Sitting in the larder
> Eating an apple pie
> I dive in
> And get pulled under
> Like a fly

The grownups laughed. I was disappointed they didn't take it more seriously. We rebelled by smoking hollow stems of hogweed.

As we grew up, more fantastical imaginings were replaced by football fantasies. I turned my vast reserves of car love towards a sport I would never really master. We built a goal from branches and painstakingly knotted a net together with orange binder-twine gleaned from straw bales. I spent hours kicking a ball around outside, alone and with friends and neighbours. One older boy, Mark, who was fourteen, attained superstar status during the endless summer of 1984 when he organised the Booton Olympics. Each day there were new races, from slow cycle to sprint. Jeremy and I and our sisters competed, with Mark totting up the golds, silvers and bronzes.

Every generation is prone to nostalgia but it is only by looking back that we see how childhood has moved indoors. In the affluent West, at least, childhood's terrain has been radically annexed.

It is now grandparents who reminisce about disappearing for

the day and only returning home for tea. In the 1980s, aged seven, I'd explore the common with my mates for company and muck about in farmyards amongst the machinery. Later, aged nine or ten, I'd cycle two miles, alone, to a good conker tree. My roaming space was large; my public play, without adults, significant. A few years ago, I interviewed the filmmaker David Bond, whose documentary, *Project Wild Thing*, revealed the progressive curtailment of a child's freedom to roam. His mother Helen, who was then eighty-one, roamed across fifty square miles of Yorkshire as an eleven-year-old. When he was a boy, in the 1970s, he moved within one square mile of home. In the 2010s his children wander freely only within the limits of their 140-square-metre garden.

An academic study of three generations of families living on the edge of Sheffield revealed the same picture. When they were children in the 1960s, the grandparents could roam up to three kilometres from home without their parents knowing where they were going. They played with twenty other children in the local woods, chucked stones into the river from a bridge, raced each other along sewage pipes, and messed around on bikes. They needed permission to go into 'town' and banned locations included hanging around outside the pub. Their children, today's parents, who grew up in the 1990s, could visit three or four places within half a kilometre without parental permission – usually friends' houses and the local playing field. Today's children, growing up in the 2010s, could go nowhere without permission. One ten-year-old boy was allowed to go alone to two friends' houses within 115 metres of home. And not only has children's roaming been curtailed but contemporary children play with far fewer peers, they have swapped public spaces for private homes, and are away from their houses for many fewer hours. A child's 'home range' is no longer negotiated between parents and children but 'imposed by the parents in a very rigorous way', the researchers concluded.

The scary thing is that, as a parent, I find nothing unnatural about this. Of course I know where my children are at all times. Of course I am constantly watching my five- and seven-year-olds, apart from when they roam unaccompanied around our fenced garden. 'Failure to supervise has become, in fact, synonymous with failure to parent,' declared the American writer Hanna Rosin. She looked at the work of the geographer Roger Hart, who followed eighty-six children around a rural New England town for two years in the early 1970s. Reading his dissertation today 'feels like coming upon a lost civilisation, a child culture with its own ways of playing and thinking and feeling that seems utterly foreign now', Rosin wrote. Hart revealed how 1970s children got together without their parents arranging it, took great pride in 'knowing how to get places', and spent huge amounts of time creating imaginary worlds that their parents never knew about.

When Hart returned to the town in 2004 as a highly respected New York professor, he found that childhood was extinct: the next generation of parents barely let their children out of their sight, and the children never did anything without their parents' permission. Hart wasn't even allowed back into the same school to interview children because the head teacher judged that his research was not related to its curriculum.

In Britain in 1970, eighty per cent of seven- and eight-year-olds walked to school unaccompanied by adults. By 1990, just nine per cent did so. I would be surprised if any did today. My family and I live 700 metres from our village primary school. Some parents living at a similar distance to us drive their children to school. I admit to a little pride that every day, whatever the weather, we walk to school with our children. Then I feel foolish because it's the most dangerous thing that we subject them to. For half an hour each day, we expose their lungs to diesel particulates you can't see and pollution you can smell. Our route is on pavements, within a 30-mile-an-hour zone, but I've shouted at cars for passing us at 50. And we have to cross three roads without pedestrian crossings. One is a busy A-road where we must wait for drivers to pause and wave us over. There is no way I'd let my children cross that road alone.

When we wonder why children have lost the freedom to roam enjoyed by former generations, we usually blame traffic and stranger danger. Four children in Britain were killed by strangers in the year to March 2018. That's about a one-in-three-million chance. But our fear of traffic is more rational. Traffic is increasing; the empty Norfolk lanes of my childhood are long gone. In the year to June 2018, 1,310 child pedestrians were killed or seriously injured in Britain, a one-in-nine-thousand chance.

Mayer Hillman, the sociologist who revealed the extinction of the unaccompanied walk to school, argues that rather than removing danger from children by making our roads safer for pedestrians, we have removed children from danger. In so doing, we are infringing the rights of the largest vulnerable group in society. The constraints we place on children's freedom foster a growing resentment against controlling parents and a distrust of

'strange' adults – 'disturbingly effective ways of inducing alienation, disaffection and anti-social behaviour', asserts Hillman.
'It is almost as if there has been a conspiracy to lower the quality
of the lives of children and to make more difficult their transition
into responsible members of society.'

Our failure to imagine how our communities could be better
if they were not designed around the car, and our inability to
control the adult freedom to drive that so drastically curbs the
freedom and security of those without vehicles, may be the
major reasons for children's loss of roaming, but there are other
causes too. Neighbours mix less than they once did; just as we
find communities of friends further afield, or online, so do our
children. As groups of children disappear from the streets, there
is no longer safety in numbers; any children that remain look far
more vulnerable. Children, like house sparrows, are communal
animals; when their populations dip below a certain number,
they suddenly scatter and disappear. There is less habitat for
them too. Public space has steadily diminished in Britain, and
so has unmanaged or unenclosed private space – derelict land,
former bombsites, scruffy woods. Austerity has seen playing
fields sold off.

The increase in families with two working parents means
that children's time has to be more organised. I say 'has to',
but my assumption here reflects my modern parent's mindset
that children can't be home alone, or anywhere alone. We fear
the opprobrium of fellow parents as much as we fear for our
children's safety. The ideology of parenting has intensified
during this century, fuelled by the anxiety and competitiveness
induced by globalised capitalism. We may shrug off disdainful

media labels such as 'helicopter parenting', but my generation of parents swallow unthinkingly the belief that parenthood is a heavy responsibility that requires us, and us alone, to constantly take care of our children's needs. We believe we know better than our children how to maximise their life chances and so we chauffeur them to adult-supervised activities (one survey suggested parents drive 5,000 miles each year in so doing) and institutionalise their play. Even in nature-rich, sensible Norway, Susanne Nordbakke found that the proportion of six- to twelve-year-olds playing outdoors without adult supervision fell from fifty-one per cent in 2005 to thirty-nine per cent in 2013/14.

There are, of course, caveats to the idea that the loss of free-range children is a tragedy. Nordbakke, for instance, found that children who undertook more organised activities actually also experienced more free play. Roger Hart, who witnessed the disappearance of the free childhood, also recognised downsides to the old freedoms. Left alone, children's hierarchies ensured some children were permanently at the bottom, or excluded – a *Lord of the Flies* scenario. Furthermore, fathers were mostly absent from childcare in the early 1970s. Increased equality between the sexes has helped ensure that today's fathers are far more involved in their children's lives. This presence can be a hugely positive change.

Statistically, the children of affluent nations are safer than ever, for which we should give two cheers. But the costs of withdrawing children from danger and risk are increasingly apparent. In her brilliant book *Kith*, Jay Griffiths argues that children need their 'kith' – from old English *cydd* – which can mean kinship but also native country, or the home outside the house. Instead, the territory of childhood has been annexed, and children enclosed indoors, mostly for adult profit. Human nature, argues Griffiths, is to be part of nature. It requires freedom within it, and closeness to it. Nature is central to our identities, our health and our growth. 'This is not about some luxury, a hobby, a bit of playtime in the garden,' she writes. 'This is about the longest, deepest necessity of the human spirit to know itself in nature.'

When I was eight or so, I discovered the joy of hunting for butterflies, a geeky little secret that I continued to pursue, with my dad, during my teenage years. Who doesn't have a difficult time as a teenager? I was solitary, fatigued, depressed and oppressed by my parents' failing relationship, for too many years. The natural world around me was a source of solace and renewal. I started running on the peaceful lanes and footpaths for three miles beyond our home. I loved these tracks filled with cow parsley in May and hogweed in July, the slanting evening light, the slow Norfolk countryside and the speed of the swifts that screamed over our roof. But I also needed to escape the loneliness of home. I needed to fledge, take flight; at eighteen, it felt like my life depended upon it.

Plenty of people move from provincial places to cities beyond and never look back. Since leaving home, I have constantly sought out the pockets of familiar wilderness that sustained me in earlier times. My university town was easy because it was a leafy provincial place whose medieval streets were much like my home city of Norwich. One of my exotic London-reared uni friends was scared by the cows grazing on the water meadows by the river in town. I survived exam-term pressure by running beside the yellow fields of oilseed rape beyond the motorway; I needed to see the edge of the city, where buildings ended and countryside began, to know that I could reach it on foot.

London, where I worked as a journalist after university, required more adjustment. When I first drove from Stoke Newington to Paddington I was astounded that I could drive for an hour and still be contained by city. My priorities were my career and my romantic life but I still required green space and constantly sought it out. The first flat I shared with friends was a ten-minute run to Hampstead Heath, which offered hills, pools, woods, panoramic views and the occasional Britpop celebrity; perfect for a young Romantic discovering the capital. From Parliament Hill, on a clear day, I could see an edge, even in this behemoth of a city. There was the basin of London and the distant blue line of the North Downs. Later, whether I lived in Islington, Elephant and Castle or Camberwell, I always cleaved to green space, blue water or brown field. My ears pricked up when a robin sang under the streetlights at 3 a.m.; my heart lifted when the swifts raced over the Victorian terraces of North London; I was the only person picking blackberries on derelict corners, apart from a few migrants from Eastern Europe who, like me, grew up around more bounteous nature than many residents of the capital.

My mind moved out of London some years before my body did.

I owe my return to a greener life to my children. As I entered my thirties, my romantic life was in turmoil and I yearned to escape the city. My failed relationships seemed a legacy of buried conflicts from childhood and my parents' eventual divorce. I kept returning to one relationship, with Lisa, that was more off than on. Finally, getting together for a fourth time involved promises that this time it must be serious; we must live together and have children. Within a month, Lisa was pregnant. With twins.

I felt luckier than ever before. What might have been complicated made everything much simpler. We required grandparental support, and both our mothers lived in Norfolk. Two months before the twins were due, we moved into a small terraced house in Norwich. We chose it because it backed onto the green thicket of an overgrown cemetery. It was one of the best decisions I have yet made.

On the night Lisa's waters broke, we heard that tawny owl calling, repeatedly, stowed in the cemetery's dark trees beyond our fifteen-metre strip of garden. I'd never heard one before from our new home, and took it to be a sign. The twins were calling too: legs thudding against Lisa's rib-cage. Eventually, they were born in a windowless operating theatre, a place of emergencies, because the doctors were worried about Twin 2's high heart rate. She was stressed and needed to come out but Twin 1 was blocking the way and couldn't get out herself.

Twin 1, Camilla, emerged into the world small, grey and bedraggled, folds of loose skin hanging off her bones like a traumatised rabbit. Despite the shock of the bright lights and the cold air she was calm, and opened her eyes wide. A minute later came Twin 2, Esme, eyes clenched and bawling robustly.

Milly and Esme were premature, underweight and confined to the hospital for the first five days of their life but, fortunately, they were allowed to stay with their mother in a peaceful room. I was surprised that two weeks passed before we saw any suggestion that they were aware of each other's presence; but then Esme examined Milly; and they began to appear more content side by side than apart. They may have been twins but they looked quite different. Milly had skinny limbs, blonde hair and skin the colour of porcelain that felt like silk. Esme was also fine-boned but more solid, with dark hair and dark eyes. From the very beginning they occupied distinct niches in the world.

During their first winter, I took them out regularly in our double buggy, to give Lisa a break and encourage them to sleep. Earlham cemetery, immediately beyond the end of our garden, was our destination. There, a grid of pathways had been laid out on thirty-four acres of high ground to the west of Norwich in 1856. The section nearest us was virtually filled with graves by the 1920s, as the city rapidly grew around it. The trees grew too, flexing their trunks, becoming mysterious. Now, behind tightly packed terraces, there was a modern version of wood pasture – dark green alleys and secret sunny glades. I don't think I've ever encountered more intrigue in such a small space. We could lose ourselves in dells of holly, take wrong turnings through holm oaks, and stumble upon unique collections of graves in odd hollows. Mostly we never met a soul. Occasionally we saw the flit of another being. Antisocial behaviour – from drug-dealing to (forbidden) dog-walking – was a problem. The cemetery was populated by other disreputable chancers too: magpies, grey squirrels, jays.

My sleep-walks along the cemetery paths with the newborns that winter and spring were magical. I was exhausted and the twins closed their eyes. 'They seem only averagely interested in wild things,' I note, naively, when they are seven months old. I wonder what of the cemetery seeped into them that winter and spring, for that place of endings is where their wildness began. Above our heads was a latticework of winter beeches. I paused under one tall beech very deliberately and gazed up; a daily ritual, a moment of worship that never failed to make me feel like I was gazing at the vaulted ceiling of a cathedral.

We could hear the hum of the city beyond; quiet Sundays were interspersed with an aeroplane engine revving at the airport three miles away. In the foreground were the ever-present robins, the only bird singing in the depths of winter, followed by blackbirds at January's end. In February came my favourite marker that winter's days were numbered, the see-sawing of the great tits. No matter how raucous our babies before I took them out, they were at peace inside the cemetery; they never once screamed their heads off, and there was plenty of screaming at home.

Most of us don't consider urban cemeteries, but the older, more derelict ones combine a reverence for the lives of previous residents with reverence for the urban wild. The dead become trees and live on. Winter is a time to gravely read the stones, as Morrissey once sang. In the month before the girls were born, I had scoured the graves for names, hoping to glean inspiration from the Susannahs, Elizabeths, Harriets and Hannahs. The men are mostly Georges and Jameses. Some marvellous surnames must have fallen extinct: Henry Hornagold, Frederick Platfoot.

That first season of cemetery baby-walking was an unanticipated benediction: forced out, at a slow pace, almost daily, I experienced the unfolding of spring more intimately than I had since I was a child. When we strolled after the rain, droplets continued to fall from the trees, a reverberation from the departed storm.

The copper beeches were the kings of the cemetery, regal trees in their prime at a century or more. Before their leaves unfurled, they permitted a princely succession of spring flowers beneath: snowdrops, followed by celandines, mauve crocuses, then a purple-and-white concert of bluebells and cow parsley.

The cemetery was a local wildlife site, and some swaths were spared the weekly crew-cut by the contractors. This city ecosystem might not have satisfied scientific definitions of ecological purity – the bluebells were the heavy Spanish sort, not the slender natives of a British woodland – but it was beautiful. Unbudding leaves of tender green hung from branches like chrysalises, a droplet of water at each tip. By mid-April, every tree was exploding with joy. An avenue of limes danced with a million tiny green baubles. On wet spring days, snails trailed everywhere and black slugs devoured the delicate cream flowers of cow parsley. Little lawns between the old graves soon sprouted daisies, then buttercups. Pink dead nettle arrived, then greater stitchwort. By May, the graves had disappeared into the grass. Only an occasional fawn headstone was visible, like a curious animal. Thousands of new tree seedlings quivered upwards. Left alone, unmown, the cemetery would become dense sycamore woodland within a decade. A few saplings escaped the mowers by sidling beside an old grave; and many a Florence or William raised a holm oak, a holly or at least a thicket of bramble.

As they turned one year old, Milly and then Esme took their first steps, staggering from armchair to sideboard in our tiny front room, and then tottering further, tipsy with wonder, into the garden. I hacked a hole in the old lilac behind our garden shed and we squeezed along the side of it and scrambled straight into the 'cemepit' as Esme called it. Even before the girls could talk, they directed me where they wanted to go.

Outdoors, it was more obvious how doddery they still were. The toddling stage can be perilous, as every parent remembers. Learning to walk is a heroic feat. It's a grand strain to get up a slight slope on two feet without overbalancing. As the weather turned cold, they sped ahead of me along the paths, legs in perpetual danger of overtaking their bodies, but so mission-focused they reminded me of miniature Challenge Annekas in their matching pink jumpsuits.

The girls staggered along in different directions, at high speed. Which one to follow? The choice was dastardly. Both preferred asphalt paths to more scenic, grassy ones; both routinely hurled themselves onto the asphalt.

From the moment she was plonked outside at six months old, Esme explored by popping sand, stones and soil into her mouth. By the time she was toddling, she was still an enthusiastic earth-taster. Every few steps she would bend down and grab bits in her hands: soil, tiny dry buds, old nuts, twigs, gravel, leaves. She crammed them in her mouth. On one occasion, she emerged from a trip to the cemetery sporting a soil goatee. She interpreted objects via taste. Milly showed no similar interest. Esme's soil-munching was so determined we removed our pot plants from the living room. She never succumbed to any dirt-related sickness. Most mammal babies eat soil and among human children it's surprisingly common; the Environmental Protection

Agency estimates that children in the United States consume, on average, 200–800 milligrams of dirt each day.

Watching what she was eating outside could be challenging but it was less stressful than policing her inside, where hazardous or fragile objects abounded. The more unsuitable the thing, the greater the attraction it exerted. Esme rampaged through Lisa's makeup bag and our house toolbox, chowing down on lipstick or fingering the blades of a Stanley knife. Duplo? Much less compelling.

The allure of forbidden fruit applied in the cemetery too. Some newer plots had been squeezed in between the old graves and a few of these were still tended. It took months of slightly stern instruction to stop grave desecrations: 'picking' the plastic flowers or scattering those emerald-coloured stones laid on graves of a certain era. (I understood the appeal: I amassed a secret collection of such treasures when I played in our local churchyard as a child.)

The filmmaker David Bond recognises the potential of old cemeteries as unofficial wild playgrounds and allows his children to climb on any untended or undecorated graves. This seems a reasonable rule. Unfortunately, the graves bearing fresh flowers held more fascination for my toddlers. We avoided a couple of glades where young children were buried. Those graves were enhanced by tantalising accessories – sunflowers, teddies, windmills, wind-chimes, picket fences – and it did not feel respectful to play there. Many dead Victorian and Edwardian children are commemorated with stone statues of little cherubs or angels. The little angels in our cemetery had not fared well. Most had lost their wings. Several heads had cracked off. All wobbled if hugged. The girls regularly paid homage to one we named Little Angel. She was kneeling, and Milly and Esme asked how she had hurt her knee and attentively dressed her in their hats and scarves.

During their first walking winter the snow fell thick. Grey graves became white humps. At sixteen months, Esme had a noticeable affinity with the natural world. When she woke in the morning, she stood at her bedroom window and looked outside to the screen of ash trees at the cemetery's edge. She screamed with pure delight if she saw a cat in the gardens below, and exclaimed and pointed to the fleeing movement of a pigeon or blackbird or great tit at next door's bird table.

Esme was twenty months old when we wandered through the cemetery one day and heard a squawk. I said 'Magpie' and she corrected me. 'Jay,' she said firmly. She was correct, although I made no special claims about her skills: she regularly identified wood pigeon wooings as an owl. But Milly and Esme could soon name the cemetery's rudimentary wild species. Is this important? Yes. Learning about the particularity of things is a valuable principle, and children are adept at identifying. Plenty of recent studies find they are less likely to identify different types of tree – an oak from an ash – and are more proficient at distinguishing brands of car, or junk food. A survey of Australian three- to five-year-olds found that they learn brands well before they can read: ninety-two per cent of them could identify the golden arches of McDonald's; one of many similar British surveys found that eighty-two per cent of five- to sixteen-year-olds couldn't identify an oak leaf.

In the cemetery, our favourite places gained names. There

was Fox Hole, where a fox had dug, and Secret Den, beneath the canopy of a tree, and Echoes, a porched area behind the crematorium's chapel. A chimney stood beyond; sometimes we imbibed a waft of acrid smoke, looked up, and saw pillows of white rising from it. I was not comfortable playing with the children around the chapel but the services were rare. More often, we needed to refrain from making echoes for the sake of a homeless man, who slept on a mattress of cardboard under the eaves. I didn't think he would appreciate being woken by the girls testing the acoustics of the chapel porch.

One of the pleasures of our play was that I let them decide when they wanted to go home. Sometimes Esme beetled off by herself, heading for the little tunnel back to our garden. An hour was our usual adventure. But whenever I thought we'd become bored with these little places and humdrum routines, I was confounded by the complexity of that tiny and ever so slightly wild urban space. New treasures were revealed with each trip; new activities evolved with the seasons.

'Reindeer!' shouted Esme as we traipsed through the long grass one day. I assumed she was inventing things but the strangest utterings of small children usually turn out to be true. Young humans are naturally superb observers. I looked around and eventually spotted what Esme had seen. Two muntjac, weaving between the graves. We saw another of these portly brown beasts repeatedly throughout the winter, when there was less cover but still enough peace, and plenty of saplings for them to eat.

In our second summer, we discovered blackberries. It was a vintage year and we snacked on the bushes – 'Prickly, like Daddy's chin,' remarked Esme one day – throughout July and August.

We found early-fruiting plants and later-fruiting ones. I doubted we'd cope with the absence of attractions after the blackberries disappeared, but we moved seamlessly into collecting rosehips and then 'mushies'. It was a mild winter and there were still mushrooms to find in January, alongside snowdrops.

Esme is like a hawk but I see a need in her to affiliate with the rest of life, just as the psychologist Erich Fromm first suggested in his concept of biophilia, which was developed into a more evolutionary theory by the American biologist E.O. Wilson. He suggests that we seek connections with other species because of our evolutionary history; we feel content when we see a habitat in which we can thrive, and look to link up with other forms of mammalian life in particular. Even if we don't realise it, somewhere within us is a deep requirement for neighbourliness with other species that protect, feed and nourish us. It was not deep down in Esme; it was written all over the joy in her face, and the ease in her shoulders whenever she was outside and surrounded by other living things.

By contrast, Milly revealed an urge to collect. She loved pebbles on the beach and, in the cemetery, spring flowers. I let her pick in its wilder corners, first snowdrops and then a ration of daffodils: one per visit. One April afternoon we trailed home carrying the pink candles of an ornamental chestnut bunched with cow parsley and bluebells and passed two older girls with their dad. They exclaimed at our flowers; clearly, flower-picking was banned in their household, as it is for many children. 'Society seems to consider it almost as bestial as otter hunting,' writes the naturalist Matthew Oates. Picking flowers in a cemetery may seem even more disrespectful. If every local child visited the cemetery and picked its flowers, there would be an outcry and, perhaps, fewer flowers. But then almost no children play in the cemetery, and almost no one picks flowers.

I believe that children should be able to pick common 'wild' flowers for their personal use, although not from nature reserves. In the cemetery, we stuck to common species, and not from graves. Like all complicated social rules, what at first seems impossibly complicated to convey to young children becomes simple with repetition; it is amazing how quickly they learn what is required of them.

In time, we made our first cemetery friend: Ginger Cat. His permanent hearth was a house on our street – we never discovered exactly which one – but his spiritual home was the cemetery. He was part of its continuum of wild things: I was the tamest, my children were wilder, and before the robins, foxes and jays came Ginger Cat. He would probably have been unrecognisable to his owners out here as he picked his way through the grass like a miniature tiger, stalking squirrels with deadly gravity.

Ginger Cat began to mysteriously materialise whenever he heard our voices. If the long grass was wet, he traversed the graveyard by jumping from grave to grave like some arboreal creature. He sometimes descended upon us from above, like a curious monkey. He was a magisterial climber of trees. They were his escape route when he tired of the toddlers' attentions after regally permitting a short stroking session. Milly and Esme were less willing to let him go and it took months of careful work – and several scratches and tearful episodes – before Esme treated Ginger Cat with respect.

Another friend was the matriarch of the cemetery. She was a giant cedar, a totemic presence that was visible from the city centre a mile away, raising her head above the treeline. She had a mass of branches unfolding horizontally from her peak, a slim waist and a robe of greenery lower down. She was not flawlessly statuesque; she had grown one way, lost a branch one season and then thrown out another enormous limb to steady herself. She roared her head off on a windy day but kept her counsel most of the time. No matter how wild the weather at her peak, she kept us humble little creatures sheltered, warm and dry beneath her skirts. There the ground was covered in a bouncy matt of old seeds from her decaying cones. It was a superb soft play park. Best of all, a fox had dug two tunnels into her roots. This is Fox Hole.

Most of the time these holes were unoccupied and cobwebs crossed the darkness. But on every visit we 'fed the fox', gathering old seeds or soft brown needles and sprinkling them in the hole. We climbed the cedar's lower limbs or, rather, I lifted up each girl so they could dangle from them. We sometimes sang, or talked, but there was no need for structured games or instruction. Mostly, we hung out; the girls in their world and me in mine, all of us nurtured by this mighty living presence. If I was particularly stressed, I would touch the cedar's thick bark. She soothed me. I tried to remember to gaze up, and consider her height and age and her perspective on things.

One damp evening in May after the twins had gone to bed, I returned to our playground and sat quietly beside Fox Hole, shrouded by the cedar's curtain of needles. A blackbird sang from the top of the yew and a robin offered a short song for the day's end. A pause, and then a fox suddenly appeared from the mouth of another dark hole beneath a yew twenty yards from the cedar. Bouncing along in the grass behind was a cub with downy grey fur. The fox sauntered off, scenting the air for notes of promise and danger. The cub disappeared but then had second thoughts about following its parent on the nightly forage and returned to its earth, dallying in the entrance and finally retreating. I thought of my cubs, secure at home a few hundred yards away, dreaming in their warm nests.

Our last summer in the cemetery was a golden one. We had another child, Ted, and outgrew our tiny terrace. I spent days out with the girls, Ted strapped to my chest, at eight months a smiling bonny baby whose eyes followed the girls' every dash around Fox Hole. Ted joined in my blackberrying with enthusiasm, while the girls scooted on the asphalt paths. It was a great place to learn to ride a bike, said a neighbour who had wisely stuck to this corner of urban paradise for the duration of his children's early years.

I lacked his wisdom, or restraint. I hankered after more space. On an internet trawl when I'd finished a book and had too much time on my hands, I found an unmodernised chalet bungalow in a suburban village beyond Norwich. It was built on half an acre in 1952 and was now bordered by overgrown evergreens and an industrial estate. There was no adjacent public land but it was a short walk into open countryside. I knew that a small patch of private land was an inferior roaming ground for a child, compared with a much larger public green space. But I couldn't resist a project. Lisa was excited too. We decided to move. Looking back five years later,

I still don't know if this was the right decision. Thinking about the cemetery makes me miss it terribly. There isn't always a better wild life for us in the intensively farmed countryside than there is in the city. As I was to learn, rural children don't get out much either.

3

A Dandelion Spring

*'The best classroom and the richest cupboard are
roofed only by the sky.'*

Margaret McMillan

Laurel hedge,

Fire Circle

BOOKS

Yurt for rainy days.

Public footpath

Dandelion outdoor nursery

or dens

AB

Grandma's Cottage

Trees for climbing

Swing off the busy A-road between Norwich and Aylsham, and you bump onto a narrow lane that is Marsham's high street. It twists between small cottages, modern redbrick houses, a village hall and an old chapel. Cars have to pause and wait for each other. There's no space for a pavement. Tractors bound for the next hamlet, Little London, appear to draw in their breath to squeeze through. When the chug of tractor recedes over the hill, the only sound is the atonal chirp of a healthy colony of house sparrows.

As with every rural village, much life has left this place. Its population is dominated by older people and commuters whose houses are silent during the day. There are no shops any more. At each end of the parish stand two beautiful metalwork signs erected in the 1950s that say:

M
A
R
S
H
A
M

On the top of each one is a wrought-iron lapwing. I remember them in these parts when I was a boy, pee-witting and air-flouncing on every wet meadow. But the wet meadows are gone, the big arable fields are sown hard to the margins, remnants of hedge are no more than the fragments of the medieval city walls in Norwich, and lapwings are lost to this landscape and to the experience of every child. There is less wildlife in such intensively farmed countryside than in cities; out here, wood pigeons and pheasants are our only ubiquitous companions.

At least there are plenty of children here. Unlike many rural villages, Marsham has clung on to its tiny Victorian school with its orange bricks, peaked gables and tall windows. In 1993, it was about to close until unexpected political ructions at Norfolk County Council caused a change of administration and a last-minute reprieve. Since then, its roll has risen from eighteen to capacity: thirty-five children. Marsham is alive, vow the village hall regulars at 'Meet & Mardle' – Norfolk dialect for passing the time with chat.

The orange-brick school sits on a bank above the tiny high street. There are seventeen steps up to it, dauntingly steep for a small child. At the top, past the school's blue wooden gate, a footpath continues ahead to the open fields.

On the left is the playground and neat green playing field. On the right, behind panels of Norfolk reed, is something else. It looks like an overgrown garden tended by sprites and pixies. There's an assortment of small wooden sheds, straw bales, pallets, tree stumps and a yurt between hedges of overgrown laurel and leggy leylandii. Beneath bushy sallows and field maple, the ground is paved mostly with mud, tussocky grass and anthills, constantly trodden and retrodden by running pairs of wellies. Woodsmoke drifts from a fire that works with the breeze like a swinging censer, dispatching its sweet scent over everything and everyone.

Established in 2016, the headquarters of Dandelion Education is not picturesque. It's as ramshackle as the smallholdings carved from this sandy heathland north of Norwich. There are no beautiful trees, no lush wild-flower meadows, no lovely woodland. But it is idyllic.

The children who make up this unusual outdoor nursery are not immediately obvious. Peer over the fence, and you might see a pack of three or four, moving through the undergrowth like a family of rooting pigs, albeit dressed in primary-coloured waterproof suits. Whatever they are doing is head-down intense, and may involve sticks, foraging, fantasy and climbing trees. The groups morph and change; children draw away to be alone, swinging on a rope, or dreamily engross themselves in this or that. Busy. But calm.

After Dandelion is judged 'Outstanding' by Ofsted, the schools inspectorate, and then wins the 'nursery of the year' prize at the *Nursery World* magazine awards, it draws the gaze of television news and the tabloids. 'Nursery that swaps tots' plastic toys for power tools' is the *Sun*'s take; 'Outdoor pre-school where children are kept outside in ALL weathers and can only play with toys they've made themselves' is the *Daily Mail*'s.

Like the *Mail*'s headline writers, most of society today views outdoor living as a kind of extremism, or hardship. In approximately ten generations, we have become an indoor civilisation, accepting that the good life is lived almost entirely inside our grand shelters of concrete and glass, these inward-looking, all-human worlds over which we have complete control, for better and for worse. But being outdoors is central to Dandelion's philosophy.

The proliferation of outdoor nurseries and of concepts such as Forest School is rooted in a growing fear that the affluent world is failing its children. The wealthy West is presiding over troubling declines in young people's mental and physical health. Britain is a world leader in producing fat, unhappy and anxious children. In England, one in five pupils in their final year of primary school, aged ten or eleven, is obese. Childhood obesity is today shaped by poverty – it is twice as high in England's most deprived areas than in the most affluent regions – but childhood unhappiness appears more evenly spread across wealth and class. And various measurements suggest it is increasing.

Unicef's assessment of childhood wellbeing in rich countries put British children bottom in a table of twenty-one nations in 2001. Although Britain climbed to sixteenth out of twenty-nine nations in its 2013 survey, its education was ranked twenty-fourth out of twenty-nine. (The Netherlands, followed by Scandinavian countries, consistently lead Unicef's childhood wellbeing charts.) A more recent assessment, the Children's Society's annual survey of eleven- to fifteen-year-olds' feelings about their own lives, finds a steady decrease in happiness since 2010. More clinical measurements of objective health detect the same trend. One in eight people under nineteen in England has a mental health disorder, according to government statistics published in 2018.

Almost one in four girls aged seventeen to nineteen has a clinically diagnosed mental disorder.

Another unsettling trend, observed among American children, is a steady and persistent decline in creativity since 1990, despite studies also showing increases in IQ over recent decades. Using a measurement of creativity called the Torrance Tests of Creative Thinking, an assessment of the originality and variety of individuals' responses to various stimuli devised by the psychologist Ellis Paul Torrance, thousands of children aged from five to eighteen were appraised in 1974, 1984, 1990, 1998 and 2008. As Kyung Hee Kim, the author of a subsequent paper, put it:

Over the last 20 years, children have become less emotionally expressive, less energetic, less talkative and verbally expressive, less humorous, less imaginative, less unconventional, less lively and passionate, less perceptive, less apt to connect seemingly irrelevant things, less synthesising, and less likely to see things from a different angle.

In her conclusions, she suggested that changes in the home environment, rather than school, may be most significant because declines in creativity were particularly marked among the under-nines. She also wondered about the impact of technology and the over-scheduling of academic and structured activities, recommending the restoration of 'free uninterrupted time for children' at home and at school: more playtime.

The erosion of our children's vivacity and joy is caused by a complex constellation of factors not fully understood by anyone.

There is, however, a growing body of evidence assembled in the last thirty years pointing to green space and wild nature as one important cure.

Most of the world's population now live in urban places – more than two-thirds will do so by the middle of this century. In urban worlds, green spaces provide areas to be physically active, space to socialise and arenas for relaxation and mental restoration – the commonly accepted factors in the correlation between nature and good health. In the 1980s, the American psychologists Rachel and Stephen Kaplan famously devised the concept of 'soft fascination' to describe the restorative impact of natural environments: our immersion in green places enables fatigued, stressed and overstimulated minds to recharge. More than a hundred studies have supported this theory; it also rings true when we think about our experience of, say, the calming effect of a country walk. These ideas fit nicely with E.O. Wilson's theory of biophilia, with its suggestion that we are drawn to landscapes providing wooded grassland beside water – conditions where we have thrived for most of our evolutionary history. I'm suspicious of genetic determinism, but whether I've become dependent upon natural spaces through my upbringing or through my genes, I know this dependence to be a fact, and I see it in my children as well.

There is a library-load of self-reported evidence for the benefits of high-quality green space. A study of twenty thousand people in England in 2019 found that those who spent two hours each week in natural spaces reported significantly better physical health and mental wellbeing than those who didn't spend such time outdoors. This effect occurred regardless of whether people were rich or poor, young or old, urban or rural, or suffering from a long-term illness. And, interestingly, the benefits appear to be more pronounced the more wildlife-rich the natural space. In other words, nature reserves may provide a more potent natural cure than a park with scalped grass.

A famous study in the 1980s, which revealed how hospital patients who enjoy leafy views recovered more quickly from their operation, prompted a burgeoning field of more objective measurements of our physical responses to green space. Researchers studying Shinrin-Yoku, or 'forest bathing' – a short therapeutic visit to a woodland, which has become popular in Japan – found that exposure to forests lowered cortisol, a stress hormone, as well as pulse rate and blood pressure. Further studies have found that people who live or work in forests have a significantly higher percentage of 'natural killer' cells, white blood cells that attack tumour- or virus-infected cells in our immune system. These natural killer cells have been found to be induced by phytoncides, substances given off by plants and trees to protect them from harmful insects and bacteria. This aroma of the forest, or 'antimicrobial volatile organic compounds' as scientists refer to them, can protect us too. Even occasional day trips to a forest have been shown to raise natural killer cells' activity for more than thirty days afterwards, demonstrating how such trips may improve city-dwellers' immune systems.

The positive impact of spending time in an idyllic woodland might be obvious, but even green space in the Scottish city of Dundee in midwinter appears to have healing powers too. Scientists sent text messages to Dundee residents four times each day to prompt them to sample their saliva, which was used to measure their 'cortisol slope'. Differences in the way cortisol levels decline over a normal day reveal an individual's mental health; researchers found that the percentage of green space near home was, alongside exercise, the most significant predictor of their cortisol slope. It appeared to make individuals more mentally resilient. Other studies have stuck walkers in high-tech headsets that perform mobile electroencephalographs, wirelessly logging signals produced by the brain that are defined as 'short-term excitement', 'long-term excitement', 'frustration', 'engagement' and 'meditation'. They found lower frustration, engagement and excitement and a higher degree of meditation in the greenest of the urban environments.

Natural spaces have been linked, too, with reduced overall mortality, reduced rates of cardiovascular disease and, most notably, less depression, anxiety and other mental disorders. Increasingly, big data is providing objective epidemiological evidence for the physical and mental health gifts of nature. In 2009, researchers examined data from Dutch GPs serving 350,000 people alongside measurements of green space around each household. They found that the annual prevalence of fifteen disease clusters was lower in home environments with more green space within one kilometre. The association between green space and improved health was strongest for anxiety and depression, and stronger for more deprived people – and for children.

Plenty of other studies have identified green space as particularly significant for children's health, and this is no surprise, for childhood usually begins at home before skipping into the neighbourhood beyond. Given that children are more rooted in one place than adults because of that drastic curtailment of childhood liberty in recent decades, green space is more important than ever. In 2019, scientists analysed the green space around the childhood homes of nearly one million Danes between 1985 and 2013 and the risk of them developing one of sixteen different mental disorders later in life. After adjusting (as all such studies do) for risk factors including socioeconomic status and family history of mental disorders, they found that children surrounded by large amounts of green space have between fifteen and fifty-five per cent lower risk of developing a mental disorder. A meta-analysis of many studies has revealed the prevalence of depression in urban areas to be thirty-nine per cent higher than in rural areas, and a range of psychiatric disorders thirty-eight per cent higher. Higher levels of schizophrenia and autism are particularly pronounced in urban areas.

Even allowing for proper scientific caveats such as correlation not meaning causation, these are drastic findings. Rather like the scientific evidence showing climate change, there are occasional studies that don't find an association between green space and healthier children, but the overall weight of evidence is compellingly in one direction. Like climate change, too, we are a long way from understanding the full implications of the correlation between a lack of green space and mental disorder: how, precisely, it operates; and how it will shape the world for the adults of the future.

Scientists like to debate the 'mechanism' that gives nature such power over our good health. There is, of course, not one mechanism but an array of potential causes. As the damage to our bodies and minds from air pollution caused by petrol and diesel vehicles becomes more apparent, scientists have pinpointed links between pollution and numerous human sicknesses, including depression. Green space, with its pollution-fighting powers, helps shield us from this too. Scientists looking at how green space around schools in Barcelona enhanced pupils' cognitive development over twelve months attributed between twenty and sixty-five per cent of their gains to a reduction, caused by greenery, in traffic-related air pollution.

Pollution is part of the picture, but some scientists critique the now familiar idea that green space is good for us – and particularly good for children – simply because it facilitates exercise, socialising and relaxation. These may not be the only, or the most important, effects of contact with nature. Graham Rook, emeritus professor of medical microbiology at UCL, points out that many psychological studies are not specific enough. We cannot simply compare the experience of a park with that of a busy street. A city-dweller may be able to find restoration via a quiet cafe, a cinema or art gallery; similarly, the opportunities to exercise, socialise, avoid pollution and soak up health-giving sunshine do not necessarily require green space. Despite the surfeit of positive findings for nature, there is not yet evidence, Rook and others believe, to show how measurable short-term psychological and physiological changes we experience in natural environments actually translate into long-term health benefits.

But for all Rook's scepticism, he is a leading exponent of another series of scientific revelations that help us better understand why we need more natural childhoods. One contemporary epidemiological puzzle is why wealthy countries are experiencing massive increases in allergic disorders, such as asthma and hay fever; autoimmune diseases such as multiple sclerosis; and inflammatory bowel diseases such as Crohn's. One answer came in 1989 when a study noticed that children with older siblings were less likely to develop hay fever. From here developed the 'hygiene hypothesis'. This is the now popular truism that we are too clean for our own good – hygiene in family homes in affluent countries is preventing the proper development of our immune systems.

Rook is horrified by the popular cry of 'Let them eat dirt!' The idea that hygiene is harmful is as dangerous as the myths propagated by the anti-vaccination crowd, he argues. Hygiene has been the most life-saving advance in modern medicine. Instead, he has developed a better theory from the hygiene hypothesis, which he calls the idea of 'old friends'. Whether hygienic or not, our world is naturally full of billions of micro-organisms, or microbiota. We have more bacteria in our guts than human cells in our bodies. These organisms also reside on our skin and all over our bodies, and among fellow animals and plants. Most are harmless, some are useful to us, and a few are dangerous pathogens.

At birth, says Rook, our immune system is rather like a computer with hardware and software but no data. Early in life, it must rapidly collect data from diverse microbial sources, learning which are harmful and which are beneficial. If our body encounters a diverse range of different bacteria, particularly when young, we are more likely to recognise and respond to novel viruses. Lab tests have discovered by delivering a mouse by Caesarean section into a sterile environment that not only is a germ-free mouse a very fragile creature but its brain does not develop properly. Rook's theory is that something similar occurs in humans. If we are not exposed to 'old friends' from our evolutionary past – tiny organisms and infections – we may develop illnesses related to failing immunity, or inappropriate inflammatory responses such as our immune system attacking the contents of our gut, as occurs with Crohn's disease.

The fact that urban environments and modern lifestyles may not be delivering us the microbes we need for good health was first spotted in the nineteenth century, when a doctor from Manchester, Charles Harrison Blackley, noted that hay fever was common among rich townsfolk while farmers were oblivious to it. In this century, Finnish studies of skin microbiota have compared people living in towns with those in the countryside. There were no differences in the levels of domestic hygiene between town and country people but there was a correlation between the proximity of the home to agricultural land and a healthy lack of allergic sensitisation. The crucial fact here was not a person's 'hygiene' but their exposure to biodiversity.

Joseph Stalin helped create one of the most vivid illustrations of the importance of microbial 'old friends' when he seized control of half the region of Karelia from the Finns during the Second World War. Ever since, the genetically homogenous Karelians have been divided between Russia and Finland. The ultra-modern Finns have the economic advantage of being able to pop across the border to much poorer, traditional Russian Karelia to buy cheap petrol. But the Russian Karelians have a microbial edge. Which is as follows.

In Finnish Karelia the prevalence of type 1 diabetes is sixfold higher, and childhood 'atopy' – the tendency to develop allergies – is fourfold higher, than in Russian Karelia. Researchers have found strikingly different microbes in the guts of infants as between the two people, and markedly different microbial populations in the home. In Russian Karelia, where many people still live in close proximity to livestock, there is much more microbial diversity, and many more animal-associated strains in Russian homes than in 'clean' modern Finnish homes. Humanity's current assault on biodiversity is well documented; our attack on microbial diversity is less well understood, yet it may be just as significant for our health.

E.O. Wilson's biophilia thesis suggests that we flourish only when we have intimate relationships with other species. And here is a compelling medical reason for requiring animals in our lives: we need to be exposed to their microbes for our own good health.

Another pertinent set of studies revealing our dependence on animals are those conducted with the Amish and Hutterite people of the United States. Both farming communities emigrated from the Alps – the Amish from Switzerland, the Hutterites from Tyrol – during the Protestant Reformation, and have remained relatively isolated ever since. The lifestyles of these two communities are similar with regard to most factors known to influence the risk of asthma, including living in large families and breastfeeding for relatively long periods, high rates of childhood vaccination, diets rich in fat and raw milk, low rates of childhood obesity, and minimal exposure to tobacco smoke and pollution. Both peoples also have taboos against indoor pets. But while the Amish live on small dairy farms and use horses for transportation and working the fields, the Hutterites live on highly industrialised communal farms and have little contact with farm animals. The prevalence of asthma among Hutterite schoolchildren is 21.3 per cent, while among Amish just 5.2 per cent; the prevalence of what doctors call 'allergic sensitisation' is 33.3 per cent among the Hutterite children and 7.2 per cent among the Amish. The key difference appears to be the Amish's close relationship with horses and other animals.

A properly 'trained' human immune system seems to require prolonged exposure to 'old friends' – a wide range of microbiota during childhood. Rook's prescriptions for healthier children include fewer antibiotics, exposure to important microbiota in the vaginal passage during birth and in breastmilk, the right kind of hygiene (the parent licking a baby's dummy that falls on the floor is preferable to washing it), and a varied diet including a far wider range of vegetables than we currently consume. Children, he says, also need to be exposed to more green space. Scientists have shown the benefits of exposure to soil organisms in mice but have yet to test the benefits of wilder, more diverse green space for human microbiota. It is logical to expect that more biodiverse areas will better provide a diverse range of microbiota than manicured monocultures. Green space that is good for wildlife is good for animals like us.

I have no knowledge of microbiota when Ted becomes the first member of our family to attend Dandelion at the age of three. Dressed for all weathers, Ted is driven for twenty minutes twice a week through the lanes to Marsham. We had hoped to send his older sisters to Dandelion too, but when they were nursery age Dandelion was based at another site too far from our home. Ferrying children to an outdoor nursery by car is an irony of our times, when traffic has so radically curtailed their freedom to roam. But there are limited alternatives in hollowed-out rural places: the ten-mile return journey from our home to Marsham on public transport – via trains and buses – would take more than three hours.

It's when I ferry Ted to Dandelion that I remember my similar commute nearly four decades earlier. Mum used to drive me twenty minutes to a nursery beside the primary school in Aylsham, a rural market town not far from Marsham. I have only a flicker of a memory of a busy indoor room in 1979 but I remember the journey in our blue Ford Cortina estate vividly, taking the bouncy, twisty B1145, which locals call 'the quarter to twelve', through a Norfolk landscape that was revolutionised during that decade: hedgerows grubbed up, meadows ploughed, and fields enlarged into arable prairies, growing wheat, barley, sugar beet and oilseed rape for the European Union's (then the EEC) food mountains. The countryside looks similar today, only the labourers have virtually disappeared and the tractors have quadrupled in size.

In Ted, I see myself as a small boy. He's got the same thick, straight brown hair and he's quite serious and self-contained. Adults are often amused by his gravely delivered statements of fact, which are very clearly enunciated. Like me as a child, like most children, he hates change. Unexpectedly, however, he adores the first few weeks at Dandelion. 'I love forest school,' he says, holding it close like a precious toy – something unique for him. He's visibly proud of himself, and each day brings home something he's made during supervised tool-work sessions such as a piece of wood with ivy leaves or a conker nailed to it.

Within weeks of starting at Dandelion, Ted is astonishingly

independent. He wants to do everything for himself: serve himself a drink when he's thirsty, master the difficult art of doing up buttons, pack his own bag. In the jargon, he's developing resilience.

Soon, however, storm clouds gather over my hopes for his outdoor education. On each journey home, before Ted flops asleep with exhaustion, I ask about his day. Who did you play with today? 'Emma and Hayley,' says Ted. I ask about his friends. His friends, he says, are Hayley and Emma. I'm surprised that about two-thirds of the twenty or so Dandelions are girls. I imagined there might be more boys, of the energetic can't-sit-still-cliché kind, for whom free roaming in such an environment is so liberating. But the problem is that Ted isn't playing with girls or boys: Emma and Hayley are his teachers, and no matter how brilliant they are, teachers are not best-friends material for a three-year-old.

Emma Harwood and Hayley Room left their jobs as primary school teachers in 2014 and set up Dandelion Education. Their vision was a unique version of an outdoor 'Forest School' nursery, where children and teachers are freed from the confinement of the classroom. Emma is a blonde woman who looks much younger than she is, and is instantly likeable; one of those warm, gentle, smiley people who light up nurseries with their love of children and saintly good humour. I later learn she is deceptively strong and has been vegan for years. Hayley is a decade younger, pale-skinned with great corkscrews of strawberry-blonde hair. There's a hawkish glint in her eye, I think; fierce, in a good way. But after a few weeks dropping off and picking up Ted, I realise that Hayley is also hilarious, very droll, very dry, and always looking for amusement, with the children, herself, and Emma. They are a brilliant double act, which is accentuated by their habit of wearing matching bumbags and orange waterproof jumpsuits.

Every parent has that heartbreaking few days, or weeks, when a child starts nursery and is weepy and bereft; Ted's bout of sadness starts at the end of his first term. When Emma and Hayley gently start coaxing him to become more independent and play with his peers, he begins to hate Dandelion. Each week becomes a tumultuous struggle to get him there. 'Is it forest school today?' he'll say after breakfast, when we can delay the news, and the putting-on of salopettes, no longer. 'Don't want to go to forest school,' he'll repeat, ad infinitum. Sometimes this mantra of resistance continues for the whole duration of the drive. Tears intensify.

It becomes harder, not easier, to leave him. One day, I have to stay with him. We sit on a log. Distraction usually works, but not today. He's inconsolable. Despite being so gentle and loving, Emma can't drag Ted's attention away from his own misery. Then Hayley comes over. Within a few minutes, she's hooked him into a conversation and floated him off the rocks. I slip away.

Back home, Lisa and I are wobbling. Ted clearly does not like Dandelion. Is it the right place? Is he cold? Is he eating enough? Perhaps he hates the outdoors. What parent cleaves to ideology when it comes to their children's comfort? I worry about green zealotry. My eagerness for our children to be outdoors as much as possible, my conviction that this must be better for them than today's conventional childhood, might be as damaging as forcing a homesick child to attend boarding school. Lisa thinks we should change nurseries. The local nursery is within walking distance. It has a perfectly nice outdoor area with a play boat and a tree. We decide to wait and see.

In the afternoons, when I collect Ted, I peep over the fence to see what he's doing. He's usually apart from the others, staring into space. Not unhappily. But adrift. I've often felt like that in big groups of people. On the edge, looking in. It doesn't bother me these days; I can be apart, because I'm a grown-up. But I want Ted to be comfortable in social situations. He plays with his sisters at home. What's stopping him playing with others here?

After Christmas, in the depths of winter, unexpectedly, every-thing changes. When conditions at Dandelion are the toughest they will ever be, Ted is fine. He loves 'forest school', again, only less in a show-mum-and-dad-how-great-I-am way and more quietly, more genuinely. He's made a friend, Amelia, and they do everything together. Sprawling imaginative games that Ted explains but I can't quite follow. She's an older girl, rather like his sisters. Ted is settled.

Emma and Hayley's many terms as teachers in state primary education have led them to a vision of schooling rather different from the dominant form in Britain today. They have seen how children learn through play, and always have done. Ancient Greek children made balls from pigs' bladders. Young Romans played with toy soldiers. Jean-Jacques Rousseau led the Romantic movement's recognition of the value of play. 'Let all the lessons of young children take the form of doing rather than talking, let them learn nothing from books that they can learn from experience,' he argued.

For all the Romantics' veneration of play, though, the British schools that emerged from the Education Act of 1870 that gifted compulsory universal education to five- to thirteen-year-olds were as dour as their Victorian architecture, windows so high that no pupil could be distracted by anything other than sky.

From the moment this formal, government-provided schooling began, there were dissenters, those who championed an alternative concept of education that placed the health and imagination of the child at its heart, in the form of outdoor schooling, woodland schooling and versions of today's 'Forest School'. These alternative educational models were also born of a growing repulsion for the cruelties of the industrial age and a mounting antipathy to urban life. The mood among many of these thinkers in the latter decades of the nineteenth century reminds me of today's upsurge of anxiety about new technologies and good old global capitalism. The outdoor-schoolers believed that education was not simply the new state schools' mechanical recital of the 'three Rs' – reading, writing and 'rithmetic – but that it should be a path towards self-realisation, freeing the natural nobility of the child and her imagination, as well as providing clean air and space and fostering good health.

These same beliefs also gave rise to a golden age of children's literature.

From Richard Jefferies' *Bevis: The Story of a Boy* (1882) onwards, children's inner lives were portrayed with a new sympathy and authenticity in fiction, alongside the idea that the higher freedoms of childhood could be realised in nature. The heroes of the children's books of Charles Kingsley, Lewis Carroll, Kenneth Grahame, Beatrix Potter, Edith Nesbit, J.M. Barrie and A.A. Milne wander freely, encounter talking animals (if the animals aren't surrogate children already), magical events and fantastical worlds. These authors did not see children as the miniature adults-in-waiting envisioned by didactic earlier Victorians but as enlightened innocents, possessed of a higher state of consciousness. It was not for adults to shove facts into *them*: the wise infant could tell us grownups about ourselves. As William Wordsworth put it, 'the Child is Father of the Man'. This Romantic view of childhood took a strong hold on many imaginations in late Victorian times, not least because it offered adults an escape from the brutalities of the age of the machine and from a gnawing pessimism over imperial rule. But there was also a growing conviction that we had to do better for the poorer children in newly urban Britain.

The Fabian Society that Edith Nesbit co-founded was soon home to another progressive thinker, Margaret McMillan, who with her sister Rachel devoted her life to improving the welfare of slum children. McMillan published numerous works on child health and welfare. In *Education Through the Imagination* (1904), she wrote: 'When the youth of the country have left the schoolroom, when they are out in the open of industrial life, competing with educated workmen of other lands, mechanical training and formal attainments will not carry them far.' Ten years after McMillan's treatise, she and her sister founded an open-air nursery and 'training centre' in Deptford, South London. The children played, ate and took naps outdoors. During the first six months, there was only one instance of illness among thirty pupils.

The Scouts, founded in 1908, have been the longest-running popular British – and international – movement promoting the wellbeing of children through physical activities outdoors. After the First World War came a proliferation of breakaway groups objecting to the Scouts' militarism and rigid hierarchy. These included the Woodcraft Folk, founded in 1925 by the freelance journalist Leslie Paul, who was inspired by nature writers such as Richard Jefferies and Fabians including William Morris and H.G. Wells. The Woodcraft Folk provided camping adventures for city children, recruiting girls as well as boys, and emphasised children thinking for themselves, while learning about pacifism, feminism and early environmentalism. Its campers were taught to think globally; they helped arrange Kindertransport to rescue Jewish children from Nazi Germany and later protested against apartheid in South Africa. Jeremy Corbyn, the Labour leader, attended their summer camps when his son joined a local group in North London.

In Europe, the first *skrammellegepladsen*, or 'junk playground', was created in Copenhagen in 1943 by a Danish architect who observed how children played on bombsites. The landscape architect Lady Allen of Hurtwood encountered the playgrounds by chance on a lecture tour and brought the idea to Britain. The first anglicised adventure playground opened in Camberwell, South London, in 1948. Almost half a century later, it was another visit to Denmark that reignited the outdoor schooling movement in Britain.

In 1995, students studying nursery education at Bridgwater College, Somerset, went to Denmark to see Danish nurseries run on Scandinavian *friluftsliv*, or 'open-air life', principles. They were inspired to establish a similar approach in their college's nursery. Since then, in Britain, a blueprint for 'Forest School' has been established by a charity, the Forest School Association.

It promotes child-led learning in woodland or other natural environments, with the opportunity to 'take supported risks' and a holistic approach to learning which aims to foster 'resilient, confident, independent and creative learners'. In practice, usually, this means learning to use tools to make things out of wood, tree-climbing, hide-and-seek games, teamwork such as shelter-building, learning about wildlife, and opportunities for discussion and reflection – and hot chocolate – around a campfire.

Whatever activities are on offer, the children choose and are free to develop their own ideas, adventures and imaginative elaborations. Thousands of teachers and nursery practitioners have been trained by the Association, and 'Forest School' has been enthusiastically taken up in weekly sessions at some state primary schools as well as by a growing number of nurseries for pre-school children. Like many, Dandelion's teachers have Forest School training, but their nursery is not run on formal Forest School lines because it also incorporates philosophy lessons and other learning inspired by Emma and Hayley's experience in conventional schools.

The growth of Forest School and other outdoor alternatives derives from contemporary anxieties about children's mental and physical health and their increasingly insular indoor lives, but also from perceptions that mainstream schooling has returned to the Victorian age. I'm a child of the 'trendy' state school teaching of the 1980s – a grammatical education somehow passed me by – but that was a short-lived moment of educational freedom in which individual teachers could determine what students studied within their subject areas, and children could learn via a greater liberty to pursue their own interests.

The 1988 Education Reform Act put a stop to all that. The state schooling we have today is a choice-based market system of education constructed around a rigid 'National Curriculum', with a strong emphasis on formal learning, testing and 'league tables'. The same system can be found across many other Western countries. In England and Wales, under governments of all political colours, learning in state schools has become more structured, less experiential and less topic-based, with more time devoted to maths and English to the exclusion of other subjects. There is certainly no space in timetables for the nature walks I was taken on by my primary school teachers. Since the early 1990s, every seven-year-old and eleven-year-old at English state schools has had to sit 'standard assessment tests', or SATs, to measure their attainment. Proponents of testing argue that it has restored the acquisition of important basic knowledge to state school children, and say the tests hold schools to account and give parents the ability to make informed choices about where to send their children. Critics argue that this exam culture, the pressure of testing from seven and the narrow teaching it requires, has contributed to the mental ill-health of Britain's young.

The logic of giving parents choice is that when schools are seen to fail, we will withdraw our children from them. As stories of break-time being cut or primary school children being intensively coached for their exams over the Easter holidays proliferate, so increasing numbers of parents are removing their children from formal schooling. In Norfolk alone, between 2012 and 2018 there was a doubling of children being home-educated, to 1,452. Invariably, some refuseniks seek out Forest School and other forms of outdoor education. A few join Ted at Dandelion.

*

I am the second member of my family to become part of Dandelion. In the spring, I start volunteering there, one day each week. I must first obtain a Disclosure and Barring Service (DBS) check, a piece of paper to prove I don't have a criminal record and can work with children. Then I have to read the Dandelion staff pack: any teacher will be familiar with rules and regulations, but their labour-intensiveness is a shock to me. I skim through fifty documents assembled by Emma and Hayley and typed up in school-teacherly 'Marker Felt' font, a book's-worth of words covering everything from accidents and first aid to intimate care, touch policy and whistleblowing. Child protection is everything.

As a volunteer, my work is very circumscribed. I'm never to be out of sight of another member of staff. I can't be alone with a child. I can't take them to the toilet, serve food, share food or do work with tools. Most importantly, I must abide by a closely regulated form of physical contact: touch is a normal part of human interaction, says Dandelion, but the 'Dandelion hug' is sideways, never front-on, and usually initiated by the child. If a child wants to sit on an adult's lap, this must never be between our legs. Instead, he or she sits side-saddle, well away from any private parts. If a child wants to hold hands, this won't be resisted, but must always be open-palmed, not fingers intertwined. Children are not to be carried or lifted at any point. They are never helped up or down trees either, but must learn to climb them alone. Most of the protective and loving-dad stuff I do unthinkingly with the children at home is banned. It sounds austere and joyless.

The day I start, it's cool and breezy and I feel as nervous as a nursery-age newcomer when I ding the bell by the gate and

Emma welcomes me in. I'm not sure what I can contribute. Another Dandelion rule is that parents are not allowed to volunteer on the days their children are present, so there's no Ted for company. But there are twenty-four other Dandelions, including five-, six- and seven-year-olds who are home-schooled and come into Dandelion twice a week for a taste of communal life with peers.

I wear a name tag that comes with an emergency whistle, and preposterous layers of clothes: long-johns, cotton trousers and waterproof trousers; wicking T-shirt, long-sleeved T-shirt, jumper, down body-warmer, down jacket and waterproof jacket. Even in May, I will need them all. Occasionally, after Whitsun, the layers can be peeled off to what we might wear in our centrally heated homes.

My first job is to help one of the teachers, Tracey, with the risk assessment. Each day, a handful of children volunteer to put on fluorescent jackets, grab clipboards and inspect dangers around the site. What sounds like satire is a smart way to get children thinking about how they keep themselves safe. They have a sheet of A4 with drawings of things to check, and tick off. A couple of the more serious three-year-olds join us. (Each week, I struggle to recruit a willing team; the older children spot it for what it is, a chore, and only the younger ones can be cajoled.)

We start by testing that the yurt ropes are secure, and then we go inside the yurt to press the fire alarm button, check the fire extinguisher, inspect the little wood-burning stove and go through the contents of the first-aid kit. The yurt is the only piece of indoors at Dandelion. It's a sturdy, semi-permanent tent and its round interior feels like a deeply restful human nest.

The centrally placed stove is surrounded by a fireguard, sofas, rugs and shelves of picture books. The children can ask to go in at any time and chill out, snuggle down, or warm up. But in my year at Dandelion we use it only once, during a peltingly rainy day. Inside is not part of Dandelion's language, horizon or consciousness.

Perhaps it would be different in wetter western Britain. Norfolk is a dry county. I'm amazed at how rarely it rains properly on my one day a week. When it does, the children are dressed for it, and happily play in the rain, as dismissive of drizzle as ducklings. Inside-reared children can adapt, very quickly, to life outdoors. During the year, I meet just one child out of forty who complains that playing in the rain is a hardship.

After we've checked over the yurt, we tour the site, pulling on the swinging ropes to see that they are securely tied to the trees, and that the tree branches are sturdy and safe to climb. The wambly limbs of the overgrown laurel hedge often bend and break from all the climbing. The 'forest school area' is encircled by coppiced sallows, birch and field maple, with a few seedling oaks and hazel beneath. These trees need checking for climbing but also for fungi. We must assess if any we find are potentially poisonous or not. Eager eyes are cast over the multitude of logs and tree-trunk wedges dotted all over the site; by the music area with drums are the two composting toilet huts, the mud kitchen, and the play area with its gutters and water-filled trugs.

Finally, we must consider the safety of Dandelion's spiritual heart: the fire circle. The fire is front and centre, burning all day and in all weathers in the drum from a washing machine. It's encircled by tree stumps with planks between them for seats, and then a protective fence. We sit around it at snack time, when there are games, stories and eggy bread or crumpets with hummus or marmite. The first and most important of many Dandelion songs that Ted learns guides him safely around the fire and its tree-stump seats:

Dandelions go round the outside, round the outside, round the outside
Dandelions go round the outside until they find a seat.

Today, Hayley has deliberately scattered newspaper inside the seating area, close to the fire. Josh, one of our three-year-old risk assessors, spots the paper, we pick it up, and Dandelion is declared safe for play.

I'm a father of three but I've never worked with children before. After an hour on my first day, Hayley tells me I have to get low. I am a clumsy Gulliver, looming over the Lilliputians; wise teachers kneel, crouch, sit. Ted recently borrowed my camera and the pictures he took startled me. The world looked so different from his height. I was struck by how the grownups towered over him – distant Olympians, apparently authoritative and judging, by virtue of our great height.

Most of the Dandelions are wary of me at first, and freak out when I mention their name. 'How do you know my name?' they say, eyes narrowing at this adult voodoo. I explain I've heard others say it. I'm struck by their deep absorption in the present moment. Unlike adults, children do not pay attention to much beyond their immediate horizon.

At one of my first sessions, I help another teacher, Labone, make 'journey sticks' with the children. This is a lovely concept. The children find a stick and then walk around collecting leaves or whatever takes their fancy, and use wool and scissors to tie their finds to the stick. The finished object looks like it should be brandished by a Green Man or a white witch, a stick with special powers.

Cherry, do you want to make a journey stick? 'No,' says Cherry, and vanishes.

Rose, do you want to make a journey stick? 'No,' says Rose, sprinting away.

The Dandelions race around, a thunder of wellies on dry ground.

One group is busy with a collection of pallets, which become a ship and then a spaceship. Another lot are hanging out in the laurel hedge. Labone and I feel like chuggers in a shopping mall. The concept of a journey stick is a little complicated, and not easy to sell. Full of morning sprightliness, the children aren't in the mood to make stuff. But Josh, who has long eyelashes and a serious mien, agrees to. He's soon all quiet concentration against a backdrop of jumping and shouting. He chooses leaves very carefully from my offering of hazel, field maple, dead nettle, sallow and red campion – and then trims a small piece off each leaf. He ties them to the stick using very short pieces of wool and blue ribbon. Another older, louder boy, George, who is six and mixed race, dashes by and seizes Labone's prototype journey stick and says it's a sword and then a lightsaber. Josh decides his now beautifully adorned stick, with five leaves and flowers tied to it, is a 'lightsaver' too.

Then he pauses and reimagines it. 'This is my memory stick to remember the baby who died in mummy's tummy.' He says this gravely but he's pleased with his handiwork and trots off to put it safely by his bag. It's the first of a number of occasions when children, particularly boys, unburden themselves of deeply emotional parts of their family life to me. Such revelations seem to arise very naturally when we're engrossed in physical tasks.

Dandelion is completely off grid. There is no power, no gas, no electricity, no plumbing, no running water. At the end of each day, staff run a hosepipe from the primary school next door and fill a big tank with water. From this is decanted drinking water, water for the play areas, and emergency bucketfuls that stand by the fire. Another teacher cleans out the two composting toilets.

It takes me a while to realise that there are virtually no plastic toys at Dandelion, and absolutely no branded items. My not noticing is significant, not because I'm myopic but because it suggests that this stuff isn't as important as we believe. It reminds me of a big winter snowfall a few seasons ago. No one in my neighbourhood could drive for four days and the roads were revealed as a vast public space, a resource for pedestrians, cyclists, sledgers. Not having a car was no big deal. It taught me that we drivers could do less of it without much effort, just as we could buy less and use less energy. Still, we all submit to the ease of convention and routine; I know I do.

A place like Dandelion sounds like punishment for a toy-loving toddler but it actually satisfies the most ardent collectors and gadget-lovers. There is loads of stuff. Beside the low kitchen unit with basin and taps that don't work are old plates, a gravy boat, pots, pans, utensils, spoons, spatulas, ladles. There are gutters for pouring water down and tyres and wooden pallets and slices of wood that the children can rearrange. An old limb of corkscrew willow stuck into a tree stump is hung with paintbrushes, sieves and buckets. A flat log table bears watering cans, buckets, a teapot and dishes. Containers hold bark, shingle and pine cones. There are rope swings, wheelbarrows (normal ones and child-size ones) and a music stand: five logs bound together with blue binder twine like the frame of a tepee, from which hang two steel drums, waiting to be struck. A construction area is equipped with trowels, spirit levels, tape measures and broken tiles and bricks. Everything is either a 'real' adult tool or object, or a loose part. Most purpose-built toys, I realise, strongly direct a child towards a limited range of uses. They are 'closed'. Loose parts are profoundly 'open', to be turned into anything the twisting kaleidoscope of a child's imagination can devise.

There are a few toys in Dandelion, such as the venerable, slightly damp rocking horse in the meadow. Books lie on various straw-bale reading areas: *A Kid's Guide to Keeping Chickens* and, somewhat incongruously, *Big Rig*, a picture book about trucks. A wooden Wendy house called Grandma's Cottage is the closest Dandelion comes to being twee. It is adorned with a pretty painting of a fox curled up asleep among some flowers alongside the words, PLAY EXPLORE IMAGINE LEARN, which must be for the benefit of parents because most Dandelions are too young to read. Adults drop down on hands and knees to enter, and inside are wind-up lanterns hung from the walls, a woven Moses basket and pillow, a toy stove, a table, two seats cut from tree trunks and a quartet of cuddly toy animals – slightly grubby from their life outside. The children don't pay them much attention. On the walls, cards with children's faces drawn on them demonstrate emotions: scared, sad, happy, angry, excited, tired, loved. There is still some plastic, but with a purpose: plastic tweezers, plastic compasses, plastic hand lenses, plastic containers for water.

Dandelion is stuffed with stuff. And, despite the children performing a daily 'tidy-up time', moving around the site like a supervised plague of locusts, it takes two members of staff two hours to clear up at the end of the day, wiping mud from spatulas and returning pine cones to baskets.

Norfolk springs are nothing like the soft unfoldings of summer experienced in the south-west. They are cold and grey and scoured by biting north-easterlies. Low clouds scud across the sky and the wind sprints across the big arable fields and straight onto the Dandelion site, whipping through the gaps beneath the straggly leylandii, which were planted thirty years ago to stop the breeze and have outgrown their usefulness.

I seek out the warmth of a pile of straw bales that cascade over the hummocky grass and the anthills. These bales were once firm and golden but in three months outdoors have become as beige and saggy as exhausted commuters on the Tube. They are too heavy to lift in their new life as sponges that acquire every raindrop and slowly disintegrate, releasing bright filaments of straw like an exploded star. Still, miraculously, they hold heat and slowly transmit it. On a cold day, it's like snuggling against a human body. I warm my hands by stuffing them into the bales.

A few weeks later, Emma and Hayley arrange for a delivery of fresh, dry bales. They are flaxen and dusty; an August day encapsulated in orange twine. It's mercifully warm work, helping heave them from flatbed truck to gate. Balers can be set to produce different densities, and these rectangles are firm, well packed and surprisingly heavy. The Dandelions sense excitement and gather round our tumbling pile of golden blocks. Then, with minimal supervision, the children decide to team up and begin heaving them across the site, past the fire circle and into position in the meadow. Maisie, who is four, robust and as blonde as the bales, lifts and pushes one over all by herself, laboriously rolling it all the way, before returning for another.

The children decide how the new bales are to be arranged, although we grownups cap the height at three. They become a castle, with bridges, a tunnel and gaps to traverse; then a climbing frame and soft play, more forgiving than plastic or metal. A whole afternoon of jumping and imagining.

The grandest climbing frame is provided by the trees. One of the Dandelion guidelines that made the deepest impression on me was the one about never helping children up, or down, a tree, so I'm momentarily discombobulated when I first spot Joe far above my head, way beyond where I would be comfortable, in a sallow. I have to resist the urge to reach up to assist. Drones may give us a tree-climber's view of the world today but they don't provide the glory of the climb. Joe is proud of his achievement. He gets down easily as well, even though he's wearing wellies.

Elsa, a diminutive three-year-old, is one of the keenest climbers. She's not a 'brave girl' climber, either. Just a climber, among adults and other children. Scaling trees is not gendered. James, although older than Joe and Elsa, wants my help to climb Joe's sallow. The rules are clear. I bend them slightly by putting my boot on the ground by the tree trunk, so he can stand on the boot and gain a couple of centimetres to put his other foot onto the first bough. It's a stretch, but Elsa can reach it easily. James is taller but he can't, or won't: he only comes once a week and has not yet developed his peers' physical confidence. It's an interesting example of how outdoor nurseries enhance coordination; even the simple act of walking on uneven ground all day is a challenge for someone reared on carpets and pavements. The physical environment is always going to be more taxing outdoors. It is a compelling, constantly changing and endlessly fascinating structure for play.

There are no big screens on site (I'm quite surprised by the number of films my children watch in class during their first year at primary school), but Dandelion staff carry tablets. These are mostly used to take photographs of the children and their activities; the children can take photos with them too – Ofsted inspectors like forest schools to tick a technology box. And the influence of stories told on screens is all-pervasive. Many of the children's games feature imaginative material provided by the commercial world.

On one occasion, the children ask me to be a zombie and respond with delighted screams when I begin lurching towards them with my arms outstretched. James is obsessed with *Star Wars* and turns any conversation towards it. Ruby talks about *The Boss Baby*, a film she saw at the cinema. On one occasion, Josh says he's Spider-Man; then he goes sailing, as he reimagines what he watched on a *Swallows and Amazons* DVD at home. The Swallows are a group of good children; the Amazons are bad but they become good, he explains.

For all these outside influences, the quiet power and immediacy of the natural world make it the strongest influence on play. 'It's snowing,' shouts Maisie with delight, as they play on the bales. Specks of white float on the cool north-easterly. None of these children are old enough to have experienced proper snow but this is the next-best thing, thousands of seedheads from dandelions, drifting on the breeze.

Some months before, Dandelion's chickens were snatched by a fox, and I'm given the exciting task of buying some new ones. I drive a few miles to a house by the main road where a man sells hay and hutches and guinea-pigs and hens. A 'machine' bird costs £14. She'll reliably lay one a day, more or less, three hundred in her first year, a few fewer in the second, and then she'll keel over and die, the hutch man tells me. She is pale brown and no-nonsense, and the hutch man expertly wrangles her into a cardboard box. The children already have a name for her: Daisy. Then I'm told to buy a 'plodder'. She will go on for years, but lay fewer eggs. She has iridescent black feathers which can mysteriously gleam green and purple. She's Feather.

I bring them back to the site, as happy as Father Christmas. The chicken house is waiting for them and so are the children. After giving the newcomers some quiet time in their new house, we let them roam the site. Feather is cautious and steers clear of the children. Daisy is more confident, and gets picked up regularly. I tour the site on my hands and knees with various Dandelions and help them move the logs that line the little pathways. Beneath are woodlice, worms, and lots of tiny meadow ants frantically guarding their – larger – white grubs. It's a minibeast hunt but it becomes a chickens' buffet with gimlet-eyed Daisy and Feather at our shoulders. They jab and dart adeptly, fearsome gigantic dinosaurs to every tiny invertebrate. Even a domestic chicken must move like lightning to catch something that's alive.

When Hayley passes we chat about what the chickens like to eat, and with typical teacherly creativity she suggests that Sara, who is most interested in feeding the chickens, could devise a chicken menu. She hands us an offcut of wood salvaged from a local carpenter and a permanent black marker, and we get to work: '1. ant grub. 2. spiders. 3. slug. 4. Oops.' At least, that is what Sara's writing looks like. She draws an excellent grub, spider and slug. The sallows sigh in the wind.

At the end of my first month at Dandelion, I tally the pupils I've met so far. There are four from what appear to be quite underprivileged families but the rest probably fall into the ABC socioeconomic bracket. On the face of it, Dandelion might be criticised by those who argue that forest school nurseries are a niche concern for the white middle classes. Ambitious migrant families rarely send their children to play in the woods; they know it won't equip them for the global race. And forest school nurseries appear too expensive for the working classes. 'There's no such thing as bad weather, only unsuitable clothing,' the great populariser of fell-walking, Alfred Wainwright, is credited with saying. Today these words are a brusque clarion call to buy expensive Scandinavian wet-weather gear.

But there is no line of Audis or Mercedes or 4×4s outside Dandelion's gates. The nursery provides government-funded places whereby all parents of three-year-olds can obtain fifteen free hours each week. Local children on low incomes can, and do, attend. There are children of single mothers and a greater ethnic diversity than at comparable rural Norfolk nurseries. The children's fleece-lined wellies and salopettes – which are like mini fishermen's dungarees and totally waterproof – are expensive, but many are secondhand and there are always cheap low-tech options. Emma hoards shrunken cashmere jumpers she finds in charity shops for the children.

Many people might consider the countryside to be the last place with an urgent need for outdoor schooling. Clearly, some rural children spend more time among other species than most city kids. But the landscape for children around here, as I mentioned before, has utterly changed in three decades, and no child goes exploring alone, as I did. Indoor, screen-based attractions are universal and, if anything, country children surrounded by fast roads and vast privately owned fields are more likely to be trapped in their homes than city kids who live on 20-mile-an-hour roads with parks around the corner.

Class, gender and ethnicity are irrelevant inside Dandelion. The only divide I see there is between children who are familiar with the outdoors and those who are not. The very young, of course, are more oblivious than adults to class, race and gender; as in many things, they show us the way. But this outdoor world, in which possessions and brands have a low profile, seems to smooth over differences and hierarchies. And to my surprise, after I begin working at Dandelion, the age of the children quickly becomes invisible too. When I start there, my own children are five and three, but at Dandelion I can't always tell who among them are five and who are three. Many of the three-year-olds who attend four or five days a week seem more mature than five-year-olds who visit just once a week. But more fundamentally, after a while, the Dandelions don't seem like children. They just present as people. Of course, I don't forget for a second that they *are* children and must be treated with special care, but first and foremost I am dealing with just another person. Their personalities and passions are already so distinct. Perhaps this outdoor environment helps. Given so much more freedom and responsibility, children quickly learn to take care of themselves and make their own decisions. Play is very self-directed; appeals to authority are rare; and a passive need for adults – or screens – to provide entertainment diminishes.

I quickly understand why every early-years teacher says they love working with children. I've laboured alongside many sorts of people: plastic-bag factory workers (bullying banterers), book warehouse workers (lazy students), bookshop customers (quirky), market-stall customers (hagglers), posh-shop customers (entitled), publishers (terribly nice), and all species of journalist from war correspondents (adrenalised) to telly folk (friendly show-offs) and environmental charity press officers (the best kind of PRs). But children are the nicest of all.

Over the weeks, I get to know every child at Dandelion before I meet their parents. I can't help but develop a picture of their families but when I eventually encounter each parent at the gate, I struggle to see much trace of the joyful child in the harassed adult. We think of children as half-formed prototype adults, but children here seem to be an advanced life form. I don't intend to be mean: if someone got to know Ted before me, I'm sure they would experience the same fleeting comparison, and find me somehow diminished, malformed or at least weathered by experience. There are two children I don't initially warm to: one boy appears to have no social skills whatsoever; another appears to be a whiny drip. (When I read back this part of my Dandelion diary at the end of my time at the school I'm amazed because, a year on, I've grown to like both boys; they may be unconventional but both have fantastic imaginations and deeply kind hearts; I was wrong – they were not.) Even so, the most difficult children are not as tricky as difficult adults. The children are overwhelmingly enthusiastic, sunny, passionate and unpredictable exemplars of living in the present. Apart from bags of charm, their finest qualities are their directness, openness and honesty.

When I first meet Ruby, she gazes at me, with a mesmerised half-smile. I wonder what she finds so interesting. 'Why do you have funny teeth?' she asks. 'Why don't you go to the dentist?' Ever since my teenage brace failed, I've had the kind of crooked teeth that Americans would never tolerate. I've never felt self-conscious because no adult ever mentions them. Children do. 'Why do your teeth point straight out?' asks Sara on another occasion. Later, my own children start calling me 'wonky-yellow-toothed Dad' with unconcealed glee.

I'm sure the children in a cramped indoor nursery are just as nice as the Dandelions. But I suspect they don't behave quite so nicely. The children at Dandelion are constantly busy, but it all happens in such a spacious environment that they are much calmer than the children I see in conventional schools or nurseries. As with the absence of plastic, or screens, I don't really notice the most astonishing absence of all at Dandelion:

when a child cries, it's a foreign sound. My ears instantly prick up. There are fewer tears here than when I'm at home with my three children for a day. Some days, there's barely one meltdown among twenty busy small persons.

I've been into enough traditional nurseries to know that this is deeply abnormal. Is there less conflict at Dandelion? 'Massively less, absolutely massively,' says Emma. When I ask other Dandelion staff in private, they say the same thing. Everyone who has worked in an indoor nursery says that conflict management is almost constant. 'It seems to me that [in conventional nurseries] we've made spaces for conflict,' says Emma. 'There's lots of toys to fight over, there's not enough space, there's too much bloody noise.' A fair proportion of children at Dandelion have presented with attention deficit hyperactivity disorder in other nurseries, and their despairing parents have found this outdoor space keeps them calmer. Emma would like academics to measure this, but she knows it is common sense: 'If I put you in a room not much bigger than a living room with eleven other adults and filled it with a lot of plastic, eventually you are going to shout at each other. We know children don't usually empathise until they are eight. When you're little, if you want that plastic toy, you're going to get it by hitting the person who's holding it. Then somebody is going to shout at you – but actually nobody has given you any other way to get that toy.'

There are still plenty of possessions at Dandelion, and I notice newcomers are less adept at sharing, but Emma thinks the character of the stuff reduces conflict. 'If James loses his stick, that's a really important stick, but actually there are quite a lot more so for most children there isn't anything to overly worry about. You might want to keep that chipped mug for a little bit but it's not like wanting to have a bike, is it?' Conflict reduction is also about Dandelion's high staff-to-child ratio and their staff's emotionally intelligent approach to conflict management. Hopefully, says Emma, children's anxiety is reduced because they 'know that adults mostly will step in and listen to you if somebody has done something'. Children find it devastating if they are not heard, or misunderstood, by adults, which is easy in a busy nursery. 'As a child, you're not listened to,' says Emma. 'You literally don't have a loud enough voice and if you talk back in schools you're told not to. It's unjust as well. That completely floors children.' Dandelion's boundaries are as strict as a conventional school but I notice how even 'misbehaving' children are listened to, carefully.

Being outdoors does not automatically instil peace and love and tranquillity. Nevertheless, I'm struck by how the children's natural enthusiasm for making the most of the present is enhanced by the extra space, air, and copious places of security – little dens, huts, fairy houses or glades – where adult or child society can be fled, for a moment, if required. Pigs pop into my mind again; many of us are uncomfortable with confining these intelligent mammals to tiny concrete pens indoors when they could live a tactile life in the mud outdoors. Animal welfare is high on our political agenda; factory farming is frowned upon. What about child welfare and factory schooling?

The most amazing thing I notice during my first weeks at Dandelion is its effect on me. At each day's end, I'm elated. One part of this elation is spring, the lifting of the light, the creeping warmth, the leaves unfurling, the mad orchestra of birdsong, the explosion of life and possibility. Another part is learning new skills. But the largest component is sheer physical pleasure, the glow I get from fresh air and action. I hadn't imagined that working in a nursery would provide the long, sustained release of adrenalin that hitherto I've only experienced after a day walking in the hills or a long stint of strenuous gardening. Afterwards, I am extremely physically tired and extremely mentally relaxed. I sleep for ten hours at night.

When I ask Hayley what surprised her about starting Dandelion, she says, 'how exhausting it is. Teaching is exhausting anyway but being outside, in the fresh air, is utterly, utterly exhausting.' And yet she also finds it a more creative place. 'I get a lot of ideas outside, and when Emma and I are outside we fire off each other.' It has reduced her tolerance for indoor work. 'Just going into a school to use the photocopier makes us go, "Uuurrrrgh, I can't bear it." Working in the study at home as well, I get a sedentary feeling. I definitely feel more stressed if I'm in the office all day. Jangly. I just need to go outside and breathe a little bit.'

If this is the effect on adult bodies and minds, it's likely to be more pronounced on children. Ted falls asleep seconds after his head hits the pillow after a day at Dandelion. This alone could probably persuade many parents of the merits of an outdoor education: it helps children sleep well. How much are put-upon parents' lives enriched by having well-exercised, well-rested, well-sleeping children? All of us, of all ages, are so much happier if we spend a fair chunk of our waking hours outdoors. It is how we used to live; it is how we are meant to be.

4

Nests, Chicks, Death – and Stuffing

'Without death, there is no time, no growth, no change . . .
If we avert our eyes from death, we also erode the delight
of living. The less we sense death, the less we live.'

Iona Heath

Spring sparks a fever in nature and a fever in us. April, the first warm day for nearly a fortnight, and the air is filled with birdsong. The growth spurt of grass is visible between days. Garlic mustard and cow parsley leap skywards. The sunny faces of primroses beam from every hedge bottom. A pair of oystercatchers pipe-scream as they shuttle over our house between feeding grounds and their nest. A heron flies low overhead, crankily changing its course when it sees me. A coal tit makes a frenzied call; blackbirds perform synchronised worm dances on the lawn.

Milly and Esme, followed by Ted, are in that golden period between five and ten, when their independence is growing but puberty is still beyond the horizon. No one guesses Milly and Esme are twins because they look so different – one blonde, one dark – and from the very beginning they have responded to identical stimuli in contrasting ways. Both have the same early-years experience, the walks and then free play in the overgrown cemetery. Milly enjoys it, but Esme nurses an intense curiosity about the natural world, and a need to run free within it. They've developed their own interpretation of their distinct identities. 'I like arts and craft and playing indoors because I've got thin skin,' reasons Milly, 'and Esme likes nature and outdoors.'

We moved to our new house in a suburban village because it has the sort of big garden that was such a gift for me as a child. But it represents a compromise: I'd rather be completely in the countryside and Lisa prefers the city. Instead, we find ourselves in a suburban in-between, living beneath a flight path for helicopters servicing off-shore gas platforms in the North Sea.

There's a small branch-line railway passing by and the air hums with traffic from nearby roads. What sounds particularly unpromising is that we live beside an industrial estate housing a vast cool-storage warehouse for potatoes, a luxury yacht factory and a pair of financial advisers. The potato warehouse emits a soft hum on warm nights, the boat factory periodically closes as ownership shifts between hedge funds, and the financial advisers are presently jailed for defrauding elderly clients. But living next to an industrial estate is a revelation. One hundred boat builders are our alarm call, their cars thundering down the lane outside at 6.45 a.m. A great calm descends, though, when the estate gates are locked each evening and weekend. The warehouse's long out-of-hours renders its surroundings a peaceful realm for herring gulls, muntjac deer and hedgehogs. The nearby houses were mostly built in the 1950s and their generous gardens and mature hedges are ideal terrain for songbirds. There's a fragment of woodland and waste ground beyond, where a tawny owl woos and a buzzard skulks.

I cut down an overgrown Lawson's cypress hedge and a towering Lombardy poplar, plant native hedges and fruit trees and let the lawn grow wild and long. My gentle rewilding still necessitates occasional weeding, and while I futilely extract a tangle of ground elder from the herb bed, a male blackbird lurks behind my shoulder. Its beady eye is so fixated upon this alluring patch of freshly dug soil that it doesn't notice a larger predator at its back.

Esme wants the blackbird. She's crept up holding an extra-large butterfly net like a Faroese seabird-hunter, ready to swoop. Nothing escapes her gaze on this irrepressible spring day. She stalks the garden like a feral cat, rampaging with spring. The season's urgency has taken hold of her and she wants to be outside all the time. She spots an orange tip in the garden before I do, and another brimstone. Both are naturally flighty butterflies and evade her net.

If I didn't know Esme, I might assume she was inventing the things she finds. It's astonishing how much drama unfolds before her eyes. The professional wildlife guide seems to have a knack for making implausible stuff happen; it looks like sorcery, or luck, but of course it's time in the field. Most of us miss so much. True naturalists see more because they are interested and focused upon the present moment. Esme is interested. And exceptionally present.

The oblivious blackbird hops closer to me. Esme lunges. The blackbird catches a hint of movement in its peripheral vision and darts sideways. Esme swipes a second and a third time, and each time the blackbird scuttles neatly away but remains mockingly close. Esme huffs with frustration. 'I want a bird, I want to stroke a bird,' she says.

This desire is strong. Many children crave it. To hold a warm, quavering bird in our hands, to touch its soft feathers, to gaze into its eye; this intimacy is the reward for caring for anything. And most of all, more than anything else in the world at this moment, Esme desires a chick.

*

Nests, baby birds, death and taxidermy. It is not quite the circle of life but it's an accurate representation of springtime for the birds around us. We celebrate spring as a time of new life but for most creatures it is dominated by death. The human race is the predominant species because we are by far the most successful at swinging the odds of infant mortality so decisively in our favour. Other animals are not so fortunate.

I don't fully realise the seasonal carnage until we move into our new home, with its hedges thick enough to house birds' nests and children sharp-eyed enough to keep a close watch. We have two pairs of dunnocks in our garden, although one pairing of this notoriously polyamorous species seems to be a trio. These busy, attractive little grey-brown birds mostly nest in the snowberry hedge, although they are careful never to enter it at the point where they make their nest. I'm routinely surprised in winter by old nests that I never knew existed back in the spring.

I'm late for the school run one day because I promise Esme she can look inside the dunnocks' nest we have found in the middle of the hedge, only a metre above ground. We've not had a good nesting season. The first dunnock nested early, in March, before any leaves had sprouted from the snowberry, and its two chicks disappeared while we were away over Easter; I'm sure they were too young to fledge. A robin deserted its nest in the open-fronted box we put up in a yew tree, leaving six tiny speckled beige eggs behind. I hope that the blue tit fledged from one of five nestboxes we optimistically erected around the place, but

I'm not confident because the spring turned hot and dry, and heat and drought seem worse for chicks than wind and rain.

A blackbird we call Whitey because there's a smattering of white feathers on her wing like spilled paint naively built her nest in the ivy beneath the top of a fence, within swiping distance for one of the neighbourhood cats that constantly patrol our garden in early summer, despite my futile cursing and shooing. Whitey's first nest was destroyed when it had two chicks inside. Whitey's second was much better placed inside a bramble patch. Her two babies looked fine one hot evening when the sun set upon them. Both chicks were dead the next day, and I kicked myself for not feeding them, as Esme had suggested. I think they had overheated, but perhaps their father (the male blackbird is usually the main feeder) had died or deserted them.

The dunnocks' nest is a bowl the size of half a large orange, woven together from hundreds of grasses and the skeletons of last year's leaves, the sort that resemble a mayfly's wings. There are soft tendrils of green moss too, but the central cup is lined with blond and white hair. Some looks human and some looks like it was gathered from the feral white cat that is the nesting birds' main tormentor. Inside this immensely pleasing, nurturing shape are three pointed turquoise eggs, unhatched. Among them sits one large chick.

Each day, we check on this precious only child. Unlike with the blackbird, we never catch a dunnock parent on the nest. The adults melt into the hedge, unseen, before we loom close. We peer inside, careful not to stay long. But looking isn't enough for small children. Esme desperately wants to touch the chick. She craves to hold it in her hand, feel the kiss of its down and stroke its trembling body. The naturalist Chris Packham once declared that children must be 'stung, slimed, slithered on and scratched'; for that, they have to poke, prod, touch, explore. This chick is feathered now, although it lacks the wing or tail feathers to fly. So I relent. Esme stretches out her hand to touch the chick. It deftly avoids her by bouncing from the nest into the hedge, falling through the branches like a cartoon character. The chick has vanished. We are late for school, so I drag a wailing Esme away. She wants to hold it but she's concerned about its welfare too.

After the school run, I return to the hedge and scrabble around, stricken with guilt. At last, I see the chick's dark body quivering in the leaf mould inside the base of the hedge. I stretch in and my hand closes around its deliciously soft warm body. So this is what Esme wanted to feel. I pop it back in its nest, it sits there, and I sigh with relief and apologise. I hope it will be OK. The next day, we peep in again and the nest is empty. I suspect the chick has fledged and is now being tended by its parents, but there's no sign of the youngster or its parents helicoptering around it as we've seen blackbirds and blue tits do in our garden. Writing the biography of a chick is so often frustrating because we can't provide a full story. We blunder around their life-and-death struggles, not knowing if we are culpable or not, hoping for a happy ending.

Esme redoubles her efforts to possess a chick. She suspects I'll constrain her with my adult rules, so she's hatching her own plans. In the garden one day, I notice that a garden chair has been dragged to a spot beneath the beech tree. On top of this chair is balanced a child's wooden desk chair. Someone has stood on this wobbly tower and lifted the lid of the nestbox. Sure enough, Esme spotted a coal tit entering the box and, as diligently as a magpie, has been checking for chicks. There is nesting material inside, but no eggs; unfortunately, Esme's rummaging may have dissuaded the coal tits from settling there.

Later, she turns her attention to the most exciting new nest of all. We have an open shed where I park my car. For a few weeks moss and leaves have accumulated over the wipers. On top of a long wooden plank stowed in the eaves appears to be a growing pile of old leaves. It takes some days before I catch sight of a robin darting out of the shed. The female robin (she's the nest-builder; the male helps by feeding her) has constructed a horizontal skyscraper of moss and leaves more than a metre long. Robins are renowned for nesting in improbable locations, from postboxes to coat pockets. (The following year she will create a beautiful nest inside my bike helmet that hangs in the garage.) But I'm struck by the size and ambition of this nest.

Esme is desperate to see the eggs but I'm not sure where in the nest they are, and also I don't want to disturb them: robins desert their eggs extremely easily. A few days later, Esme comes running. She's felt the eggs and all is well, she says, because they are still warm. She climbed onto the roof of the car and dabbled her fingers through the nest until she found them. She now demands to check on the nest every hour. I haggle her down to once a day, and no touching. We reverse the car out of the shed so no cats can use it like Esme did, and bring in a stepladder. She climbs up to show me the eggs' location. Before I can reiterate the 'no touching' rule, she's darted a hand in and is holding an egg to show me. Oh no! The robins are definitely going to desert now. We quickly retreat and, thankfully, the robins hang in there.

Chicks hatch. We see their necks, straining and wavering like triffids, yellow beaks constantly seeking nourishment. Esme counts four. An ornithologist friend reassures us that birds are unlikely to desert once they are invested in feeding their chicks. The belief that our scent will cause the parents to abandon their nest is a myth: most birds can't smell well, if at all. But disturbance *is* an issue. And my friend tells me that the act of ringing chicks has to occur before they are old enough to become 'jumpers'; this is where we went wrong when Esme stroked the dunnock chick – it was already a jumper.

We check the nest almost daily and I tell Esme she can hold a chick when they are a bit bigger. Finally, I guess they are old enough to be held but not old enough to jump. Esme reaches in and draws out a chick, cupping it in her hands.

'Oh it feels so lovely,' she sighs. 'Hello chick.'

It is floppy and hapless and ugly, lightly feathered in grey and brown, with no trace of orange and an unexpected tinge of blue. After a minute, Esme puts it back and I'm relieved to see a robin hovering by the hedge.

The next day, we peek in again. Disaster. The chicks have gone. The little cup-shape in the centre of the great pile of moss and leaves is empty. How? Why? Was it us? No cat could possibly get them there, and we haven't seen any magpies or squirrels around. But wait. We peer again. In the gloom, we can just see four necks waving in a darker spot, further in from the edge of the plank at the back of this capacious horizontal construction. The mother has moved them, beyond the centre of the nest and further into the darkness. We can't reach them so easily now. Clever mum. I'm still worried that we've disturbed this vulnerable family, so we leave them in peace.

It rains for a few days and then we check again. The nest is definitely empty this time. I check online. Robin chicks are feathered by ten days and they fledge at fourteen, when they are still flightless. So they should be safely gone. There's no sign of any birds in the hedge outside. I thought we would see youngsters being fed by their parents, but the robins have outsmarted us.

I ponder how I can sate Esme's desire to nurse a baby bird. Perhaps we can wait until she is a bit older; a ten-year-old we know has several pet wood pigeons she has rescued from cats or storms. We should probably just have a go, but for all the internet guidance it does not look easy to keep a helpless chick alive, and all we find in our garden is a procession of dead ones. We stumble upon a bizarre substitute for live chicks after I spend a day watching wildlife with the photographer David Tipling. While we are crouched in his purpose-built hide beside a woodland clearing, a female chaffinch thumps into the glass we're looking through. We find this small brown bird warm and dead in the leaf litter. I've never seen a chaffinch so close up before and it's anything but brown: there are green feathers on its back, a patch of lemon-yellow on its wing and the softest sky-grey down on its belly.

I take it home for Esme. She holds it and strokes it, enthralled. For the next twenty-four hours, she and Rosie-Rose, as she calls her new pet, are inseparable. But this spell together is not so blessed for Rosie-Rose, who steadily becomes less lifelike: Esme cradles her so much that her neck breaks and droops and her soft neck feathers get bedraggled from constant stroking. We have so far resisted our offspring's urging for pets – three young children are enough dependants – but I feel I owe Esme an attempt to preserve Rosie-Rose.

I find the name and number of a taxidermist who lives nearby. I've interviewed a couple of taxidermists for journalistic assignments and they are a diverse breed: there are eloquent young artist-taxidermists who make expensive artworks and appear in Sunday supplements; there is also the traditional type, who are as wary as a badger catching a whiff of human. Taxidermists know that plenty of animal lovers are hostile towards their craft, and some rogue animal-stuffers are caught with illegally killed birds of prey or exotic species traded without the requisite paperwork. So this one, Benny, is monosyllabic and noncommittal on the phone. Nevertheless, I arrange to pop round a few days later.

Comforted by the promise of immortality for Rosie-Rose, Esme allows me to pop the bird in the freezer until we call on Benny. He lives in a low cottage, down a long track, beside the woods. There's a pick-up truck in the driveway. I feel apprehensive as I take Esme and Rosie-Rose in hand and knock on the door. Benny's cheerful wife directs us to his workshop, behind another door. We open it, call out, and step into another world.

Esme's eyes widen as we gaze around the small front room. Frozen mid-motion, like a filmic special effect, are dozens of creatures. Beside our feet stands a hare on its hindlegs. A curious young fox, its ears too large for its face and its fur still downy-soft, is darting towards us. Another, larger, fox is carrying a red-legged partridge between its jaws; a third is curled up asleep. A hedgehog is about to amble off. On the shelf to our right is a jay, poised to bury an acorn held in its beak. Beside it perch a garrulous-looking magpie and a trim sparrowhawk with a wild yellow eye. There's a pheasant, a pike, a snowy owl and a stoat, and some smaller birds too, including a robin about to hop down from an overturned plant pot. Some ageing birds of paradise encased in the Victorian era do not look like they have just paused the business of being alive, but everything else does. 'Dad! Dad! Dad!' exclaims Esme as she takes in each animal.

Benny, a cautious-looking, sturdy countryman of late middle age and possessed of sharp blue eyes, emerges from a back room, bringing a strong smell of preserving chemicals to the glass counter. I gabble apologetically about the smallness of the task, explain how Esme is attached to this bird, and hand him the small, stiffly frozen, unpromising-looking corpse. Benny holds Rosie-Rose up to the light and turns her gently.

'Yep, I can do something with her,' he says.

I make a bit of small-talk and compliment him on the animals. I fear he thinks I'm some kind of inspector so I try and reassure him by saying I've always liked taxidermy and I've got an old taxidermied badger at home. Benny doesn't say much.

It's Esme who wins him round.

'Dad! Dad! Dad!' Esme wants to show me something else she's spotted.

'She's noticing everything,' says Benny, admiringly.

'Do you know what this is?' He points to a barn owl.

'A tawn— no, a barn owl,' says Esme, correcting herself.

'Have a look in here' – and Benny gestures us to follow him into the room next door. It's even fuller than his small showroom, a storeroom of orders awaiting collection: floor to ceiling with buzzards, otters, peacocks, woodcocks, partridges, black grouse, red grouse. Benny specialises in birds.

'Did you notice this?' He points to a small stripy snail shell by a hedgehog. Esme quickly makes the connection, spotting the snail on the base of every beast in the room.

'It's my signature,' says Benny.

He can't tell me exactly how much Rosie-Rose will cost, perhaps £40; or precisely how long it will take, he's busy and it might be a month, but I can ring in a few weeks and he'll let me know. I feel as impatient as Esme to return to this magical cottage in the woods.

Taxidermy may be enjoying a fashionable decade or so but it is not to everyone's taste. If it was, perhaps more animals would be shot to order, even though there's enough roadkill to fill everyone's front room with badgers and foxes and pheasants, if they so desired. Taxidermy is associated with trophy-hunting, with killing and cruelty; it is often seen as a symbol of our subjugation of other species. Where a taxidermied animal comes from matters, and I believe it is defensible if they are found dead after striking a window or being hit by a car. I don't believe I have the right to buy dead animals just because they look nice. But I like having taxidermy around. I like animals, alive and, sometimes, dead. I like the feeling of living among them, and being able to touch these object-animals and think through them.

Children are fascinated by taxidermy, without reservation. When mine are babies, I notice they are far more transfixed by taxidermied animals than by animals on the television or computer, or in the pages of picture books. Even virtual reality and 3D images cannot be touched. Taxidermy can. It is only an inert, lifeless form of nature but it may help develop more intimate relationships with the living world.

Our children come to know the softness of a tawny owl's feathers and the brilliance of a starling's iridescence through taxidermy, and they know this in the most powerful way possible – from their own senses. First of all, though, they become casually familiar with the size of a badger, the wiriness of its coat and the sharpness of its teeth. They have not yet seen a live one but they grow up with the long-dead beast I bought, in a rush of blood to the head, at an online auction. This poor animal is set in the snarl of a creature being hounded by dogs, drops of blood painted on its teeth. I suspect it spent many years in an old country pub: it is still suffused with stale smoke and yellowed with nicotine. It is not an uplifting representation of its species, or of its hunters.

When the children are tiny, they are not sure if Badger is alive or dead. Ted asks several times about the status of this immobile animal, which looks and feels real. Bizarrely, without any encouragement from me, they start borrowing Badger from my study. He (we think – his underside shows no traces of nipples and his genitalia vanished where he was stitched together) disappears with them into cupboards for hours. There, in a sett together, they dress him up and nurse him, curing imaginary ailments and breakages. Later, they take him to the bath and wash and shampoo him. They shove food into his mouth – grass and nuts and, most bafflingly, chewing gum. They meticulously brush his teeth, again and again. Badger is the nearest we have to a particularly compliant dog or cat.

We encounter more kinds of taxidermal life when I take the children to the Castle Museum. Norwich's main museum, situated inside the Norman castle that looms above its pedestrianised shopping streets, was my favourite city excursion as a small boy. In the decades since I first visited, the natural history exhibits have been freshened up, with added interpretation and electronic bird-calls, and yet the stars of its two glass-lined corridors and one high-ceilinged room remain pretty much as I remember. One corridor contains scenes of local taxidermied wildlife; another houses the beasts that Victorian and Edwardian trophy hunters brought home. The high-ceilinged room is filled with dead birds.

The children have been a few times but not as often as I would like, and I take them on impulse one day after they have refuelled with beans on toast on their return from school.

'Can we go to the bird section?' asks Esme, 'because – da-da-dah!' She fishes out her pocket guide to birds. She's also brought guides to insects and fungi. This is a field trip for her. We purchase our bargain £2 'twilight tickets' and run in, skidding along the polished floors, voices echoing. We have the last hour at the museum, deliciously, almost to ourselves.

'I love this one. It's my favourite,' says Esme as we career into the Ted Ellis Norfolk Room. It was named after a brilliant local naturalist who memorably described his Norfolk Broad heartland as 'a breathing space for the cure of souls'. His room is a corridor between floor-to-ceiling glass cabinets which contain six dioramas of Norfolk wildlife. These are lifesize displays that place three-dimensional objects – in this case, taxidermy but also branches, leaves and reeds – before a painted background and trick the eye, via a curving back wall and a tilting floor, into interpreting the whole scene as a three-dimensional picture. Money was raised to employ landscape painters to create these images in the 1930s. When they first opened, the museum blurb claims, they were the finest in Europe.

Although the English countryside has been transformed since the 1930s, these dioramas, surprisingly, hold true. We can still find similar scenes, and similar wildlife, in the world a few miles from the Castle Museum. One diorama depicts the marshlands of Breydon Water in the Broads. A wherry, a traditional sailing barge, is painted on the background; in the foreground, on mudflats and in the water, are a taxidermied heron, a great black-backed gull, a dunlin, a redshank and several wigeon. Some of the birds are in flight, positioned by invisible threads.

The children rush along and press buttons to listen to the birdsong. A multitude of calls – the screams of terns and the booms of bitterns – cascade down the corridor. The bittern stands among the reeds in a general representation of the Broadland marshes, which also features a dragonfly, tiny but broad-bodied, a chaser. Ted and I pause to look more closely. Its blue body touched up with paint is nowhere near as vivid as it is in reality. The kingfisher is a disappointment as well. The lights are dim to stop the animals fading but we cannot replicate the shafts of sunlight that set fire to its iridescent feathers in real life.

Nevertheless, there is something deeply engrossing about these scenes. I can stare at the North Norfolk coast diorama for hours, with its whelk-egg capsules on the sand beside nests of common and little terns. Beyond is a painted salt marsh of purple sea lavender and the gentle rise of farmland. Ted studies a bird 'with a stone in its mouth'. Esme identifies it as an oystercatcher; she recognises it from when I excitedly point out their spring forays over our house. And Ted is correct: the bird is holding something: the taxidermist placed in its beak a small mussel, part of its coastal diet.

The red squirrel is the only one of the stuffed creatures that is now extinct in Norfolk, but many of these animals are much rarer in our neighbourhood today. We have little chance of casually encountering water rail or jack snipe or woodcock or waxwings, although Esme has caught sight of a flash of a water vole. At least the wildlife in the image of a Norfolk 'loke', a dialect word for a lane leading into a field, has endured. This was my favourite scene as a child because it is a cosy tangle of bushes, here set in autumn. A hedgehog and a rabbit rootle through the red and brown leaves scattered across the earth; above are a song thrush, a blue tit, and green and great spotted woodpeckers. Ted's favourite thing lurks, immobile, in the undergrowth: a fly agaric fungus.

The children ricochet onwards like billiards, in amongst the entire zoo crammed into the three dimly lit rooms. Each specimen, from the bush duiker to the beast I remember from childhood, the polar bear, standing taller than the tallest adult and swiping a tiny common seal with one hefty paw, can trigger a thousand conversations about species' niches worldwide; each is a lesson in biology, ecology and conservation but also a spark for our imaginations, kindling stories and greater flights of fancy.

Children continually make fabulous connections of the kind most adults would consider an occasional Eureka moment. I'm also constantly taken aback by the precision of children's comparative observations. Ted studiously avoids the human skeleton which troubled him on his previous visit, but pauses by a Chinese water deer. 'Fangs!' he exclaims. 'Do they drink your blood?' Then he points to a skull.

'Dad! You've got that one!' he says. I won't have, I think, but I check the label. It's the skull of a gaur, or Indian bison, the largest surviving bovine species on the planet. Ted is correct, because in my study is the skull of a cow that I found on the island of Eigg. Later, he and Milly immediately identify a lappet-faced vulture they have seen only in a picture book by Julia Donaldson and Axel Scheffler.

Critics of these old-fashioned facsimiles of animals say such collections are a group of objects, not a community of subjects. They are killed, pinned and fixed; stripped of their dignity, reduced, objectified and commodified. There is a danger that taxidermy simply teaches children that animals are curiosities, separate from us. All this may be true, but I'm not sure it's how children experience it. Our children don't love taxidermy per se. They simply love animals.

The one that Ted meets closest up is in an exhibit of 'circus' animals, a curator's creative device to display what the internet knows as 'crap taxidermy'. At Ted's eyeline is a leopard with unnaturally protuberant glass eyes. He puts his face as close as he can, hot forehead resting on cool glass. He murmurs for a moment, as if in prayer. Something mysterious passes between boy and the mounted and preserved century-old skin of a leopard.

'The leopard is saying hello to me,' explains Ted matter-of-factly before moving on.

We reach the bird room, high-ceilinged and packed with grand glass cabinets.

'Did they kill every single bird in here or did they find some of them dead?' asks Esme. She is distressed by the scale of this slaughter. 'That's why there aren't any in the wild any more,' she concludes. Milly shows me a hobby, because she's heard me talk excitedly about seeing this bird chasing dragonflies on the Norfolk Broads. 'It's tiny,' she says. Tiny is disappointing. She's right. When anyone hears tales of a fantastically fierce raptor, they want giant birds, wings outstretched. The hobby's wild majesty is not its size but its dynamic movement, its cut and flash and mastery of impossible hunting feats such as taking swifts on the wing. Here, the taxidermied hobby is tidily perched, bearing no sense of its explosiveness or even the shape of its scimitar wings. The bird room does deliver mighty, in the form of a sea eagle set high in a cabinet. It makes us step back and exclaim because, just as when we get close to a grounded aeroplane, it seems almost unfathomable that such a large creature can fly.

The glass-topped table that most draws in Ted and me contains a display of nests, which are as inviting as the dioramas. As we gaze we imagine our way into these homes of other beings – the circle of a skylark, the shallow weave of a teal, and the enclosed den of the long-tailed tit, miraculously woven from feathers, moss and cobwebs, which give the nest elasticity and allow it to stretch to contain eight, ten or even twelve chicks. Children are great connoisseurs of nests. 'A nest is a circle of infinite intimacy,' writes Jay Griffiths in *Kith*. 'Every generation of children instinctively nests itself in nature.'

Children need to nest. The first thing our children do when

we stay at another house is work out where they are sleeping, and fashion their home for the night from their duvets and soft toys. The most memorable sanctuaries of my childhood are my nests: the hedge bottoms and bush hearts where I squatted unseen and watched the world beyond.

In an era of parental surveillance, we forget that children also require privacy, of which nature is a great provider. I've built a couple of dens for the children but these rarely catch on for more than an afternoon; children need to discover and name their own places of retreat. If we tell Esme off, say, at meal times, with some Edwardian parental plea to remain at the table for a minute after she's bolted her food, she runs away. Away is our garden. She hasn't run further yet, but I expect she will.

Sometimes, I surreptitiously watch her after she flees grownup oppression, and see how she hides like a fawn in the long grass of the meadow, lying down and gazing at the sky or bending over, medicating her pain with absorption in another species, stripping the seeds from a piece of grass or trying to catch a grasshopper. She needs a nest in nature: its safety, security and freedom.

Often, she heads for the Maze. When we moved into our house, we inherited a featureless lawn and after I removed the overgrown conifers we lost the only good place of concealment. I set about making amends, cutting cavities inside existing shrubs that can be colonised by the children. Native hedges grow slowly but, on an impulse, one day I bought 150 fast-growing sallow saplings, 20 centimetres high, for 27 pence each, and planted them in a spiral. It is soon the best addition I make to our home. A muntjac steals into the garden in winter and munches a few saplings, but most survive. Three summers later, the Maze becomes an authentic three-metre-high tunnel, winding round three times. I bend the sallows over the top and tie them together. Adults can no longer squeeze through its sides and must take the one, hidden, entrance point and then walk round; children still burst into it from all sides during chasing games.

It becomes their sanctuary. Ted enjoys a residency in the grassy bower at its centre, invisible to the outside world in summer. The only traces of his occupancy are the temporary middens of toys he deposits there. I don't realise the bonds he has formed with this place until he berates me for chopping down one of his favourite trees and says, 'Don't you *dare* ever cut down the Maze.' I take inspiration from Ted: when I'm stressed, I enter the Maze and lie there for a few minutes, cocooned by the spiral and soothed by the delicate oval sallow leaves, the sunlight slanting through, the astounding beauty of it all. John Clare and other early writers on nature are said to have possessed 'ditch vision'. It is every child's view of the world, and children can help us recover it. Lying in the Maze, I'm reminded of those wonderful lines from the Irish writer Patrick Kavanagh: 'To know fully even one field or one land is a lifetime's experience. In the world of poetic experience it is depth that counts, not width. A gap in a hedge, a smooth rock surfacing a narrow lane, a view of a woody meadow, the stream at the junction of four small fields – these are as much as a man can fully experience.'

Six weeks and a brief phone call after our first visit, we return to Benny the taxidermist's cottage in the woods. I've brought all three children this time. His workshop is just as interesting as the Castle Museum.

'I'm quite pleased with how it has turned out,' he says, opening a cardboard box on his counter.

Rosie-Rose's lately bedraggled form is immaculate. Her eyes gleam blackly. She is perched on a short stick, surrounded by moss stuck to a little plinth.

'Don't let the children touch her or she will get ruined,' he advises. I don't tell Benny that I fear this will be impossible.

We chat and I mention I write about wildlife. 'I thought you were a teacher,' says Benny. He tells me more about his animals: most, he says, come from gamekeepers. Birds of prey must arrive with paperwork to prove they have not been illegally shot but found, for instance, on the road after being struck by a car. His clients tend to be country people who want a memento of this species, or of that day's shooting. He also undertakes work for other artists.

He shows us his work tables in a larger room behind the counter. There's a chest freezer full of labelled carcasses. Four foxes stand on his work benches. These are being set to pose like people, on their hindlegs. This anthropomorphism is not to Benny's taste, but a fashionable London artist has ordered them.

We take Rosie-Rose home and I let the children hold her. Rosie-Rose perches on Esme's bedside table and receives strokes, conversation and love. After a couple of days, she still looks unruffled. Esme begs to be allowed to take her to school, so we agree. That afternoon, Rosie-Rose arrives home a transformed bird. I hardly recognise her. It's the morning after a raucous night out: she's hunched and tousled, dangling one leg off her perch, tail irrevocably bent. I feel guilty about Benny's craft, but three years later Rosie-Rose still perches on the window-sill by Esme's bed. She's recognisably a chaffinch even though she's missing a wing and her feathers have faded to grey-brown in the sunshine.

A precedent has been set, and whenever Esme finds a dead bird, she asks to have it turned into taxidermy. Most are too decayed or pulverised by cars but I stow promising specimens in our freezer and see what Benny reckons. Over the years, we will commission Benny to taxidermy a starling and various roadkill: a grey squirrel, a tawny owl and a polecat. The squirrel is a disappointment: Benny does a beautiful job, its grey tail is primped and fluffy, but the squirrel reveals to me that its bounce is its most attractive feature, and this is only found in life. The polecat is glorious, and until I found this one squashed on the road to Dandelion I had no idea this brown-and-silver mustelid – the wilder, beautiful relative of the ferret – had recolonised East Anglia. Esme discovers the starling laid out on our lawn, inexplicably unblemished, with none of the signs of trauma we associate with sudden death. She decides she wants to give the stuffed bird to her friend Josie, who was impressed by Esme's chaffinch and pestered her mum for something similar. Josie loves it, and takes it into school one morning. The teacher tells her mum that Josie can't show it to the class because some children might get upset. They might also start asking questions about death.

Just as we've become more distant from other forms of life, so we've become more distant from death. Most of us no longer kill what we eat or wear. The slaughtering of livestock is kept beyond our gaze, just as our own dying is often shielded from the living.

We've become adroit at avoiding death. Becoming more intimate with other nature is one way to recreate a healthier relationship with death and the dead. The experience of the lives and deaths of other animals offers children all kinds of opportunities to think about death, although the reaction of Josie's school suggests that it is adults who require this rather more urgently.

Not every school is the same. One afternoon, while playing in the shade of Dandelion's sallows, I catch a flit of movement near a bat box hammered to the sallow trunk and realise that blue tits are nesting there. The bat-sized slot looks too narrow but I peer in and see chicks inside, yellow feathers shining. Unfortunately the nearest chick to the entrance is dead, so I spend ten minutes jiggling with a stick to fish it out. The chick is a pitiful thing, recognisably a blue tit with a trace of yellow and blue feathering, a few days away from fledging. It has been very dry; perhaps the parents couldn't find the astounding number of caterpillars their offspring need to grow and thrive.

I show it to Emma and Hayley. They agree it looks sad but pop it in the primary school's fridge next door. 'It'll give us a chance to talk about death,' says Hayley brightly. Emma points out the absence of decay in life today. 'Children don't even see vegetables rot, because vegetables just go in the bin.' Indoor life is sterile, but Emma says they don't need to self-consciously discuss death with the children at Dandelion: outdoors, it is encountered quite naturally, and can be experienced in an undistressing way.

When Emma and Hayley show the dead chick to the children everyone talks about it with great interest, pondering its life and death, and the possible fate of the other chicks still being fed in the bat box. Children have a natural sympathy for the young of other species. The Dandelions decide to bury it and compose funeral songs. These are not overly sentimental. 'This is the way we bury the bird, bury the bird, bury the bird,' they sing to the tune of 'Here We Go Round the Mulberry Bush'.

This absence of bother about death is another small revelation for me; children are neither squeamish, mawkish nor fearful about dead things, until we teach them to be. (Although I remember as a child the moment I first grasped the concept of death, and how I cried inconsolably at the thought of my own passing; these feelings were more honest and true than my current position of pushing death to a faraway recess of my mind.) The deaths of animals, particularly pets, may be a real tragedy for small children but they are also a gentle rehearsal for the bludgeoning hit of loss when a human loved one dies. The rituals matter too. Taking grief seriously, giving it pomp and ceremony, consoles us when someone we are close to dies, and so it is with pets. Pet funerals are vivid memories from my childhood. Our mouse graveyard eventually stretched across a whole flowerbed. The death of our dog was my first experience of genuine adult grief. Mum cried but Dad could not and we felt sorry for him. I can still hear the hollow thud as Dad's first spadeful of soil hit Mishka's stomach after she had been laid out in the hole at the bottom of our garden. How small our German short-haired pointer suddenly looked. There was something profoundly comforting about putting a corpse into the ground. It just seemed right. Back to the soil, a natural end.

Several weeks later at Dandelion, I'm surprised by the contents of the Mystery Box. This is a game we play at snack time, when we gather around the fire circle for a story. The game begins with another catchy Dandelion rhyme, this one to the tune of 'This Old Man':

Mystery Box
What's inside?
What's the secret that you hide?
Are you hard, are you soft, are you squidgy like a bear?
Ask a question if you dare.

The children learn the difference between questions that are open (many answers) and closed (one answer), and ask five questions to guess what's inside the small wooden box.

'What's the initial phoneme?' is the standard first question, and Emma or Hayley write it on a hand-held chalk board: T—

'What does it do?'

'It lives in damp places.'

'What's the second letter?'

'To—'

'What colour is it?'

'Greeny-brown.'

'Is it a toad?'

The box is opened. It's a dead toad. The children don't recoil. They want to see it. 'But don't touch it,' says Hayley. 'It's decaying.' She found it on the site; probably another victim of the dry, warm June.

I think we should touch dead things, we need to feel the matter of the natural world much more, but I love how Emma and Hayley embrace the opportunity to discuss death. It's something we could all be brave enough to do.

*

At home, my family's brushes with mortality via baby birds continue. We pull our own dead blue tit chick from a nestbox and I admire how Esme flinches less than I do. She is pragmatic about dead chicks by now, although burying them is an important ritual. Tears fall only when she opens the nestbox and finds all the blue tits have fledged: empty-nest syndrome comes early to her.

Although the nesting season is over for most birds by July, the wood pigeons and collared doves, indefatigable twenty-first-century success stories in the pantheon of garden birds, continue to make romantic wing-flapping gestures at each other. It is only when we find a broken collared-dove egg on the drive that we realise a foolish-looking dove has made a pitiful, threadbare nest, more gaps than twigs, above our outside light, under the eaves of the house barely two metres above ground and directly over the well-used path to our front door. Now Esme spies a large grey chick, rearing up and flopping around in the nest.

I'm working away for a few days while Esme's desire for this chick incubates and grows. Finally, she snaps. She finds a bamboo cane, stretches up and pokes the nest. Prod, prod. The chick comes tumbling down. Now Esme's devastated. What has she done? She calls for mum. The sun will soon set and the temperature will drop. The chick is quite large and plain grey, with a slightly bovine look about it. Esme wants to put Chicky in a box, keep it warm and feed it. She and Milly and Ted get to work, digging for worms, which they deduce – wrongly – is this chick's food. They offer some to Chicky but it doesn't want to feed. It prefers its mother's vegetarian 'crop milk'. Lisa decides it is best to put the chick back in the nest. She and the children get a stepladder, add some hay to its threadbare home, and return the chick, with some worms in case it wants to eat. There is one other chick in the nest and it is dead, so Lisa removes it for burial-by-children.

I return that night, and am relieved to learn that the chick has been re-deposited in the nest. Birds are usually tenacious in returning to their young even when badly disturbed. The next morning, however, Chicky is dead. Esme is furious.

'I knew we should have kept it and looked after it,' she says through tears. I feel guilty because my grandma, who devoted her later life to rehabilitating and releasing injured badgers, owls and buzzards, would have known how to save it. Only later do I discover that collared doves' mothers do not sit on their chicks at night when they get older but only return to the nest periodically, to feed them. So the chick was not abandoned but must have died of the injury it sustained in being hoiked from the nest.

Esme climbs the stepladder with me, and picks Chicky from its nest. Its beak sags open, and she wonders, several times, how it could have been alive yesterday when it is dead today. We all struggle with this impossibility when we grieve. Worse is to come. As we bend down to bury the chick in the flowerbed beside the nest, the mother dove flutters onto the eaves above her home. She coos, tentatively, head on one side, and peers into the nest before stepping back, uncomprehending. She is looking for her last child and, unfortunately, its killers are the foolish humans kneeling in inept grief below her.

5

Dipping into Ponds

'Children use animals as a gymnasium for their own emotions.'

David Attenborough

The first sunny day of the Easter holidays, the air still cold, and Milly, Esme and Ted are hunting for chocolate eggs in Nana's garden.

My mum has hidden a silver trove of sixty small eggs at the base of dwarf daffodils, crocuses and grape hyacinths in her small garden. The children are racing against each other, eyes darting, hands lunging, buckets swinging, engrossed in the surprisingly difficult task of finding every foil-wrapped egg. And then suddenly, we all become distracted by a more spectacular haul of treasure that shines as the sunlight slices gold into the dark water of Nana's pond.

The garden is a resolutely ordinary rectangle in a 1990s redbrick housing estate. It has a pretty young silver birch, a small cherry, a clematis climbing over a metal arch, a sun-lounger, a diminutive wooden shed and a compost heap behind it. There are blackbirds and wood pigeons: the usual visitors. In the middle of the lawn is the circular pond, two metres in diameter. The pond is exceptional.

We routinely tease Mum about her powers of exaggeration so I'm dubious when, a week before, she claims there are two hundred frogs in her pond. Today, however, a few days after the conclusion of surprisingly noisy mating rituals and the laying of spawn, there are still fifty. Most are enjoying a post-coital sunbathe. Every now and again, one turns and performs a languid breast-stroke across the dark waters.

Where do they come from? Where do they go? They don't reside here all year round. There wouldn't be space for more than about five in Nana's garden. And these mating grounds, created only after the house was built, are sealed off by the house and road at the front, wooden fences mounted between concrete pillars at the side, and a bank, wire fence and huge hedge at the bottom. Neighbouring gardens are mostly inhospitably close-cropped lawns and decking, without much cover for a frog.

Every year, however, the frogs emerge from their suburban hideaways and make their pilgrimage to Nana's pond. We kneel by the water, as if in worship, where the brown sheaths of yellow flag iris will soon burst with green. A few of the frogs are flag-iris brown but many are sky-after-dusk blue, blotched with dark grey. The males are noticeably smaller than the females. Occasionally one dinky male half-heartedly pursues a female swimmer and attempts to cling to her back. Mostly, the great mating ritual is over. The remaining frogs congregate around their produce: great clumps of spawn. These are multi-celled grey shapes with hundreds of black eyes set in jelly like an alien monster. They flex and undulate, yielding but not breaking as the frogs scramble around.

The frogs are docile in the sun, and some of them look baggy and exhausted, loose folds of skin flapping where they once housed hundreds of eggs. Our knees are wetted by the miniature marsh at the pond edge but Esme and I reach in and grab a frog or two. It's hard to hold them for long. Each one feels like a seaweed-covered stone, cool and slippery, and they squirm like a mouse, peeping from our cupped hands with eyes that glint in the sunshine but are as black as their spawn. Each eye is surrounded by a socket of gold, giving them an affluent, monocled look. We usually interpret their down-turned mouths as disapproving or grumpy. It is easy to see why frogs and toads have been so heavily anthropomorphised, particularly in children's literature.

This cultural image of frogs and toads probably obscures our view of their real nature. When I see a toad, I always think of foolish, incorrigible Mr Toad, a byword for decadent aristocracy in *The Wind in the Willows*, and the clever but fantastically conceited Detective Toad in another splendid old children's book, Marjorie Beevers' *The Great Mr Toad*. My children love Ed Vere's *Grumpy Frog*, a picture book about a frog who insists he is not mean or grumpy ('this is my resting face') but is actually both. The nature writer Richard Kerridge admires toads' 'portly dignity' and the way they sit watching the world with what resembles patient rumination, 'like elderly people in front gardens'. He also accepts that such observations often obscure what is true about the actual species, although he believes that anthropomorphism can also inspire an affinity with the natural world even when its factual premise is shaky.

Children are besieged by talking animals on television, in computer games and in picture books. It would be a miracle if we were not all influenced by these portrayals of wild animals, because we've piled certain attributes onto innocent creatures with the heaviest of trowels since Aesop. Wolves are wicked, foxes are cunning, badgers are bossy, peacocks are vain, snakes are tricksy, cows are slow. Browsing through our children's bookshelves, I find that 138 of 178 fictional picture books have animals in leading roles (including a few extinct or mythical beasts, such as dinosaurs and dragons). Just forty of them are solely about people, or machines. Even allowing for my parental purchases betraying a biophilic bias, that is an astonishing predominance of the animal kingdom in our stories. If anything, cultural anthropomorphism is intensifying in an era of extinction: traditional fairy-stories are usually led by a human hero, with animals taking up supporting roles, whereas most contemporary classics – Julia Donaldson and Axel Scheffler's *The Gruffalo*, say – are wholly about an animal world.

Of course most animals in children's stories are underdogs – unseen, unheard or unheeded in an adult world – and so these talking animals may simply be substitute children. But I agree with Richard Kerridge that anthropomorphism can help us (and our children) relate to other beings in nature, and pay closer attention to them. It can inspire greater empathy or simple curiosity: my children and I have progressed from reading about Ratty to researching water voles on the internet. I don't notice their sense of a real frog or toad being warped by any literary or cultural teachings. They don't think toads resemble old people or that frogs are foolish and mean. Children are mostly far too attentive to the precise qualities they observe in a real animal; it is adults who are more likely to make lazy connections to fictional ones.

Frog stories may stoke our sympathy but it is only when I hold the real things with my children that I notice the spectacular webbing between the toes of their rear legs, which is the source of their speed and grace when they return to the water. I don't dare squeeze them and so with a wriggle and a slide they force themselves out of my hands and jump – desperately seeking the safety of the pond. Terrified by their short time encased in a warm dry palm (we should have wetted our hands), they disappear into the rich accretions of mud in the bottom of the pond. This sediment swims through your fingers, feels delicious, smells pungent, and gives life to all kinds of amazing creatures.

We put our buckets of chocolate eggs in the shade and take the cheap fishing nets from Nana's shed. Most nature reserve wardens roll their eyes at pond-dipping. Even the boundless enthusiasm of bright young education officers who work tirelessly for wildlife charities wavers in the face of their hundredth pond dip. And yet, lowering a net into murky water and seeing what you come up with is an enduring activity. It is reliably scheduled into school trips to 'engage' children in nature. Pond-dipping is the oldest of chestnuts, but as a brilliant old-school Fleet Street newspaper editor (who, coincidentally, resembled a permanently amused toad) used to say when he dispatched me to write a particularly clichéd story, the thing about old chestnuts is that people love to collect them every year and roast them on the fire. Hoary old chestnuts work. Pond-dipping is a supreme pleasure for people of any age.

Every time we visit Nana, we go pond-dipping. Today we fish well away from the spawn because we don't want to damage it with our prodding nets. The spawn seems less successful if its large clumps are picked up and fall apart, although the feeling of spawn between the fingers is a ravishing sensory gift.

The children plunge their nets into the water and bring up hornwort and mud and a multitude of aquatic life, which they slide into the shallow water of a large plastic tub for our admiration. Some of the freshwater snails are circular coils like a Cumberland sausage, others have perfect seashell-like forms. There are tiny beetles that resemble water-loving woodlice. There are pond-skaters, diminutive invertebrates that zip across the water, and water boatmen, which are more ponderous and move like a rower brandishing a pair of oars. Deeper lie more thrilling finds. We haul up the bulky grey larvae of several dragonflies, sinister bodybuilders-in-miniature brandishing tools for clasping and devouring small prey. The most thrilling find from the muddy deep is a large shiny black beetle that moves with fury through the water and pounds the sides when we release it into our container: a great diving beetle.

Esme picks it up.

'Owwwww!' she screeches and drops it back into the tub. 'It bit me! I hate those beetles.'

There's no trace of a bite mark but no reason to disbelieve Esme. Her eagerness to handle animals has seen her receive a tiny nip from a spider once or twice, but she knows very precisely the most dangerous wild animal in Britain – the adder – and when she asks about others I remind her of the risks posed by domestic dogs rather than the stings of nettles or wasps, which are harmless to the vast majority of us. Esme has picked up bumblebees and not been stung, and remained unreddened after handling caterpillars that supposedly cause a nasty rash. Most natural hazards are overstated.

Our favourite pond resident is a ferocious-looking but less

fearsome figure: the common newt. Scores of newts hang in the water, four legs suspended as if held by an invisible string, the most marvellous dragons in miniature. Each scoop of the fishing net brings up one or two of these languorous, easy-to-catch creatures. The females are gingery brown with a hint of olive; the males are more showy, during the breeding season growing a fine crest that runs the length of their body like a Mohican. Flip them over and their bellies are a vivid leopard print of orange, cream and the darkest of browns. Their delicate-looking feet are translucent and tiny and yet, with a few subtle sculls, capable of holding their bodies motionless and upright in the water.

'Newty newty newt-newt,' sings Esme to herself as she takes each newt from her net and puts it on the grass where it writhes wetly before she plops it into her own plastic measuring jug.

Milly is more tentative. She asks me to dabble my fingers in the muddy residue at the bottom of her net after each fish caught. She is an expert fisher but wants me to pick out her finds. Doesn't she prefer to do it herself? 'I'm not very good at holding them,' she says. 'I'm worried I'll hurt them.' Esme is dexterous with animals but sometimes too confident; Milly, who is quietly self-assured about most things, from meeting new people to dancing at friends' birthday parties, has less faith in her abilities with minibeasts. Eventually she holds one. She does not squirm like a newt, but she still worries about its fragile hands and feet. There may be mutual fear here but both newt and Milly emerge unscathed from their meeting.

Esme has now caught half a dozen of the creatures and is trying to hold them all in her hands. The collective noun, a knot of newts, perfectly describes this writhing mass of wet bodies that glint in the sunshine. I try the knot experience; the newts feel cool, busy and dainty in my palm.

If she had belonged to a previous generation, Esme would have probably kept newts in a tank at home. Now, we worry about the scarcity of such garden treasures. The death of one newt hangs heavy on our consciences. When Esme was a toddler, it was a struggle to persuade her to put them back. We've had to take one or two home a few times to soften the blow of parting, later releasing them into our garden. A couple of years on, Esme wants an array of pets as ardently as ever but has learned to accept that wild animals belong in their natural homes.

As the sun lowers and the wood pigeons start wooing, it's time to go home. Esme picks up each newt. 'I'll miss you,' she says. And kisses it. 'I'll really, really miss you.' This sounds sentimental but she's also no-nonsense. 'Come on,' she prompts as one laggardly newt resists returning to the stirred-up soup of Nana's pond. Each newt gets a personal send-off. 'You're my very favourite,' she says, with showbiz insincerity, to more than one of her cluster.

We have the space in our garden for a pond. Anyone with any outdoor territory has a space for a pond. And anyone with small children shudders at horror stories involving babies and ponds. For a while, Lisa resists my desire for a pond on the rational grounds that plenty of friends with babies visit and we would need to fence off any open water.

Eventually, one afternoon, I dig a pond where we can see it every day, just outside our kitchen window. Lack of time has inhibited my ambitions, so I spend one hour cutting out an oval of turf a metre long and half a metre wide and excavating a small hole. I secure a £3 pond liner down with leftover bricks. It is not pretty.

But this unpromising project rapidly becomes more attractive. I pour rainwater onto the liner and drop in handfuls of pond and duck weed from Nana's pond. Many ornamental pools are fitted with fancy pumps but a wildlife pond doesn't need anything – aquatic plants keep the water clear. I drop in some of Nana's frogspawn too. Within days, creeping buttercup – a pleasant golden flower dismissed as a weed by the gardening establishment – is pushing out tendrils, covering the unsightly exposed liner and bricks at the pond's perimeter. Later, I find frogs and common newts in the garden and within weeks they have discovered this small wet hole in the ground.

We are half a mile from a river and a lovely ribbon of wet valley that becomes the Broads. I periodically see a heron flap overhead en route for these wetlands but our pond is too close to the house to attract such a cautious bird. Besides, another figure stalks its perimeter: Esme.

On garden patrol, Esme can seem more bird of prey than human. She perceives the natural world around her so quickly that fleeting events for us – the flash of a sparrowhawk overhead, for instance – appear as if in slow motion for her. I seldom spot anything before she does. After school, without pausing to change out of her green-and-white checked summer-dress uniform, she runs round the side of the house to grab her blue fishing net from the long grass where she last flung it. A few brutal, deft dredges later and she's holding a frog. Instant gratification. One day, a year after I dug this tiny pond, she catches three frogs, several newts, a pond-skater and a great diving beetle. I'm astounded by the great diving beetle and wonder how it found this tiny wet place. There is only one pond I know of in the neighbourhood, in the high-school gardens, a block away across a main road.

More typically, Esme seeks out her favourite frogs. She extracts them from the dark-grey sludge in her net and, hands cupped, brings them into the house, like a cat with a shrew.

'Guess what I've got?'

'A frog?'

She nods. 'Petal.'

Or 'Billy.'

Or 'Freddie.'

She opens her cradled fingers, fractionally, and a sleek yellow-brown head and two anxious eyes peer out.

She is proud of Freddie because she believes he is the first frog she has caught completely independently. How does she know it's Freddie? 'Oh, he's got spotty legs,' she declares airily.

One evening, after bolting down her tea, she races outside then quickly returns to the kitchen.

'We're now a family of eight,' she announces. I do a quick calculation in my head: five humans plus two guinea-pigs – these we got for the girls' sixth birthday. So there's one newcomer.

Esme holds up a frog. Freddie?

'No, it's Barry,' she says. 'He doesn't have spotty legs.'

Esme can be timid in social situations but she is strikingly assured with wildlife. She savours the freedom of the natural world and has developed a naturalist's skills but also self-esteem. Over time, she has become a deft handler of animals. The price is a few squished creatures along the way – frogs, crickets, snails and the occasional hand-caught small white butterfly – but if we think with our hands, as crafts people often say they do, then we commune with our fellow species through our hands too. Our touch is a form of worship and kinship and care, and the basis for a more fulfilling relationship with other animals.

For the whole of May, the animal that Esme returns to almost every afternoon is Petal. She has identified it as a female after studying the mating frogs in Nana's pond. She knows the males are smaller and thinks they tend to have dark-grey patterns on their lighter-grey bodies. Petal is more yellow-green, and Esme believes that makes her female, and her favourite.

Petal is a peerless pet: as subservient as our guinea-pigs but possessing feet that are a lot less scratchy. I'm a bit puzzled that Petal stays so loyal to the tiny pond, when she is fished out so regularly. The constant dipping is taking its toll on this small pool, which increasingly resembles a bit of recently dredged ditch. The weeds have disappeared. Not much can thrive in a permanent churn of mud and stagnant water. There can't be a newt or any dragonfly larvae left in the sludge. The children's nets catch only small leeches. These are smooth and black and, when momentarily trapped in the net, can wriggle like miniature octopuses through the tiniest of gaps.

Esme strokes Petal's head. A few months before, the frogs were always leaping from her hands. 'Careful,' I shout, as she dives after them; I say careful a lot with Esme, and I shouldn't. 'People are always saying "You'll squish them",' she says as she expertly transports one from the back garden through the house to release it in the pond. 'I hold them with my gentle hands.'

Petal does seem content in Esme's grasp. One afternoon she

shows me Petal by opening her hands wide, and still her pet does not jump free. Does Petal have Stockholm syndrome? Is she tame? Or so traumatised she can't move? Esme croons conversations with her. I see them in the garden hunched together, girl and frog, and wonder what they are communicating, what miracle of childhood I have grown away from for ever.

I'm working in my study when I hear a wail from downstairs. It's that time of day. The children are tired after school, and hungry before tea. The sobbing is Esme. I can't quite tell if it's a squabble or a banged knee, but Lisa is comforting her. I carry on working. Some minutes later my door opens. Esme is red-eyed, her cheeks rendered matt by dried tears.

'Petal's dead.'

Heaving, racking, shuddering sobs.

Has our little wildlife pond become a death trap? There's a rising toll of mysterious fatalities. A few days before, Esme found a dried frog on the lawn. It was as thin as newspaper and smelt like a long-dead fish. The day before, she found another expired frog while fishing in the pond. Now this. A third. I can't help speculating that excessive squeezing was the cause of death.

How do you know it's Petal?

'Her colour.'

And is she definitely dead?

'She had stuff coming from her mouth.'

I agree to come downstairs. 'After tea you can make a gravestone and we can bury her.' This consoles her.

We search the garden for a memorial and choose an offcut of wood from the woodpile. 'I'll get a Sharpie,' says Esme with the brand-awareness of the modern child. I didn't even know she had one.

In green Sharpie, she writes:

grav for Petl
my Pet frog.
I Love her
Esme

And finishes with an emoji: a face with a down-turned mouth.

We look at Petl. I've been wondering if it's yesterday's dead frog, which Esme let sink back into the pond goo. But it does look like Petal. We choose a patch of turf near the water that this frog loyally refused to leave, probably to the detriment of her health. Esme doesn't want to touch her. 'She stinks,' she says unsentimentally but not harshly. I lever up the turf with a spade and place Petal below ground and we say our goodbyes.

Later that year, after much negotiation with Lisa, I dig a second, larger, oval pond within a couple of metres of our little one. I buy marsh marigold and yellow flag iris, and line the edge with turf rather than bricks. Into this we pour more frogspawn and weed from Nana's pond. The pond is soon a meeting place for the entire garden's wildlife, including Esme. Blackbirds and sparrows bathe in it. Wood pigeons greedily glug back the water. Common darters flit over.

By June, the frogs are spending more time in the long grass that has grown up around both ponds. There's a heatwave, but when we weave our fingers into the roots of the grass we find them damp and cool. The grasses bloom with sheaths of peppermint seeds. Ted collects the seeds in a little plastic tub and gives them to me as a Father's Day present. Stripping a grass-head of its seeds, and feeling them scatter drily in your palm, is a sensory pleasure I'd forgotten from childhood.

The bigger pond is not an unequivocal triumph during the heatwave. My sole yellow flag iris dies. Then two more dead frogs appear, floating, face down in the pond like murder victims. Soon afterwards, we receive a surprising visitor. The most surprising thing is that I spot it before the children. A head glides across the pond. I idly follow it as I clear tea from the kitchen table. I assume the head is a frog's. But it keeps sliding out of the water. A newt. But then the head keeps coming. What? A snake. A snake in the pond.

'Grass snake in the pond!' I yell.

At least, I think it is.

Ted, Esme and I hurtle out of the door and round to the pond. Nothing. No sign. I gingerly part the grass with my hands. Ted looks keenly. Esme stomps about. I tell her it's only a little snake, and we mustn't tread on it.

Snakes have never been part of my natural experience. I can count on the fingers of one hand the number of grass snakes and adders I've seen in my whole life. My grandma once showed me the grass snakes that writhed over the warm clippings on her compost heap. She seemed to conjure nature out of nowhere. Rather like Esme, in fact. Her garden, beside a wood above Lake Windermere in the Lake District, was full of improbable wildlife, from red squirrels to roe deer. Those fat, olive-coloured snakes of Grandma's seemed huge to me as a child.

This snake is smaller and has vanished. Then I glance back at the pond. There it is. Hiding under a fringe of grass overhanging the water. Ted and Esme zoom in and loom over it, and this small reptile whips from one end of the pond to the other, seeking an escape. We draw back, and let it creep out and slip through the grass like liquid, disappearing into the bottom of the snowberry hedge.

'We must go and hunt for its nest,' says Esme decisively. I persuade her to let the snake rest in peace.

On another hot day two weeks later, I glance out of the kitchen window and see the snake in the pond again. I call Milly, Esme and Ted and we watch it from the window. We have a fine view. It has a pursed expression on its face as if set in disapproval, and a dainty collar of black and white around its green neck. Definitely a grass snake.

I lift the children up so they can see it better. Esme has vanished. Suddenly she appears outside the kitchen window, darting, reaching. She's grabbed the snake. She is holding it up. I run out of the door and round the corner. Esme is caressing the snake, utterly delighted, its tail wrapped around her wrist. I'm disconcerted by what she's done – by her confidence, her skill, her fearlessness. The snake seems fine, thank goodness, and emits a pungent smell as a deterrent. 'Rotten onions,' says Esme with a child's typical precision.

After we've admired it, she releases it into the pond and it slides away, rapidly. As it flees us, it causes total panic for one frog, caught by surprise: it leaps away from the disappearing snake in terror. We look online and decide it is not a baby but a male, which are markedly smaller than the females. We hope there's a nest somewhere. And we hope we haven't scared the snake away from our pond. For the world of snakes has gained a fan for life.

During the weeks when portly black tadpoles still sunbathe in the shallows, Ted and I spot our first froglet in the pond. Esme may have annexed wildlife for her identity, but Ted is growing into an outdoor person too. Attending Dandelion nursery has made him noticeably more independent than he was before. He is far braver than I was as a child about heights, fearless about climbing trees, and completely careless of rain or other unfavourable weather.

When he cried as a baby, I would take him outside and wander around talking to him about the trees or the birds, occasionally pointing to this movement or that. He would always calm down. My parents used to place my crying sister under the boughs of a weeping willow. So many people and cultures use similar tactics. Mohawk mothers commonly take their crying babies outside and whisper to them, pointing at something in the distance. Traditional techniques for soothing babies trickle into modern technology too: the internet is awash with natural-sound files, such as babbling brooks or birdsong to pacify small children.

When Ted was eight months old and I took Milly and Esme to the cemetery behind our old house, he bounced along in the carrier, facing outwards, and joined me picking blackberries. To this day he remains keen to pick berries. Formative experiences resonate throughout our lives.

Ted expertly scoops up the first froglet before I see it. This minuscule amphibian is beautiful, a tiny scale model of a frog, complete with olive skin delicately speckled with black. Its hands and feet look too small to be real. If they were made of plastic or china or even metal they would snap off instantly, but the froglet is fine in Ted's hands. We begin a collection.

'Come here Froggy,' says Ted in his falsetto, and scoops up another. He collects six of the tiny jumping creatures and is very proud. He wants them as pets and I anticipate problems; he's recently kept a ladybird in a jam jar for an inhumane two days, and imprisoned a cricket too. But no, I explain where they need to be, and Ted is content. Letting them go into the pond is a pleasure too: the water seems to animate and frame their movements as they swim away on a tidy breaststroke.

I let Ted do some dipping in our big pond, as a treat. In four or five sweeps of the net he catches pond snails, skaters, water boatmen and, best of all, another great diving beetle. 'That's the one that bit Esme,' he says, remembering our pond-dipping session at Nana's at Easter. He has only seen a diving beetle once before in his life. We humans have an impressive aptitude for precise observation, just below the surface and ready to be deployed again, should we ever need to hunt and gather our own food.

One hot summer's day, Esme is busy patrolling the Maze when she shouts for me, urgently. Somehow, buried in the parched grass, she's found a tiny dark-grey snake, the thickness and length of a biro. She hasn't grabbed it, as normal, because she is not yet sure if it's a grass snake or an adder. Smart. We look closely, take our time. There, around its neck, is a looping pattern of yellowy-green – it's a baby grass snake. Esme picks it up.

It feels smooth and cool on her fingers, and it seeks out each one, coiling around them, twisting between.

'Can I keep it as a pet?'

'Ezzie, it's a wild animal, we don't really know exactly what it eats. And it belongs here, in the garden.' Again, I'm braced for a tussle, but like Ted she's unexpectedly accepting.

We walk round to the pond, taking turns to hold it. I understand why Esme does not want to let go. There's something magical about an animal so small and neat and self-contained. Mammals seem messy and chaotic in comparison. The baby snake is tasting the air, flicking its tongue, working out what Esme's hands are, and why it is confined in them.

After a couple of minutes that pass slowly, she kneels and releases it into the pond. The creature snakes off through the water, figure-of-eighting across the surface, elegant and free.

6

A Dandelion Summer

'How to begin to educate a child. First rule, leave him alone.
Second rule, leave him alone. Third rule, leave him alone.
That is the whole beginning.'

D.H. Lawrence

Barley ripples in fields like an inland ocean. On Dandelion's meadow, stray fronds of barley wave in warm eddies beside the slender clubs of grass seedheads. Hops rampage in the hedgerow, the sallow leaves have darkened and shady spots deepened, rich in possibilities for dens. In the garden, maize and runner beans stretch towards the sun and newly planted fruit trees wilt in the dry. The dirt pathways are dusty grey and almost as unforgiving as concrete. Every child is slathered in suncream and wears a sunhat with a rear flap to cover the back of their neck. The flaps bounce as the children run.

The chickens own the place now. Daisy and Feather bustle around, constantly on the move, much like the children, scraping their feet back and forth in a constant search for little insects, bugs and grubs. They've become cockier, and have to be shooed into their house before lunch because they've taken to strutting around the table to cadge food or peck a child's boot. The children are established as well. Most have been here for nearly a year; many seem ready for school. My heart sinks a little to think of these characters so confined.

Ruby, who is nearly five, is the matriarch of Dandelion. She has dark hair and might have been called a tomboy in an earlier time. She has been here since she was two and knows all the Dandelion rules but doesn't always listen to teachers who haven't been here as long as she has. The other children listen to her, though, and obey if she instructs them to do one of the regular chores.

Ruby shares Esme's fascination with other forms of life and I obediently follow her around the site lifting logs so she can acquire what she calls 'a collection' of woodlice. She holds them in the cage of her right hand and says they tickle. She opens her hand a crack, and there are six inside, including several that are the biggest I have ever seen.

Her deftness with animals is a source of pride. 'I'm the chicken whisperer,' she says – a title casually bestowed upon her by Hayley. Ruby is the only child who can pick up Daisy. She holds her adroitly, preventing her wings from flapping and keeping her calm. Then she marches around, other children trailing behind to beg a chicken cuddle. Ruby explains that she is gentle with Daisy because 'she's special and she's private'. One day, Ruby finds an egg, laid outside their cage in straw littered by the bales. Later, she is uncharacteristically tearful. Why are you crying? asks one of the teachers. 'I want to be a chicken,' says Ruby. Why? 'I just want to lay an egg,' she sobs.

'Deers' ears!' shout Emma and Hayley when they have an announcement to make. The children learn to pause wherever they are, and cup their hands to their ears. Then it's tidy-up time, when they move through the site like a small murmuration of starlings, pecking and picking, sorting and straightening. Only then do I realise what carnage they've created in a couple of hours, and how this level of creative mess could never be tolerated inside. Outside, however, it is tolerable, and the starlings soon tidy it up.

Just before lunch, there's a session in front of the 'phonics wall', which is where letters are written on a chalk board fixed to the side of a garden shed. For this, Emma has invented a song which she and the children perform to the tune of 'The Time Warp':

It's just a word to the left
And a word to the rii-iiiiight
It's a word on a page
And a word out of sii-iiiiight
It's the Phonics Wall
Where you read and write your own nay-aaaaame
Let's. Do. The Phonics Wall. Again.

Emma is delightfully am-dram and her sense of humour is absurdist. She also plays the straight person to Hayley's satirical dry wit. So much of their work is deadly serious; the responsibilities on their shoulders are enormous, and I notice how almost every parent – including me – is constantly grabbing them to talk about this or that minor developmental worry, as if their child is their only pupil. Every teacher will recognise this myopic parental pressure, but not many also run the school they work in as their own start-up. As the year passes, I notice how hard Emma and Hayley work. They have no administrative help, they answer emails all hours; and they are constantly repairing their outdoor site themselves. Despite – or perhaps because of – these burdens, they are a comedic double act when they work together with the children. They make each other laugh, constantly.

'I had to sing then, and I was a bit out of tune,' says Emma to everyone after she performs a song from a picture book.

'It *was* a bit embarrassing,' chips in Hayley.

'Have you chosen the right word?' asks Emma.

'Wait a minute, I'll just spell-check it,' says Hayley, pretending to glance down at the tablet in her hand. She pauses. 'Yes,' she says, deadpan. 'That's the right word.'

On another occasion, they joke about eating the children, and the children join in the banter, threatening to eat Emma and Hayley instead.

'You wouldn't want to eat me, look how dirty I am,' says Hayley, pointing at her legs – she's wearing shorts and today has mud on her knees.

'We'll baste you first, you'll be fine,' says Emma quickly.

'We've spent a lot of time in hotels in beds next to each other, working,' reveals Hayley when I ask how they set up Dandelion. At first there was the relentless training, fact-finding missions, and research trips away. 'We're like Morecambe and Wise when we're working together, like a little old couple.'

Dandelion began one summer's day in the deep shade of the flowering magnolia tree in the garden behind Emma's modest semi-detached house in the Norfolk countryside. She had grown up in Wales, moved to Norfolk and taught reception classes at a rural primary school for twenty years. There was one boy who struggled at school but loved tying knots. 'Me and the children would just step over the fact that he'd tied all the chairs, all the tables, all the doors. He tied everything together because he was into knots,' she says. Emma allowed him to learn by following his own interests. It worked. She got away with it, she thinks, because it was a small rural school and the local education authority had forgotten about them.

Parents told her it worked too. They came from miles around to put their children into her school. One parent was Hayley. 'Hayley came in with Jens, her husband. I remember thinking, you are both really tall and really beautiful, like giraffes,' says Emma. Hayley began to work as a teaching assistant at Emma's school and they became friends, and played with their children together in the evenings. 'We must have talked about our beliefs about education before, but I can just remember that conversation under the magnolia tree – it's all going wrong, and this is where it should be, and this is what it should look like.'

By this time, Emma had quit her job. She disliked the way her school was following national trends: a myopic focus on the core National Curriculum, testing, rote learning. Five-year-olds in Year 1 were tested in phonics. One morning when making Christmas cards with her class, she was told she must do spelling and grammar instead. 'No, clearly you can do just as much spelling and grammar when you're writing Christmas cards or Diwali cards,' says Emma.

Hayley grew up in Leicester and began her adult life by dropping out of university because she wanted to explore the world. She tried many different jobs – pubs, restaurants, cleaning, psychiatric nursing assistant, teaching assistant. 'There aren't many sectors I haven't worked in,' she says, typically poker-faced. 'Apart from the sex trade.'

Whatever job she did, she always ended up working with children, in schools and nurseries. She and her husband moved to Norfolk because their youngest daughter suffered from terrible eczema, and this was eased by being close to the sea. After she met Emma, she studied for an Open University degree and qualified as a teacher. She first taught at a city school where there were seven hundred children. The head teacher didn't know the children's names and Hayley didn't know all the staff. The school had a traffic-light system to measure progress (green = good, red = bad), and one year Hayley got hauled into the head's office to be interrogated about why a little girl in her class had not moved from 'red'. 'I said, "Well, that's because you don't have a place on your grid that says, 'no longer sits under the table miaowing like a cat'." That's what she did when she first came to me. By the end of the year, she was sitting *at* the table. But they didn't want to know about that.'

Hayley took a post at a smaller school. There were still thirty to a class but fewer pupils overall, and everyone knew each other. She found it more creative and nurturing. The head supported her wish to train in Philosophy for Children, known by acronym-loving educationalists as P4C, and Hayley introduced it into her classes. The schools inspector loved her philosophy class and the school was rated 'Outstanding' – top marks – by Ofsted. The head allowed staff to be creative and teach via topics.

But with the 'Outstanding' rating came new pressure to maintain it. In 2010 the ripples from the change of government from Labour to the Coalition, bringing a Conservative Education Secretary determined to re-establish more 'traditional' teaching, were felt in Hayley's village school. 'We were told that the creative curriculum had gone out of the window and so now our teaching must be more fact-based and we had to teach Ancient Greece in Year 3,' says Hayley. 'Suddenly those things that you love, like philosophy, get squished. I just don't get this system today. And if it's crushing me creatively and spiritually, what's it doing to these children who are full of ideas, absolutely jam-packed with hopes and dreams? And all we're doing is saying, "Hmmmm, you're rubbish at maths."'

Hayley had developed the philosophy as far as she could in the state system. (She knew she got bored easily. 'I found an old report from primary school – "Hayley has lots of ideas. She doesn't always see them through." That was really funny. I needed a creative outlet. And I do like a challenge.') Typically, neither she nor Emma lays claim to the original idea for Dandelion: they say it evolved in conversation. They saw a chink in the education system: what is called the 'Early Years' (before five-year-olds join Year 1 in school) offered a space where they could teach in a way they believed in: nurturing confidence, facilitating emotional development, giving pre-school children the freedom to learn.

They were both still working full-time, and spending their weekends inventing a school from scratch. They cite influences from many schooling philosophies – Reggio Emilia, Rudolf Steiner, Montessori, Forest School – but they are both doers, and rather than following a prescribed ideology they created something new that combined Emma's interest in Forest School with Hayley's passion for philosophy. Hayley says Steiner and Montessori settings are 'fantastic', but she thinks their ideas 'haven't evolved to meet the needs of today's children'. Nor has the state system. 'We really need to be thinking about children's mental health and understanding the world as it is today, outside of all the loveliness that we create in our Montessori, our Steiner, our Dandelion.'

They found a small field owned by a primary school and set up Dandelion. 'The local authority said, "Nice idea but nobody will come",' says Hayley. Council experts thought parents wouldn't understand their concept. And there were a million tiny bureaucratic obstacles: for instance, inspectors, they warned, would want to know how the children were going to step up into the composting toilet. At first, Ofsted ruled they could only open for a few hours each week. Emma and Hayley wasted most of their business loan on advertising that brought no inquiries at all. Emma's partner, Tony, who is also a Forest School practitioner, warned them they had bought too many plastic toys. 'It felt like we had to completely rethink everything,' says Emma, 'moving from a classroom that's very safe and static and regimented, to completely outside, and completely following the children. In a way, it's a huge joy. You're absolutely driven by what the children need and what they want.'

Ofsted-related delays meant they opened Dandelion's doors at the worst time of year: midwinter. A handful of children turned up at their dark and boggy field. Each morning, Emma and Hayley arrived at 6 a.m., drained the water out of their bell tent – their only shelter – and lit the fire. Understanding the practicalities of working outdoors was a huge learning curve, says Hayley. At first, they put everything inside a shed each night. They realised they needed fewer toys and more real objects, which they could leave outside and replace with more charity shop items when they weathered.

I was one of many parents who showed up for an open day one idyllic autumn morning, woodsmoke drifting across the site, Emma cooking dampers on the fire. Slowly, word spread; Emma and Hayley built a devoted fanbase. 'Every time somebody signed up we thought, wow, we can't believe this,' says Emma. Some parents drove their children forty minutes from Norwich to attend.

After a year at their first site, they found their Marsham base, which was closer to Norwich and so more easily accessible – for us too. We thought it was too late for Milly and Esme because they were starting in reception, but we signed Ted up. I followed Ted, and later, going against convention, Esme and then Milly began their Dandelion experiences.

Working at Dandelion repeatedly reminds me of the simple vitality of being outdoors, which I expected. But I was not expecting to be shown how to be a better parent. Dandelion sets boundaries and maintains discipline in an eye-opening way. Staff never, or almost never, say 'No' or 'Don't do that.' I struggle with the latter in particular. 'Don—' I repeatedly find myself starting, and stopping, rendered inarticulate by such a simple principle. Staff don't say 'naughty' and never say 'good boy' or 'good girl', or even 'good job' either. 'Good girl!' spits Hayley. 'I wouldn't say that to my dog.'

I'm a parent of the praise-them generation and at first I'm forever saying 'Well done' and 'Good work' to the Dandelions, as I do with my own children. Hayley pulls me aside and explains how such general comments are unhelpful. I must be more specific. 'I like the way you've built that wall' is just about acceptable, but more neutral, descriptive comments are better: 'You've overlapped the bricks in that wall so it will be strong.'

I'm struck by the creativity I encounter at Dandelion, in the teaching and in the children too. The technological magazine *Wired* confounded expectations a few years back when it named the best toy in the world as the stick. It's a practical tool and a magic wand for the imagination, a 'loose part' with no designated role, and so it can be adapted to almost any.

There's a game that Emma and Hayley sometimes play where they ask the children to collect a stick, gather around, and tell everyone what their stick *really* is.

'This is not a stick, this is a crutch for an elf.'

'This is not a stick, it's got zombies' skin on it,' says Luka.

'This is not a stick, it's a giraffe's false neck,' says Alfie.

'This is not a stick, this is a snowy stick, it can make it snow,' says Maisie.

'This is not a stick, it's a sword,' says Seb.

'This is not a stick, it's a man's leg, a real leg, he's died,' says Hayden.

'This is not a stick, this is a lamb's leg,' says Willow.

'This is not a stick, this is a witch's stick – it will fly,' says Rex.

The trouble with imagining alternative uses for sticks is that most frequently a four-year-old boy will decide that this is not a stick – this is a gun. Or a sword.

'Do you want to collect a stick?' asks James when we are playing. 'I have a big stick collection at home. They are weapons. Did you know I went hunting in Portugal? I shot a wolf and we took the skin, and then we could eat the animals that the wolf had been eating.' What did James eat? 'The wolf meat.'

For the boys, sticks are indeed mostly to be pointed and fired. Dandelion has a rule: no gunfire, not even pretend guns. Bows and arrows? Preferable, but not ideal. Swords? Just about retro enough to be OK, as long as they are held low and not wielded with force. But disarmament is a losing battle with most of the boys. They love shooting me dead. They adore watching me die. Power and mastery are exhilarating for small lives that have so little. And they are as reluctant to put down their weapons as a doomsday prepper. I search for a compromise: how about a stick that fires ice? Or lava? Eventually I shift the play from shooting to a chasing game called shark tag. But Rex continues to fire his stick at me. 'We are fighting-fish,' he declares. I admire his tenacity.

On another occasion, I fail to enforce the no-guns and stick-pointing-downwards rules. Peaceable Hayden aims his gun, bazooka-style, at a passing helicopter. Eventually Emma has a little 'chitty-chatty' with the gun-toters, who include one gun-toting girl. Emma and Hayley hear about one nursery that introduced a gun licence, which children had to obtain for their imaginary guns. If a child broke the rules governing use – no firing at other children, for instance – their licence would be revoked.

The Dandelion teachers pay attention to the children's chat about guns because that tells them a lot about home life – for instance, if they are playing age-inappropriate computer games. If they persist with gun games at nursery, Emma and Hayley instigate a philosophical discussion about the proper uses of guns: 'The children might say, "We'll use them to kill animals for food",' says Hayley. 'OK, well, is there another way we can kill animals for food? We could have a spear, we could create a trap.'

I never hear a teacher's raised voice during a year at Dandelion, but one summer's day I listen to Hayley reprimanding a six-year-old boy, who is home-schooled and struggles to integrate himself with Dandelion's routines. 'Rex, you are making the wrong choice,' she says. 'Don't keep saying sorry. Think about making the right choice.' Discipline at Dandelion is enforced by encouraging children to reflect upon their behaviour and work out for themselves the consequences of their actions, what choices they have, and why they would be wise, sometimes, to do things differently. It is what psychologists in other spheres call a person-centred approach, and it's amazing how very young children quickly work things out for themselves. What sounds wishy-washy in theory is uncompromising in practice.

Gentle-mannered Emma is often called upon to conduct chitty-chatties with challenging boys. One boy, Cole, is a little sprite, with a dainty square face, piercing blue eyes and a pierced ear. He looks old beyond his years, like a diminutive eighteen-year-old, and I can almost imagine him astride a motorbike. He's restless, won't stop, can't concentrate, struggles to talk, and has grave difficulty following the rules, but when his little face cracks into a smile it's a ray of sunshine. He's as graceful as a darting hare, moves through Dandelion like mercury, and takes up a lot of Emma and Hayley's time. Emma is constantly talking things through, hugging him so a confrontation doesn't become upsetting, and relentlessly reinforcing his good behaviour.

One of Dandelion's little routines is putting a child's name to the tune of 'Celebrate Good Times': singing 'Celebrate Cole – what did you do?' when Cole does something good. He grins. He performs fine feats of tool-work with proper grownup tools, as well as casual acts of astounding physical agility. But I rather fear for Cole. He loves Dandelion and yet it's hard to see how he can thrive at a test-obsessed, bums-on-seats primary school.

At Dandelion, the most structured learning of the day comes at lunchtime, when the older children sit around a long low table, beneath a tarpaulin to keep off the rain, and eat their packed lunches. At a conventional setting, lunch is a break for the adults, who stand back and talk to each other. 'What a wasted opportunity,' says Hayley. 'There's no discussion about the food that they're eating and what it does to your body, no discussion about "Oh there's a lot of packaging in your lunch today, let's talk about the environment."' At Dandelion, the adults sit down with the children, like at an idealised family meal.

The children's boxes and bags contain no conventionally packaged treats because us parents have been cowed into withholding crisps and chocolate from the packed lunches. Hayley and Emma have never banned junk food but they did send an email or two about it, and used to return crisps and chocolate uneaten. So now conscience-pricked parents supply their offspring with sandwiches or flasks of warm pasta, and fruit in washable plastic tubs. The biggest treat is a yoghurt or a small box of raisins. During one summer lunch, some months before the popular outcry about plastic caused by Sir David Attenborough's *Blue Planet II* television series, with characteristic fearlessness Hayley and Emma go on the warpath about the plastic around the children's lunches. There is very little single-use plastic per child, but they gather it up, take a photo and publish it on their Facebook page, seeking to shame parents into changing their habits.

'How much of our rubbish will go into the sea?' Hayley asks the children. They already know all about turtles getting tangled in plastic.

'I would be really sad if a turtle came in my living room and threw some rubbish on the floor,' she says. 'I'd chase after him.'

She pauses, with immaculate comic timing.

'I wouldn't have to run very fast.'

The children are always told to eat their carbohydrates first. 'Why?' asks Hayley, who has that teacherly indefatigability towards questions. The children know the answer: carbohydrates give them energy.

When the eating slows, she starts their Philosophy for Children session. Dandelion has the necessary kitemark to practise P4C. Like so much at the nursery, it's a revelation.

'Put your thinking caps on,' says Hayley, twisting and pulling a floppy green hat firmly over her buoyant curls. 'My ideas are so big today I can hardly get my hat on. Or maybe it's just my hair.'

'What's your name again?' asks James.

'James, you've been coming here for two years. Give him a clue,' says Hayley to the rest of the table.

'Huh-huh-huh,' say the group, on cue, revealing their knowledge of phonics.

Hayley turns to James again. 'Right then, Bernard,' she nods.

She begins by getting the children to list the five rules of philosophy. (The fewer rules, the better, she says. 'How many rules are there in school where you don't really know why there's that rule, but you know you've broken it and you're not sure why?')

The children know them all and list them: listen to whoever is talking, look at whoever is talking, think about each idea, care for others and for yourself, and be respectful of others and other views. 'We can't say "Ha ha, that's a silly idea",' says Ruby. I have heard Ted make exactly the same declaration. It was one of the first new things I noticed him saying when he started at Dandelion.

Hayley announces that the site was broken into over the weekend, and the thieves (teenagers, they think) wrote rude words, broke a window and stole the best things they could find – some permanent-marker pens.

Then she asks: 'Is it ever OK to steal?'

The children take it in turns to talk, and each speaker nominates the next. They all say that it is wrong to steal.

'But what if you need to steal a ladder to rescue a friend stuck on a roof?' she asks. A couple of children now waver, and say that in certain circumstances it might be OK to steal. The crucial word is 'because': they are learning to give reasons. Hayley excels at the most important skill when facilitating these philosophical discussions: remaining poker-faced. The conversation leader must respond neither negatively nor positively to any comment, but simply repeat the child's answer. A positive response, even an 'mmmm' of surprise or a nod of encouragement, signals the 'right' answer to a child, when there is no right answer.

Over the year, I feel fortunate to listen to Hayley's philosophy sessions. She has a genius for it. She thinks her natural tendency is to go 'pick, pick, pick – poke, poke, poke' towards other people's statements. I tell her she is so quick-witted. 'My husband would say "challenging",' she laughs.

She fell in love with Philosophy for Children 'because it levels the playing field', she says. 'If you are a child with additional needs, who might be dyslexic, academically you could struggle, but in philosophy it is not about your ability to write or to multiply, it's just about your ideas. It shows children who struggle and children who don't that actually we've all got valid ideas, and just because we can't write our idea down doesn't mean we're not capable of deeper thought than a child who is incredibly gifted at writing.' She strongly disagrees with that old cliché that children are sponges who soak things up. 'That means we have to fill them with something – what we think they need to know, or what they should be good at. In my mind, education is extraction – extracting the strengths of the children, drawing out what's already in them or helping them grow what's already in them. Not squeezing them.'

Philosophy for Children has been around since the 1960s but it has not had the impact of Forest School. Very few nurseries use it. Hayley believes it helps children understand themselves better and develop empathic skills long before the learning manuals predict. 'Who was it who said, "You don't know what you think until you say what you think"? The children can learn about each other, themselves, the world around them. They develop all the skills they need to become respectful and tolerant and sympathetic and empathetic.' (I'm very struck by the impact of Dandelion on my children's ability to respect others and their expectation that others will respect them. Aged five, Ted returns home from his mainstream school one day devastated because, he says, when he tried to explain something to a teacher, she 'talked over me'.)

Hayley tells me that one of the nicest things a parent ever said to her was how much confidence she had given her son. And yet the state school system's constant testing of pupils is, for her, teaching them to fail and generating anxiety and mental health problems in a whole generation. This belief is borne out by an ugly rash of data.

But Hayley's convictions are also rooted in personal distress, 'seeing what the school system did' to her youngest daughter. 'She was incredibly creative, and gifted and talented in sport – sprinting and gymnastics. And then she went to high school and she wasn't particularly good at maths and they hammered her and hammered her. She was given extra lessons, sessions in the holidays, put in bottom sets where other children's behaviour was poor. It completely crushed her.' Hayley's daughter is now in her twenties but ever since high school has struggled with social anxiety and painful eczema. 'At the same time, I was working in primary schools and I could see it coming – watching those children "failing" and seeing their self-esteem plummeting and anxiety growing. I thought there was a better way to educate children.'

Emma is particularly interested in raising girls and boys as equals. The schools system, and wider society, are failing girls badly. We know from a 2018 government survey that almost one in four girls aged between seventeen and nineteen in England suffers from a diagnosed mental disorder, with half of those girls saying they have self-harmed or attempted suicide. Emma worries about what happens to her Dandelion girls when they enter the mainstream school.

'We hand over these incredibly strong girls who know that they can climb trees, use tools and move heavy things. The children go to philosophy, so they've got a voice, they are used to speaking, they are used to being heard, and they are going to go to a school where people may not be so mindful. Those girls are going to become what our society sees as girls, rather than human beings who are powerful and resilient and vocal. As a society, we're closing girls down. I wouldn't want to be a teenage girl nowadays. I want them to be able to say, "I'm a girl and I'm strong," and once they reach fifteen or sixteen, or even eleven, you also want them to say, "Don't touch me because I'm going to rip your head off." You want them to be safe and strong. Because a lot of girls aren't safe and strong.'

The site's scents in summer are richer, the plume of woodsmoke more delicious. We have had months of dry weather. The rain, when it comes, turns torrential. Thunder and lightning. None of the children appear scared but, for the first time since I begin volunteering, we retreat to the yurt. It's warm from the woodburner and humid from the wet children. Everyone must be quiet in the yurt; if they shout they have to go outside again. Mostly we read stories but Ruby plays 'cats' on the mat by the fire.

Outside, dusty Dandelion is thoroughly dampened. The fruit trees look happier, and in no time a handful of sour blackcurrants ripen on a stunted bush. The children put on their waterproof suits, and the creation of an enormous muddy puddle becomes the defining activity of the day. A jacuzzi-sized hole in the ground is filled with pails of water. When one or two children hit upon an irresistible idea such as this, the others are attracted like filings to a magnet; newcomers usually add their own flourish or sideshow to the play.

The popularity of Peppa Pig, the cartoon piglet who makes great play of donning her yellow wellies and jumping in puddles with the approval of both parents, has made muddy-puddle fun a protean activity that most people encourage. It's quite appealing, to express our inner pig. The children spend ages mixing the mud in mugs, pans and buckets or shaping it like clay with wooden spoons, ladles and spatulas. Joe and Herbie want to throw mud pies at each other, but throwing is forbidden. Another boy, who struggles to play with the others, starts kicking the mud. This is satisfying. Splats fire in all directions and cover other children and me. This boy needs a little chitty-chatty. But the mud loosens things up. James, who is ethereal and delicate and prone to grave announcements about his ill-health, is beaming. 'I've got mud on my face,' he says. 'Mummy will be so pleased.'

It is overcast and cool but no one wants to take refuge in the yurt again. The rain returns towards the end of the day, just when Emma has handed out big sheets of paper and paints to encourage a calmer activity. We have the three primary colours, red, yellow and blue, and each child is given a small piece of waste wood for a palette. We retreat under an old parachute, which is also coloured red, yellow and blue, and sit on straw to paint. Drops pitter on the parachute and drip onto some nearby nettles, which dance with ants busy 'milking' greenflies. A lark sings in the distance. Summer term is at an end.

7

The Joy of Caterpillars

'A child's mind is constellated with animals as the night is with stars.'

Jay Griffiths

Esme's eyes are fixed on a small rabbit, lolloping quietly between tufts of marram grass. She loves to shimmy down and, commando-style, creep up on them. She wants to catch one, and keep it as a pet. But rabbits are not nearly as common in the countryside as they were.

Crawling, she's three metres away when the rabbit skips off. Overhead, a big bird takes fright when it sees us, and Esme is distracted. 'That's a herring!' she exclaims, animated. 'That big seagull, it was a herring!' She means heron.

I carry the same field-guide to butterflies I used when I was a child in the 1980s. On excursions like this I would trot behind my dad, but Esme races ahead, doubling back to report her finds.

'I've seen a coloured beetle, and a peacock over there.'

Wings closed, black outline like a shark's fin rising from a grey-green carpet of crunchy lichen, the peacock butterfly is basking in the sunshine. Esme inches forward, having mastered the slow approach required to get really close to butterflies. She can almost touch it, but then it zooms off, flashing maroon velvet wings and blue eye-spots. We retreat and the butterfly loops around and returns to its favoured spot. She pencils a tick beside its page in the guidebook.

It is a fine summer's day and I've taken Esme to the warm, thyme-scented tawny sand dunes where I first fell in love with butterflies. The drive down the track to the pine woods where the north Norfolk coast turns south into the Wash feels like we are leaving the mainland behind and entering an almost-island. Holme Dunes would have become a beach suburb like Skegness had an interwar developer not run out of money. Later, the land was requisitioned for military training during the Second World War. Bunkers, and the occasional unexploded bomb from firing practice, are periodically exposed on the sands. In 1965 the Norfolk Wildlife Trust bought 526 acres, and the dunes, salt marsh, pine woods and grazing meadows became a nature reserve. With sea to the north and west, Holme is first landfall in autumn for many wind-blown migrating birds, who find sanctuary in the woods and food among the silver-leaved sea buckthorn with its rash of orange berries.

Every summer for most of the 1980s my parents, sister and I would spend our two-week summer holiday in a flat inside the crumbling Edwardian house that is now the reserve's HQ. Holme is a heartland for me, a cherished place of deep memories where I made dams on the beach with my sister, where I learned to catch a ball, where I witnessed a heron's titanic struggle with an eel; and where I first went, with my dad, in search of butter-flies. Our lunchtime foray together to look for the then rare brown argus sparked a lifelong love of butterflies. They were my conduit into the natural world, and a rewarding source of companionship with Dad that we still reprise. Holme is special, and I rarely come back, in part because it exerts such a pull on my heart and these memories can be disorientating.

Esme is more outwardly ardent about butterflies than I was. She sensed at an early age they were of particular interest to me, and has made this interest her own. Just as they did for me and my dad, so they allow Esme and me to spend a bit of time together alone. All children yearn for parental attention and a respite from sibling rivalry, and Esme visibly blooms when she has an adult to herself. Most of the time, we go out as a family but we try to spend some one-on-one time with all three children. Today it is just me and Esme.

The air smells of warm pine and fresh salt. Most birdwatchers head to the landward side of the track, where wooden hides overlook scrapes of shallow water on the meadows. Snug and facing south, these hides turn their dark slits inland, towards gently rising terrain and the flint tower of Holme village church. Curlew probe the mud and avocet sweep their bills through the water, and smaller waders, redshank and greenshank, pick-pick at the mud for food. Over the meadows comes frequently a quartering barn owl or marsh harrier, flying low and very deliberately into the wind so as to slow its aerial survey of supper in the reedbeds.

We take a small path along the sheltered dune slacks, where dainty flowers, knotted pearlwort and bird's-foot trefoil, grow among a low sward. A skylark sings in the breeze above our heads and there's the melodic pee-witting of a lapwing above the meadow, a sound that swoops like the bird. At our feet, sand wasps, neatly waisted black insects, excavate holes in the dunes into which they insert their prey.

'Meet you at the top of the dunes by the lane I've found!' Laughing, Esme's gone. She loves the space of the dunes, their little pathways, how rapidly she can lose sight of an adult. She's pushing at boundaries now, yearning for more freedom. Out-of-sight is delicious.

'I've seen a butterfly!' she calls from a distance. 'There, look, on that dandelion.'

A white one. A green-veined white.

'Knew it,' she says, 'we're on a mission. Up the mountain,' and she's running again, along the little sandy paths that zigzag through the spiky marram.

Then, 'Just seen something interesting!' Esme drops onto her hands and knees to inspect. 'Dad, it's red with stripes.'

It's a small copper, a swift jewel of the dunes.

'I thought it was a skipper, not a small copper.'

Skippers and the small coppers are all lightning-fast little butterflies.

Esme runs over the dunes haphazardly, a butterfly in human form, and we alight upon an area of longer grass, where handsome, stocky grey Konik horses graze. I prevent Esme touching the electrified wire just in time.

'Dada?' She's pointing. 'They look like garden tiger moth caterpillars but I don't know. I saw them in this little white bundle.'

A scrubby piece of wind-sculpted hawthorn is decorated with a thick, slightly grubby cobwebby muslin. Breaking from this web are dozens of tiny wandering caterpillars. They've virtually stripped the hawthorn of its tender spring leaves. Esme quickly has four of them on her left hand. Two ascend her arm. She notices how their small furry heads sway from side to side as they walk. They have long gingery hairs and two small orange-red spots at the end of their bodies.

'They feel tickly and they feel nice,' says Esme. 'Come on, little guys.' She pauses. 'Daddy, can we take one home? I really want to. Could we just take one little tiny caterpillar?'

She loves nature, but she also wants to possess stuff. Relentlessly. Like those hippies who grew into acquisitive entrepreneurs, she's a wildlife-obsessed materialist. I explain that visitors aren't allowed to collect things from a nature reserve.

This rule, when something is so plentiful, does not make sense to Esme. 'I don't think they'll notice that we have any in our rucksack. We could just pick a little hawthorn and put it in our rucksack with one caterpillar.'

When I was little, I reared caterpillars with my sister. It was another use for the tanks that housed our pet fish, which died after two weeks. Caterpillars were more robust. We reared large and small whites on cabbages, and peacocks and small tortoiseshells on nettles, keeping the tanks in our leaky-roofed conservatory. As I grew older, my focus shifted to butterflies, but now, through my children, I am reminded of the joy of caterpillars and their lives of hunger, toil and growth. The cobwebs of caterpillars are the highlight of Esme's day. Only later, calling in at the reserve HQ, do we learn from Gary Hibberd, the warden, that they are brown-tail moths. They weren't around Holme in my childhood but this species has moved north, and thrived, as the climate warms. On the internet, I read alarming reports of how this 'pest' can cause terrible skin rashes. Perhaps we were lucky, but Esme had them crawling all over her arms for ten minutes and her skin was unblemished.

Scaremongering about toxic caterpillars is a modern iteration of the appalling press the caterpillar has always received. Christian butterfly collectors saw only themselves in the miracle of metamorphosis. Caterpillars were industrious but greedy worms, like us, and their journey from repugnant grub via a coffin-like chrysalis to winged angel showed us a hopeful passage to a better afterlife. Even so, the Victorian butterfly enthusiast Edward Newman published a poem describing these lowly 'maggots' thus: 'selfish their striving, hideous their bearing, ugly their figure'.

Eric Carle's picture book *The Very Hungry Caterpillar* is as much a fixture of early childhood as cots and nappies. A fragment of memory takes me into the distinctive smell of the little library in my home town of Reepham where I gazed with delight at the caterpillar chomping a hole through the deep-purple plum. Like all the best animal heroes of children's literature, the hungry caterpillar is a child, gorging on party food, feeling sick, and then changing – that wondrous metamorphosis – into an entirely different being. Some teenagers, like butterflies, go from grub to winged angel in a matter of weeks.

The Very Hungry Caterpillar features in my children's early years too, but real caterpillars have been harder to come by. Dozens of small tortoiseshells and peacocks gathered on the garden buddleias of my childhood in the 1980s and 1990s. Three decades on, my buddleias are mostly desolate. Something drastic has happened to these once common garden species. Lepidopterists do not know the precise cause of the tortoiseshells' and peacocks' declines. It is even more vexing given that both species' caterpillars devour the stinging nettle, a plant that is probably more common today than at any time since the last ice age, thanks to all the nitrogen produced when rain combines with vehicle emissions, and the nutrients from farmers' well-fertilised fields. Pesticides and climate change are driving the loss of common insects in a way which we have yet to fully understand.

The caterpillars that my children first got to know are orange tips. As I relaxed my gardening style in a desire to attract more wildlife, garlic mustard germinated all over. Its other name, jack-by-the-hedge, must refer to how it surges from shy low leaf to knee-high plant in a couple of supercharged days. While the male butterfly with its orange-tipped wings patrols the garden before the garlic mustard pops out its pretty latticework of white flowers, the plainer female, which actually possesses a gorgeously intricate marbled green pattern on her white underwings, only emerges when the flowers are blooming. On these she lays her eggs.

The eggs begin as a luminous yellow-green but soon colour up to poisonous orange. They are the size of a pinhead and I point them out perhaps twice before Esme, predictably, becomes more adept than me at spotting them.

'See something – I really do, oh my gosh, oh my gosh!' she exclaims, peering at a big patch of garlic mustard. Her egg is the shape of a rugby ball and stuck neatly on the stem of the tiny white flower.

The caterpillars begin as microscopic yellow squiggles with black heads. Each one sits alone on its spray of flowers. The first-time mother somehow intuits that her caterpillars will be fratricidal, and lays her eggs well apart, so the siblings won't devour each other in their race to become winged fairies. We search our garden and find a dozen eggs on different plants.

Esme wants to rear them inside, but they are so close to the house I persuade her we can observe them in the wild. Every day or so, we check on the caterpillars. They move through their instars, or stages of growth, like actors changing costume from one act to the next. When a caterpillar sheds its first skin, it slides its body away in one direction while the old black skin around the head rolls off in the other, as if guillotined.

Larger now, the caterpillars are slender sticks of peppermint green with a paler peppermint tinge to their base. They don't match the yellow-green leaves of the garlic mustard. But they don't spend much time, if any, on the leaves. Instead, they lie along the seedpods of their host. Each caterpillar is superbly disguised. 'It's like a tiny runner bean,' observes Milly.

Gradually, we notice how the seedpods vanish, eaten by the caterpillars. Then the caterpillars disappear too. We want to watch them pupate, but they elude us. We can never find their spectacular green alien spaceship of a chrysalis into which they disappear in June and do not burst from until the following April.

So the first caterpillars we rear are painted ladies, which I buy in a kit over the internet. Plenty of schools do this, so I figure it must be OK. The six tiny creatures arrive in a small plastic jar with a layer of brown honey-like goo at the bottom. According to the instructions, they must remain in the jar until they pupate, which they do on the jar's lid. It's an unsatisfying, hands-off experience, although Milly and Esme do reap the delight of releasing the painted lady butterflies into our garden. As soon as they are freed, these powerful migratory insects roar off, ignoring all the tempting nectar sources I've painstakingly planted for them, and disappear over the horizon in seconds. I vow to do better next summer.

This, fortunately, turns out to be an unusually good year for caterpillars. The Broads around our home are a wet and fertile place, and pillowy mounds of nettles grow on the banks beside the drainage ditches. In certain spots, nettle forests drip with writhing communities of black peacock caterpillars, whose spines shine silver in the sunlight. The nettle is the best butterfly food plant in Britain, supporting five species. There are also conspicuous gatherings of another communally living caterpillar, the yellow-green-black small tortoiseshells. Less visible are the red admirals: these live alone inside a luminous green tent they construct by biting a nettle leaf in two, then sewing the two halves together.

I'm keen to collect some caterpillars for the children but those I see are on nature reserves. It's illegal to collect rare species of butterflies, or caterpillars, and we must not take any plants or animals at all from a nature reserve – a rule that sits uneasily with small children's urge to explore the wild world around them.

At four, Esme had a butterfly net, and she was soon proficient at swishing it through the air and ensnaring butterflies. One spring day, in quick succession, she caught seven speckled woods, a common woodland butterfly doing well in the changing climate. She deduced that everyday members of the brown butterfly family – particularly ringlets and gatekeepers – are easy to catch. The browns jink through open meadows fairly slowly; they are less zippy than the blues, coppers and skippers and, unlike the large and small whites which take fright at the slightest human movement, they are also fairly 'tame' and allow you to admire them. (White butterflies behave as if they know their pest status among brassica growers.)

Esme soon assembles a 'collection' of live butterflies in her pop-up 'butterfly house', a mesh-and-fabric cylinder that came with the painted lady caterpillars. Her relentless acquisition of butterflies requires close monitoring at first, but her initial desire to keep them as pets for days on end diminishes and she begins to release them in a timely fashion, after mere minutes of possession. Perhaps she identifies with the butterflies; both need to fly free.

'I'm fed up with boring old meadow browns,' she declared at five. 'I want to catch a fritillary.' She would sit on the rug in my study and pore over my old guidebook. She was drawn, as was I, to the big, glamorous butterflies. Her favourite pages depict the purple emperor, the shimmering iridescent marvel of our oak woodlands in July, and the dark, brooding Camberwell beauty, a rare migrant which I have never seen in Britain, except in my dreams into which it periodically floats. She also loves the swallowtail that entranced Vladimir Nabokov as a boy: 'As it probed the inclined flower from which it hung, its great powdery body slightly bent, it kept restlessly jerking its great wings, and my desire for it was one of the most intense I have ever experienced.' Nabokov dated that swallowtail as the beginning of his passion for butterflies.

Esme holds similarly intense desires, and repeatedly asks if we can go catching swallowtails. Every June, we seek them out at our local patch, How Hill, a nature reserve fifteen minutes away. The exotic flash of Britain's largest butterfly makes the boggy wildflower meadow beside the River Ant resemble southern Europe. Esme sees a swallowtail about as regularly as a common peacock, so she struggles to grasp that this long-tailed celebrity is one of Britain's rarest butterflies and protected by law. Even when butterfly collectors are not hunting a protected species, swishing a net in public in the era of digital photography is about as socially acceptable as smoking on a train.

Esme's desire to collect is heightened by the fact that for some years Lisa and I resist the children's continuous pleas for a real live pet. Milly and Esme are desperate for one: fish, mouse, hamster, rabbit and, most of all, a cat or a dog. Esme interrogates me about the pets I had as a child (all of the above). Why then, she asks, can't we have one? Lisa and I hold out because three young children are enough to look after. I'd like a dog but Lisa, being home-bound more than me, doesn't want to become its primary carer. Lisa would love a cat, but I'm dead against it because of the feline carnage inflicted upon our bird population. As soon as Esme can write, she turns her hand to notes of entreaty: 'I want a cat, please get a cat.' She decides we'll get a cat as my surprise Christmas present, and call it Pat the Cat.

Caring for a pet is an obvious way for children and people of all ages to develop intimate bonds with species other than our own. More than one in five households in Britain are estimated to have a cat and almost one in three have a dog, with similar rates of ownership across Europe, China and Japan. In the United States, more than one in three households owns a dog.

Although there are plenty of scientific assessments of the benefits of contact with animals, from dogs to llamas, in specific therapeutic settings, the contribution made by pets in everyday life to people's mental health is less well studied. A recent review of seventeen academic papers found that fifteen reported positive aspects of pet ownership for people experiencing mental health problems. One study found that dogs increased feelings of calm and reduced loneliness, depression, worry and irritability in former soldiers with post-traumatic stress disorder. Stroking and proximity to pets have been judged to relieve depression; several studies have identified animal companionship as particularly useful for people with autism.

Pets are valued by all kinds of people because their love is unconditional and uncomplicated; they do not judge, and our companion animals often intuit when we are upset or particularly in need of comfort. Pet ownership has been found to possibly assist children's learning and social development, but there's a shortage of studies following children over time in pet and non-pet households. One recent US study concluded that any 'wellbeing' benefits of pet ownership for children – better general health, less concern from parents over their mood, behaviour and learning ability – were largely explained by socioeconomic and other 'confounding factors', and could not be attributed to the presence of pets.

There is stronger evidence for the physical benefits of pets. Walking the dog has been shown to reduce loneliness and it is also a pathway towards a kind of freedom, or roaming, for older children. This may be irrational, but we parents perceive our children to be safer if they are out walking the dog. An American study found that 'pet play' was the most common kind of play for primary and secondary school girls, and the second most popular for secondary school boys. And those older children who walk a dog or play with pets were more likely to meet the national recommendations for physical activity (an hour a day outside, according to British government sources). Children in dog-owning families have been found to be more physically active than non-dog-owning families; and dog-walking is regularly proposed as a way to reduce childhood obesity.

One study has identified dog-walking as a way to encounter more nature, although wildlife may not be so appreciative of the attentions of an off-the-lead dog. Nevertheless, Esme is desperate to recruit a pet from amongst the wild animals around us. She persuades us to pull over so she can rescue a car-struck rabbit but it has already died. She takes in a mouse that neighbours have trapped humanely in their garage but it jumps out of her plastic tub and hides inside our sofabed. We have to drag the bed outside to liberate the mouse. A few months later, I stumble upon our own gathering of blind pink grubs – like sweetshop mice – in a nest expertly fashioned from a shredded plastic bag inside an old chest-of-drawers in our garage. I don't have the heart to disturb this marvel of rodent engineering even when Lisa warns darkly of the mice imperilling various tents and tarpaulins. Esme begs for a peek at the babies but I'm worried the mother will desert them, so we wait a few days.

When we peer in the drawer again, the babies are gone. The mother has smartly relocated them. I tell Esme we will wait, again, then trap the mice humanely when they leave the nest. I scatter bird seed on a plate for the mother mouse. Each morning, I check to see how much of the food is eaten.

*

Before my sister and I progressed to hamsters, budgies and dogs, mice were our favourite pet. In our grandma's garden there was a miniature animal hospital where she skilfully rehabilitated injured tawny owls, buzzards, badgers and foxes and released them into the wild. She fed many of her charges with mice she bred herself, and when I was eight my sister and I were allowed to take home two each to keep, after Grandma had taught us the basics of mouse husbandry, such as how to pick up a mouse by the base of its tail without hurting it. Podge Beast was my favourite, a chubby brown-and-white mouse who never seemed to mind time spent in my hand. I adapted a song I learned at school from the Radio 4 programme *Singing Together*:

> Oh Podge Beast in the sun
> Willed to me by my Grandma's hand
> All my days I will sing in praise
> Of your podgy body, your shining skin

When I was twelve, I rescued a wild mouse from our cat. Its back appeared to be broken. I put it in a hay-filled box in our airing cupboard and called it Hope. She survived, hunched and crippled, and resisted any attempts to be petted or paired off with another mouse. She was an amazing athlete and every night would climb, upside down, on the zinc mesh lid I made for the tank in which I kept her. I didn't release her because I feared she would not last long in the wild, and I was more attached to her than to any other mouse. Her wild genes must have been strong because she was by far my longest-lived mouse, surviving for four years. Her departure to the sizeable mouse graveyard in the garden marked the end of my mouse-keeping days.

One morning, I find that the nightly meal I offer to the mother mouse in our garage has been polished off more thoroughly than usual. Not a single seed kernel remains. The babies must be weaned now, and hungry. I set a humane mammal trap, also known as a Longworth trap. It's a metal tube, square cross-section, that clicks into a small aluminium box. The inquisitive mouse scurries down its corridor towards some crumbs left in the metal box, brushes against a tripwire and the door slams shut. We catch one the very first night. It is small, brown and very jumpy. Adult house mice are long-nosed and not particularly cute but these young ones are adorable, with glistening black eyes and snub noses.

'It's a jumper,' says Esme as it nearly escapes our box in one bound. To my surprise, she has decided that the mice cherish freedom as much as she does, and this time she does not seek to imprison them as pets. We release the first one in the hedge on the far side of the garden. Over the next week, we catch six, a nest's-worth, and let them go in various locations. Freed, they bounce like sparks through leaf litter and hedge bottom; I'm amazed anything can catch them.

The best pets we acquire from the wild are the caterpillars, because although there's a kind of death in their pupation that requires us to let go, there follows the bonus of resurrection. Their release, as butterflies, is our contribution to the fabulously true fairy-tale of metamorphosis.

In July, I spot a circle of neck-high nettles on a derelict corner, an increasingly rare thing in a country where land is so valuable, and value extracted so keenly by everyone. These nettles have sprung up around the foundations of a vanished barn that has become a temporary dumping ground for muck and lime before it is applied to the fields. I pull over and peer at the nettles. There! Clusters of small tortoiseshell caterpillars, about half the length and a quarter of the thickness of my little finger. I pick a couple of tall nettles being munched by four caterpillars, and fold the plants and their inhabitants carefully into a carrier bag. When we get home we put them in the butterfly container and every other day I help the children collect fresh nettles, which we stuff into a small vase beside the old plants.

I'm surprised how quickly the caterpillars grow: in exactly a week they create their chrysalises, which hang from the nettles. These are creamy brown and studded with metallic gold. 'Chrysalis' comes from the ancient Greek for gold, *chrysos*; a beautiful old word for butterfly-lover, 'aurelian', from *aurelius*, is inspired by this gold effect. Despite repeated checks, we never see the magical moment when the caterpillar, fat, black and dangling, turns itself into this gold-tinted package, which looks far too small to contain a butterfly.

We also miss the hatching of the first three tortoiseshells and find them already batting against the bedroom window. One Saturday morning, Milly notices that the final chrysalis, which is hanging off a dead nettle, is now translucent. We can see the orange and brown tortoiseshell pattern of one wing pressed against the shell. We place the nettle on the window-sill in the sunshine, and within minutes the butterfly emerges, pulling its black legs out of its tiny chrysalis like a tall person clambering out of a sports car. We let it hang there in peace while it unfolds and pumps up its wings. Esme takes charge of its release, cupping it in her hands and placing it on a buddleia bloom. It opens its wings in the sunshine. For a moment I think it is an aberration, an unusually coloured small tortoiseshell, because it's so dark and furry. Then I realise I have never seen such a fresh specimen before. We admire it before it flies away.

These successes give us confidence to expand our caterpillar wrangling. We successfully rear twelve large whites that we pick from scores swarming over my kale. Our brassica-growing neighbours won't thank us for releasing these gently flapping 'cabbage whites', to wreak more havoc in their vegetable patches. Another antisocial plant species we harbour in our increasingly wild garden is ragwort. John Clare admired how this humble ragged-leafed native would 'litter gold' in late summer. But ragwort's potential to be poisonous for horses caused an unscientific panic, and sixty years ago it was listed as an 'injurious weed' under the 1959 Weeds Act. Landowners are still legally obliged to prevent such 'harmful' plants spreading onto neighbours' property.

After a long, hot day out in high summer, we pull into our drive where a large ragwort plant shines like a child-sized sun-making machine. Its flowers, buds and leaves dance to the rhythm of fifty cinnabar moth caterpillars. Each one is a tiny plump tiger that curls and waves when we draw close. Esme removes four and rears them on a sprig of ragwort in a jar beside her bed.

Later in the summer, she charges into my study. She knows she cannot interrupt when I'm 'on deadline' (super-important work) but this is super-super-important. She's carrying the most beautiful large moth. It has a broad downy body and its upperwings are marbled in brown and grey. When she touches it gently, it flashes brilliant pink underwings that reveal two huge powder-blue eye-spots with intimidating black pupils. She found it in the Maze, the spiral of sallows I planted in the garden. 'It's an eyed hawkmoth,' she says. I didn't know that, but Esme can identify hawkmoths better than me after memorising a guide she has tacked to the wall by her bed. We check online: sallow is one of the caterpillar's food plants. We put the moth back there; I hope it will lay eggs.

Hawkmoths are the honorary butterflies of the moth world. Their adult forms have fat bodies and wings that are as striking and colourful as the largest of butterflies. But their caterpillars trounce any British butterfly caterpillar for size and charisma.

Esme has a sixth sense for hawkmoths. One night, in the early hours, she comes into our room and wakes us because there's a large, olive-and-pink moth in her bedroom; she identifies it as an elephant hawkmoth. Later that summer, on a stroll to the river, she spies an elephant hawkmoth caterpillar on the edge of the pavement, bustling off to pupate. This is the most magnificent caterpillar, mid-brown with the tiniest hint of pink. It possesses two fake black eyes, complete with grey-brown eyebrows, on its chubby neck, which hoax any predatory bird into thinking it's a snake. Esme is desperate to keep it but I persuade her to put it among the leaves in the adjacent churchyard so it can pupate in peace.

There is one hawkmoth on Esme's identification chart that bewitches her more than any other. The death's-head hawkmoth is the biggest of them all. This largest moth ever seen in Britain is huge, black and furry. Its black-brown upperwings are dusted in silver and patterned with squiggles of beige and grey that look like woodworm. When it slides these wings aside, it reveals underwings the colour of freshly harvested straw. The lower part of its thorax is striped yellow and brown like a huge bee. But it is the upper part of the thorax that gives this insect its forbidding name: on the dark body, sketched in bone-yellow, is the unmistakeable shape of a skull. Unsurprisingly, this rare visitor to Britain has a witchy role in our culture. Two death's-heads were supposed to have invaded the bedchamber of King George III and sent him mad. Thomas Hardy made the death's-head a portent of doom in *The Return of the Native*, and it was a serial killer's prop in *The Silence of the Lambs* and a marketing attraction for the film.

Esme is always asking if I can look up 'Hatchimal' or 'Pikmi Pop' or some other plastic character on my laptop. So when she says, 'Can we google "death's-head hawkmoth"?' I agree. We admire the pictures and then I spot a butterfly breeders' website: fifteen death's-head hawkmoth eggs for £14.99. Shall we? I read the blurb. They are easily reared, it claims, and will feed on privet as well as their favoured food, potato leaves. (Unusually, it is an Old World species that has adapted to feed, mostly, on a plant from the New World.) We have a small privet hedge. On an impulse, we click and buy.

The translucent yellow-green eggs arrive in a small plastic tube stuffed with cotton wool. Experienced breeders glue eggs to keep them in place and use special equipment to safely manoeuvre microscopic caterpillars. I'm out of my depth. I roll the eggs onto freshly picked privet leaves in an old ice-cream tub. Each day, we pick fresh sprigs and slide them under the eggs. Some caterpillars hatch. They are tiny – far too small to touch – and so we continue to add fresh privet. Incompetently, I lose one or two when we clean out their tub. We notice that each caterpillar has what looks like a piece of cotton thread sticking up from its body – a tiny horn, or tail. The holes they make in the leaves get bigger. The caterpillars grow. Luminous green frass – caterpillar poo – starts to appear.

We have eight caterpillars. Esme loves her 'Deathies'. We all do. They have fluorescent yellow heads and shoulders and their matching yellow bodies are decorated with green Vs adorned with small black spots and a hint of purple. Their bottoms are equipped with a yellow horn, which occasionally twirls, not unlike a pig's tail.

Their markings are similar but each individual is a different size. Three are noticeably smaller. Although I'm not convinced she can tell each one apart, Esme names them all: Sallow is the largest and her favourite; the smallest is Tiny. The Deathies are fat, busy and curiously personable. They don't quail and quiver like pet guinea-pigs but are unperturbed and autocratic, as if they know their star quality.

They are also hungry. The privet sprigs are defoliated within a day. When we bring fresh leaves, they dive in with the ardour of a hungry dog at its bowl. At first we imprison them in Esme's cylindrical mesh cage, but then relax, and place their privet in open vases. They won't leave these plants as long as we maintain their supplies. They are big enough to handle now, the size of Esme's little finger. She picks them up every day and converses with them. Their skin is like silk but their bodies are tubes of tightly packed muscle-like matter. Their feet feel tacky and grippy. Sometimes all eight foray up her arm. It is a great pleasure to watch how quickly they all barrel along, shimmying their bodies with the grace of a stout but nimble dancer. When Esme places Sallow on her face, he curls along her top lip like a fat yellow moustache.

These caterpillars' capacity to grow beyond our expectations brings to mind a slightly menacing fairy-story. They keep getting bigger. They are the size of Esme's thumb. Then, they are as long as my middle finger. Two days later, they almost stretch from my knuckles to my wrist. The small tortoiseshell, painted lady and orange tip caterpillars race through their larval stage and disappear into their chrysalises sooner than I expect. But the huge Deathies like to linger. Surely they will pupate now? They keep eating. We make preparations. Eventually they will want to burrow into the earth. We put their sprigs of privet in plant pots filled with damp soil.

One day, Esme notices Sallow's body is tinged with a furious orange colour. When we touch him, he writhes angrily. His body feels different: less like muscle, more like concrete. Several Deathies go wandering at a great pace, all over the living room. One has what looks like a bruise on its body which blackens like gangrene. It dies, and smells of putrid compost. The other seven fare better, and rage a healthy orange. We place Sallow on the soil in his plant pot. He coils like a snake and then begins to disappear. It's like watching the magic maggots in *James and the Giant Peach* slip between his fingers and vanish into the soil. Within seconds, this massive caterpillar has disappeared – pffft. Better than magic.

I fear Esme will be traumatised by the loss of her pets, but she is completely accepting of this metamorphosis. If only *we* could see death as just another stage. She wonders when we'll see them again. I'm not sure. It's late summer now, and in Britain hawkmoths spend the winter under ground. However, death's-heads do not breed as a native wild species in our country; in captivity, they're under ground for about three weeks. I label the pots with however many Deathies I think have disappeared in the soil and put them in various cool out-of-the-way spots.

September is a busy month. Life moves on. I'm in the house alone, at twilight, writing at my desk, when there's a tremendous scrabbling in the corner. I jump out of my skin. Imagining a rat, I peer at the noise and see a black furry bat-like creature engaged in a heated discussion with its surroundings. The first death's-head hawkmoth.

This moth starts crashing around, and I fear for its safety. I pick it up and it fills my palm; its outstretched wings might span 12cm. It squeaks like a mouse and quakes with fury. One much-debated theory is that the squeaks mimic those of a queen bee: their purpose is to deter workers from attacking when it raids a hive to feed on honey. I take it outside, cup my hands and it's gone, buzzing like a hummingbird into the darkening sky. I'm disappointed that the children aren't around to see it and feel guilty about releasing a non-native insect into our countryside. Migratory death's-heads do reach Britain from southern Europe and Africa, but releases like mine can distort scientists' data if they are spotted and counted by moth experts. They can also potentially spread disease. I didn't think this through when I impulsively bought them over the internet. This powerful flier might just migrate southwards, but it's more likely to provide a juicy feast for a bat, which is no bad thing. Next time, I vow, I'll breed a native species such as the privet hawkmoth, which grows into an equally magnificent caterpillar.

At least Milly, Ted and Esme are around when the next Deathie emerges – again, immaculately timed as the sun is setting. We watch it pump up its crumpled wings, then Esme strokes its furry skull-patterned thorax. As it squeaks and clicks, she lets it scurry at high speed over her hair and neck. The moth's hook-like feet feel like wire. Eventually even Esme gets the creeps and shakes it off. We let it go and it sits, a brooding presence, in a plum tree before disappearing into the night. When we dig down into the soil from where it came we find the ringed shards of its empty brown pupal case, as shiny as a conker.

By October there's one Deathie left to emerge. I put the pot in our warm kitchen to help its occupant along. The fairy-tale is complete on 31 October when Esme dresses up as a witch and the last death's-head hawkmoth makes its appearance. Witch-Esme holds it and lets it wander over her as if it's a mini spell-casting demon. Then we watch it vanish into the dark with as much ceremony as we can muster.

8

Autumn Dandelions

'Hands-on experience at the critical time, not systematic knowledge, is what counts in the making of a naturalist. Better to be an untutored savage for a while, not to know the names or anatomical details. Better to spend long stretches of time just searching and dreaming.'

E.O. Wilson

'Everything is starting to decay,' declares James with a five-year-old's aptitude for making random-sounding remarks that are precisely observant and flawlessly logical. With his white-blond curls, he reminds me of an old man.

'What does "exist" mean?' he asks Tracey, during our morning risk assessment of the nursery site.

'It means things that are real, that you can touch.'

'Well, Yoda can move things around with his mind.'

'Is he real?' Tracey has a teacher's knack for turning the tricky question back on the child.

'It's a person dressed in clothes,' explains James. 'I've watched *The Empire Strikes Back* now. Do you know I can move things around with my mind? Luke can use the Force too. Well, Luke Skywalker doesn't really exist. It's just somebody pretending.'

The lengthening shadows stretch across Dandelion and announce that it's autumn. The air holds itself still. Ivy flowers send sickly-sweet perfume over the garden area; bushes talk, the sparrows hidden inside. Their chat sounds as relaxed as old country folk conversing over the wall. A red admiral dashes from flower to sky and a large white sails back and forth. The sun is no longer hot but feels like a warm hand placed upon my back.

The site is immaculate after a summer holiday of labour – Hayley's and Emma's. The fire circle has a roof built around it, and there are new sheds, shelters and plants. The vegetables have grown miraculously without the children's constant rootling, although Julie, the most green-fingered teacher, has helped by transplanting aubergines and other vegetables from her plot at home. But the first day of term still feels a little bereft. James has returned, but big, kind Joe has gone to school, Ruby has left a matriarch-shaped hole and other stalwarts have graduated too, from Edith to Cole. I particularly miss Cole's balletic genius; the energetic challenge he poses is now shouldered by his local primary school.

I guess you must become used to it, I say of the missing children to Hayley and Emma.

'I still cry every July,' says Emma.

There's one new girl I know. Esme is the third member of our family to become a Dandelion. Her joining is a big step for all of us. The idea formed slowly in our minds earlier in the year, when Lisa heard from a friend about a primary school that offers 'flexi-schooling'. This is where a child stays in their conventional state school for most of the week but spends one or two days elsewhere. It's a compromise; a less dramatic step than home-schooling. It could be the best of both worlds, or unsettling and awkward. We checked our county council website: in theory, it was possible.

Both girls had been through their reception year at school happily enough. Their state primary is our village school, St John's, which has a good reputation. Many parents from outlying villages prefer to send their children here than to their smaller village schools, but St John's is not too big either. It has one class for each year group. In their 'reception' year, pupils have 'free flow' and can move from the classroom to a small outdoor area with a climbing frame and bars for swinging from. Even so, Esme chafes against the curtailment of her freedom. Year 1, we are warned, is very different: more bums-on-seats learning. Milly is a very quick reader; Esme is better than average, we're told, but she feels the disparity with her sister, and at times that makes her fraught. We build a case in our heads.

The way our school system suddenly inflicts a five-day week upon five-year-olds leaves most exhausted, for much of the time. We hope that a couple of days out of conventional school each week will take pressure off Esme, and give her a break. She will love being outdoors, we think. We ponder the dramatic surge in Ted's independent behaviour after joining Dandelion, and his burgeoning desire to do things for himself. For someone so boisterous, Esme at five is short on self-sufficiency, and often wants an adult to help her. We mostly experience this as an insatiable appetite for one-to-one attention but we slowly realise it comes from a more profound lack of confidence. We hope Dandelion might give her the same boost it gave Ted.

We arrange a meeting with St John's head teacher, Becky Quinn. She's very accessible, considering her busy job, and ambitious for her school. Emma and Hayley come to the meeting as well. I hardly recognise them in makeup and not wearing their orange boilersuits; they are uncharacteristically serious too, although they later disappear, giggling together, into the toilets.

Mrs Quinn – I struggle to call any teacher by their first name – has never been asked about flexi-schooling before but she is open-minded and says she will investigate to see if she can make it work. Perhaps our case is helped by the fact that Milly and Esme are twins. Mrs Quinn thinks it might benefit their development to be apart some of the time, but the school's one-class-per-year grouping means it can't separate them. The main challenge for the head teacher is whether she can mark Esme as attending school; if she can't, then Esme's attendance record will be poor, and the school's attendance figures will be hit as well. But it turns out that she can record Esme as attending if the school is 'overseeing' her education. As long as members of St John's can visit Dandelion, meet its teachers, and keep track of what Esme is doing there, then it should be OK.

So Mrs Quinn agrees that we can try flexi-schooling Esme, with a review at the end of the first term. It's so simple that I don't quite realise how lucky we are. I later discover parents who have begged other schools for flexi-education and been denied, even when they make detailed cases based on their child's specific educational needs. In general, schools, understandably, believe they are the best deliverers of an education. Most are cowed by fears that flexi-schooling will affect their attendance record or funding, or set a precedent, or open a huge can of worms. So we are fortunate, and thankful.

This is the first big choice we make over our children's education. Like all parents, we worry to excess. Will two days out of mainstream school make Esme a social outcast? Will two days out accentuate the difference in conventional educational attainment between Milly and Esme and make it more painful for Esme? Will it intensify the pressure she feels? Will she actually like Dandelion?

I have part of an answer when I collect her for the first time after a day at Dandelion. There's something different about her. I had not fully registered before that when I pick her up from primary school she is often hunched with tiredness, and tense around the shoulders. Here, at the Dandelion gates, she looks liberated from stress and worry. She is exhilarated after a day outside, just as I am. For a while, after the end of each Dandelion day, she's completely wild, as if something has been released in her. I don't know what this is, but as the weeks pass it subsides, and she goes on, quietly, loving Dandelion.

So I am shocked when I talk to Hayley at the end of the autumn term and discover just how short on confidence she has found Esme. At home, she is opinionated and assertive; at Dandelion, she is often as meek as a mouse, and rarely ventures an opinion during the lunchtime philosophy sessions. 'Building resilience' is a reassuring cliché but there is self-evidently no quick fix, whether outdoors or not.

I'm a familiar figure for the Dandelions now, and gain more access to their play. It surprises me how many of the children's imaginative games span age groups, and how willingly the seven-year-olds team up with the three-year-olds. Even the two-year-olds, who are identified by the fluorescent vests they wear all the time at Dandelion, are embroiled in their elders' play. The toddlers are like newly arrived economic migrants, willing to be exploited for various menial labours. Historically, playing within sprawling age groups is normal; it is only over the last century that the educational system has confined children to their own age group.

An old favourite is digging up treasure, using metal spades and trowels and marvelling over the stones and occasional pieces of old pottery that we find. Sometimes the children bury their precious finds, picking sallow leaves to use as currency, before excavating them again. There are family games, frequently run along traditional lines. One girl adores having a 'baby' to look after and finds an old-fashioned wooden push-trolley, then tirelessly recruits different toddlers to play her baby. Domestic games are usually spiced with jeopardy or tragedy: I stumble across one in which a group of children run into their home, the laurel hedge, while someone lies still in the vegetable patch. 'Ben's dead in the lava!' shouts Maisie. The soil becomes 'lava' on a surprising number of occasions, and for different groups, which puzzles me because we're not living in fear of lava and I'm not aware of lava featuring prominently in popular culture.

Ben, who for a long time is the only two-year-old at Dandelion, is a cherubic boy with blond curls whose chubby hands are always warm. He's regularly called upon to play the baby, a role he embraces because it furthers his celebrity status within the nursery. Occasionally, the play turns a little *Lord of the Flies*. One October day, after a storm called Ophelia has passed through, the sky is a sinister yellow. I'm put in jail, behind a beanstalk-like branch – a hapless giant confronted by a semicircle of vengeful Jacks. Seb electrocutes me while the others brandish home-made bows from which they fire invisible arrows. 'Into your heart!' shouts Maisie. 'Into your eye! Into your mouth!' I must mime being massacred, many times over. During another game I have to die, and lie on the floor, whereupon I'm covered in straw.

The children take unceasing delight in my slaying. But the

repeated assassinations by the boys mean that, in accordance with the no-guns rule, I belatedly stop the game. Thankfully for me, these fantasies usually morph into something more cheerful. In one game, I join the children on their straw-bale fort, a band of knights looking to slay a dragon. Like a scent from childhood, a long-forgotten sensation floods back, a feeling of what it is like to be a gang of little people: us, in our fort-nest, against the rest of the world.

One motif of the imaginative games at Dandelion is more prevalent than any other: animals. Children are tremendous shamans and shape-shifters. Given the freedom, they enthusiastically take on the form of all sorts of beasts. The Dandelions regularly turn into cats, and there are plenty of owls and eagles too; plus a few pigs, the occasional hen, but not many deer, cows or horses. The cliché of horse-loving country girls appears to be dead, here at least. I suspect that a ruminant never makes as compelling a character for transformation as a predator. As the Oxford don Charles Foster discovered in *Being A Beast* when he attempted to live as a badger, an otter and a fox, it's easier to put ourselves into the mind of a fellow hunter.

The most popular animal shape-shift at Dandelion is to turn into a dog. Many children grow up with dogs and know them intimately, and those that don't, such as Esme, crave them. At Dandelion, the dogs occasionally have lead-wielding owners – some of the older children seem to enjoy a submissive role, an echo of their carefree toddler years – but mostly they create families of dogs with puppies, free from the interference of an authoritarian adult owner. In this sense, the dog-children are as wild as any other animal.

One of my favourite Dandelions turns himself into more unusual creatures: Ronnie has a wide repertoire of animal alter-egos, from mouse to koala. He is four, serious and round-faced, with red hair and dark eyes. He is deeply shy and the most hardworking small boy I've ever met. When he latches onto a task he pursues it with vigour. When he becomes an animal he commits as deeply to the role as any method actor. He stays in character the whole day. Animals are a mask, just as a role can be for a performer: they permit us to express what could not otherwise be expressed; liberate us from language, obligation, conformity. At 11.30 a.m. one day, Ronnie begins his new life as a mole. He crawls around on all fours, pausing to dig, furiously, with his fingernails in the dirt. He doesn't say much but occasionally gives a bark-cum-yell. 'I'm an angry mole,' he says.

This appears to be a potentially solitary vocation, but other children respond to him over the course of the day, and he makes space for them to join his game. In my mind, Esme, who is a couple of years older, is a world away from Ronnie in terms of sophistication, but in subsequent weeks she enjoys playing moles with him. I'm surprised, but should not be: other children accept his persona, and are willing collaborators in his imaginative vision. Hayley and Emma have not seen this kind of creative play in their conventional schools and nurseries. Hayley explains how teaching assistants usually set up 'role-play areas' in indoor spaces: one week it might be a Post Office, the next a vet's. Dandelion doesn't have role-play areas. 'Because there are no toys, it's open,' says Hayley, of their approach to play. 'You can be whatever you want to be, not whatever the teacher has assumed the children want to be on a Monday morning.' Emma says taking away 'closed' toys has been one of the most revelatory decisions at Dandelion. 'It has freed up their minds and it frees us up as teachers because we don't take a doll and automatically think, "Let's play mummies and babies."'

As we in the West lose contact with animals, I wonder whether Ronnie's kind of game will endure. I've never seen a live mole but perhaps he has, or perhaps his desire to be a mole has been fuelled by books or television – there's a delightfully rebellious young mole in an episode of *Shaun the Sheep*, the claymation (clay animation) series. Children don't hang out with zombies in real life, or ghosts, pirates, or non-native species such as lions, crocodiles, elephants or monkeys, and yet their games are still full of these characters, reflecting back the adult-authored culture we offer them.

It falls upon us grownups to keep animals at the heart of our culture.

Dandelion is child-led but not completely so, and as the days cool, Emma and Hayley introduce running-around games so the children get warm again after sitting still for lunch. 'Baby owls' is a game of hide-and-seek, except Emma calls out 'Twooit' and the children have to call back 'Twuooo'. Like every game, it morphs into something else, and Logan becomes Daddy Owl and announces he is fifty years old. Emma is surprised he can still fly.

One autumn day, I'm collecting Milly and Esme from St John's when their class teacher appears. She tells me Esme had a meltdown earlier because she's been moved out of Milly's group for writing. The teacher believes that she's been leaning on Milly.

The girls' relationship sometimes follows a pattern: Milly likes to do things for herself and is delighted to do things for others; Esme is a persuasive delegator, and often willing to have someone do things for her. That evening, Esme looks tense. Her shoulders are rolled in, her mouth turns down. She's clearly struggling a little at school. When I go to see Becky Quinn, she says that an academic gap has opened up between the twins. The head thinks it is because of the flexi-schooling. Lisa and I believe the gap is 'natural'; we know of occasions since they were babies when Milly picked up something first and Esme caught up a month or so later. (In other areas, Esme's development has periodically surged ahead of Milly's.) Despite Mrs Quinn's concerns, she agrees to continue flexi-schooling for now. We are fortunate to have a head teacher who is willing to entertain our experiment.

I tell Esme the good news another day when I collect her from school. I notice she has weary dark circles under her eyes. She's not visibly ecstatic, but after her next day at Dandelion Hayley tells me that she hardly stopped talking in philosophy. Hopefully, she's developing the confidence to demonstrate her extremely sharp wit and emotional intelligence when she's away from home, outdoors, and in a place like Dandelion.

Some days, Dandelion stinks. The surrounding countryside is studded with long grey sheds that breed tight-packed turkeys and chickens, out of sight, out of mind. Their manure is spread on the fields, and some has been distributed near Dandelion. A sweet, heavy stench hangs on the still air. It is the season when trees and plants shed leaves, die back and hunker down for winter.

There's less death than during the great infant mortality

festival that is spring, but outdoors it is still all around us. One day, the children find the headless body of what we think is a mouse. The children poke its gunmetal-grey fur with sticks, fascinated, wondering where its head has gone. There is a muddy tangle of stuff where its head must have been, but no blood or guts left. Dandelion's busy undertakers, Daisy and Feather, probably cleaned up the corpse. After searching the site, we locate a grubby book – they swiftly become muddy at Dandelion – containing pictures of mice. The mice have long pink tails. Ours has a short grey one. We use Emma's tablet to identify it as a vole. The children want to bury it and we dig a hole, find an offcut of wood and borrow Hayley's permanent marker (part of the essential kit she keeps in her bumbag). 'Vole,' writes seven-year-old Alfie on the grave.

On my drive to Dandelion one morning, I catch a glimpse of speckled feathers on a fast stretch of road. It takes me a mile to make up my mind and then I turn around, drive back, hit my hazard warning lights, stop in the road and jump out to identify the roadkill. I thought it was a chicken but it's a tawny owl, flattened on one side of its face and with one opal black eye squinted shut, giving it a piratical look. Its open eye is dulling. I take it to show the children.

They cluster around me at the gate. Is it dead? Can we make it better? They are not sure it is definitely dead. Some believe it can be resuscitated. They hold it, and feel how light it is, its breast feathers as soft as a kiss. Willow eventually takes it away and I'm distracted by another task. When I return an hour later, I discover that Willow and friends have taken it upon themselves to bury the bird. They did it so efficiently that Emma doesn't notice, either. We retrieve it from its grave and dust the soil off its feathers. It looks OK, considering.

That evening, I take the owl to Benny. I assume it is too flattened to preserve, but he surveys it with his hawkish gaze. It's a juvenile, he says. A young bird, probably flying away from its home range for the first time, uncertain, and unversed in road safety. He thinks he can revive it.

Alongside Esme, there are two dozen other new pupils this term. Many come from homes where parents already provide access to the outdoors, or to animals or wildlife; some keep chickens or grow their own vegetables. But a few newcomers have not yet developed an easy relationship with other species, or the world beyond our human one. One boy is competitive, and turns acorn-collecting into a fierce battle of accumulation, which reminds me of the startling fact that in Dandelion's tranquil outdoor arena so few children compete. Another boy goes 'Urrrgh' when we dig up a worm. And there's a girl who offers more of a challenge. Lily is seven years old and comes wearing an urban outfit of three layers – not enough – one of which is a silver puffer jacket. She is slightly gothic, aloof and lugubrious; Dandelion, she declares, is boring; she prefers adult company, and the indoors. I warm to her rebelliousness.

'Ed Sheeran is my knight in shining armour,' she says as she swings on a rope. 'I want to be a famous singer but my parents won't let me enter any competitions.' During her first Dandelion philosophy session, Lily is soon expressing strong views. One boy wants a pet bird but his mum doesn't want to cage a flying creature. Hayley asks: Should we put pets in cages?

The children's responses are not predictable. Gentle animal-loving Evie, who cares deeply about every living thing from a scruffy tree to one half of an accidentally executed earthworm, explains how her granny keeps birds in a cage and lets them fly around her house. 'It's OK to have them in a cage, but only at night-time,' she says.

'Is the house a cage?' asks Hayley.

'They are allowed to go where they want in the house.'

'Is that being free?'

'No,' chips in Lily.

'Are the birds free?' wonders Hayley.

'They are not free,' says Evie.

'Is that OK?'

'It's OK because they like being with Granny.'

'How do you know?' asks Hayley.

'They are happy with Granny,' insists Evie. 'I can tell because they fly around really happily and their faces look happy.' She pauses. 'Two of them are dead. One died because it got old but another died because it ate an avocado.'

I struggle not to laugh. Hayley, as ever, maintains a poker face.

I don't expect silver-jacketed Lily to be an animal lover, but she is. Cages are not OK, she says. 'I even think that zoos are cruel. They cage animals. Do you think they want to be in a cage? Leave them in the wild.'

'What if putting them in a cage saves them from going extinct in the wild? Is that still unkind?' asks Hayley.

'It isn't,' says Lily decisively. 'But if you keep keeping their babies, that's cruel.' They need to be released back into the wild, she reasons.

'What is this talk about?' asks Hayley.

'It's about nature,' says Lily.

'The big idea we've been talking about is freedom and being trapped,' says Hayley.

'We are free because we're outside,' says Logan, who is agreeably on-message about everything.

'We are not free because we're not allowed to do whatever we want anywhere,' says Lily.

'Is anybody truly free?' asks Hayley.

'Parents,' says Lily decisively. 'They can go everywhere they want.'

'What if they've got a job? – can they go everywhere they want?'

Lily concedes with a no. But I like her spirit. Defiant, world-weary and a little dogmatic; she seems like an old soul, or perhaps she has acquired a nonconformist attitude from her elders.

Over time, Lily's clothes become thicker, more waterproof, and more suited to her environment, although they are still garish. One week, she devotes hours to creating a muddy patch in the garden and getting her wellies stuck in it. Another week, she decides to create a dirt bath for the chickens. She enlists the help of a silent white-blond toddler called Wilf, and me, and we dig soil from the vegetable bed, place it in a barrow and wheel it over close to the chicken house and tip it in a big pile. As we work, Lily tells us about her chickens at home. One day, she says, her brother stepped on one of their chicks and it died. Its insides didn't look or smell nice. Helped by obliging Wilf, Lily levels the soil. When we finally let the chickens out of their house they scamper straight past us and ignore their dirt bath.

Lily seems to be settling into the nursery. She doesn't mention being bored any more, she mixes better with the other children and wittily adopts a scary, gravelly voice when she talks about the approaching Halloween. She makes perceptive and intelligent contributions at lunchtime philosophy, slurping soup and spilling it all over her silver coat. On one occasion, she tells us how scorpions can kill. On another, she declares that she does not believe in God and interrogates a peer's parroting of evangelical Christianity. 'What about hell?' asks Lily. 'Hell is a place.'

My favourite philosophical discussion ends with the Dandelions debating what they would do if they met the Queen.

We've never voiced even a mildly questioning attitude towards the Queen at home, but I have wondered if children are natural republicans because more than once Esme has asked us why the Queen is the Queen and why can't anyone be the Queen. It seems fundamentally unfair to her. So I'm quite surprised that her Dandelion peers are fervent monarchists. They talk of bowing to Her Royal Highness, giving her presents and a cuddle, and how they know she is lovely. Lily takes the conversation in an unexpected direction.

'I would buy her one million pieces of gold,' she declares.

'Hasn't the Queen got enough gold?' asks Hayley.

'You can never have too much gold,' says Lily.

'But you can't eat gold,' says Hayley. 'What would you do with it if the world runs out of food?'

'You would save it or put it in a doomsday bunker in case something happens and everyone dies,' says Lily.

'What use would your gold be if no one else was around to buy it?'

'You'd buy the only other person to be your servant,' she says. 'You would probably end up having to have children with them – if it was a boy – to start the human race.'

'What if you were a girl who likes girls?' asks Hayley.

'It's called force.'

I twitch at this conversation's alarming turn. I'm not sure any of the other children are keeping up, but poker-faced Hayley keeps her cool.

'Is it OK to force someone?' she asks.

'No it's not called forcing somebody, it's what you have to do to save the population of the world,' says Lily.

I admire her determination: a seven-year-old challenging the interpretation of a much older person who is the ultimate authority figure at Dandelion.

Hayley finishes by making the point that some girls choose to marry girls rather than boys when they get older, which is a different issue altogether, and does not actually address where Lily is: deep within her vision of an apocalyptic future.

I'm surprised when, towards the end of the autumn term, I find her lingering listlessly near the fire circle. She tells me she doesn't like Dandelion.

'Why don't you like it?' I ask.

'It's outdoors. There's no video games or anything fun. I want to go home and eat some food and play some video games. The game that we play is very addicting.'

'What is it?'

'Minecraft. I can't wait to go home. I don't like this place.'

'Why?'

'Because it's outdoors.'

The purpose of Dandelion is not to convert children to the wonders of nature. And I guess that some will never be willing converts, for all kinds of reasons. But I wonder if there is a moment when it's too late. I like to think it's never too late.

Technology is at the heart of most hand-wringing about the wellbeing of children today. If technology – in the form of hand-held screens, violent computer games and social media – is seen as a malevolent force, then nature is its good twin. But such binary thinking does not really take us anywhere useful.

There is a huge amount of interest in, but not yet much hard evidence about, the specific impact of electronic screens on children, apart from the fact that prolonged use in the evening disrupts human sleep patterns. There is even less evidence to help us understand how electronic screens affect our relationship with nature. I'm not confident that scientists or social scientists can provide us with much enlightenment here because there are so many of what academics call confounding factors. There's a myriad of variables in any individual's life; and no way to recreate laboratory-style conditions for rearing children.

In the debate about violent computer games, or social media, I could quote a critic such as Sarah Trimmer, who feared that a new entertainment for the young would 'make deep impressions and injure the tender minds of children, by exciting unreasonable and groundless fears'. Her argument was against an early-nineteenth-century edition of *Cinderella*. There is nothing new about a fear of new technology. We've had equivalent panics about the corrupting power of fairy-stories, novels, comics and television. Perhaps we should relax: the kids are all right.

I'm not quite so equanimous about online games and social media, though. These new technologies are uniquely intense and immersive. A computer game does not lead children into creating much bigger imaginary worlds in the way that a line from a book can. Social media clearly accentuate teenage self-consciousness, anxiety over body image and a felt need for peer-group acceptance. Robust data shows that most children of affluent nations are becoming more sedentary and more obese. We adults know how we feel after eight hours in front of a computer screen, particularly if we've been on social media for much of it. I don't feel particularly happy or healthy; my mind feels jagged, adrenalised, twitchy; and I don't sleep well. I don't want that world for my children.

We can probably all agree that our children inhabit a world rich in technological possibilities, but where nature too can and must play an important role. To believe we will benefit by spending more time in nature is not to shun all technological advances. Environmental charities push the idea that we must 'connect' or 'engage' with nature, and technology can help in this. I am not as convinced as some that, say, 'geocaching' – games using hand-held GPS devices – can encourage children to explore nature in ways they otherwise would not, but machines *can* sometimes deepen our experience of the natural world. Binoculars and cameras have enabled us to see plants and animals more closely and more clearly; microscopes have revealed the alien worlds of minuscule invertebrates and plants. Bat detectors, which convert ultrasonic bat calls into sounds that we humans can hear, help us gain entry into their secretive world. And social media are particularly useful in connecting nature-loving teens who in my day could feel very much alone with their obsessions.

However, there are still times when we will experience wonder, exhilaration or profound peace only if we put our phones away and exist simply as ourselves, with no technological accoutrements, in the present moment, in nature.

'It just seems so bleedin' obvious, doesn't it?' says Emma. 'As adults we know if you go for a walk, go stand in a wood, go look at the sea, your wellbeing appears to be higher, so why do we shut children in classrooms? It makes no sense. Why do we not treat children like human beings, the way that we would want to be treated, including being listened to, and not corralled?'

Emma may be an outdoor ideologue but Dandelion's co-founder is not a 'natural' outdoorsy sort of person. Hayley grew up in suburban Leicester and her vision for the nursery developed from her experience of the inadequacy of conventional schooling, and her passion for Philosophy for Children. Later, I ask her if she could do Dandelion indoors. 'Philosophy, yes we could,' she begins. 'Actually, no we couldn't because if we were inside we wouldn't be able to use philosophy in everything we do.'

The indoors is rather like a computer game, a world created by humans over which we have complete control. Indoors we may minimise risk and maximise physical comfort but we also reduce serendipity and surprise, and especially the unanticipated stimuli provided by other species. 'I had a lovely conversation with Hayden sitting on some moss,' Hayley tells me. 'We started off talking about the moss and we ended up discussing death, and time travel, just from sitting on a mossy bank . . . I said, "Oh this moss looks like tiny little stars. I'd love to go to the stars." He said, "But oh, by the time you got there you'd be dead, it would take about ten years." Oh thanks, Hayden, I've only got ten years.' She laughs. 'In being outside, you're engaging all of your body. Cognition is based on your perception, so when you're outside all of your senses are alive. No matter what kind of a learner you are – visual, oral or active – that can be met outside.'

Schools tend to focus only on oral learning, with a bit of visual: outside, says Hayley, there's 'sensory input without sensory bombardment. In a classroom you've got sensory overload – the noise, the visuals, the colours, the proximity of people to you, and the proximity of the walls; it's just too much for a lot of children.'

Being outdoors, thinks Emma, is beneficial for every aspect of a child's development, and learning. 'You've got a child who is more relaxed and more ready to learn, and they've got a bigger space,' she says. Then there are boundless teaching resources within any square metre of earth. 'If you want to teach any-thing, it's all there,' she says. Climbing trees promotes not just physical development but cognitive development too. She is particularly proud of the girl tree-climbers. 'We see children moving all the time and becoming strong. You'd think someone like Elsa is a pretty little girl with her little pink jumpsuit and long blonde hair, but if she wants to move the trunk of a tree she will do it.'

It's not just about the fact that they can climb trees, it's the way they learn to do it, Hayley adds. 'They understand that sometimes you can't just climb a tree in one go. That's huge in learning – that it's in steps, and it's OK – you can't do it all today but you can do this bit, or that bit. Tree-climbing in particular really helps with that. Oddly, I think tree-climbing is quite fundamental.'

During September, a judge for the annual *Nursery World* awards visits the site. In the years since they've opened, Dandelion has been judged 'Outstanding' by Ofsted. Historically, the schools inspectorate has been reluctant to award outdoor or Forest School nurseries its top mark because of perceived shortcomings in their technological offering. Most outdoor nurseries offer children access to cameras, microscopes or even tablets occasionally, to counter the charge that pupils are not being equipped for the modern world. This year, Dandelion has been shortlisted for 'nursery of the year' alongside five other nurseries, all of which emphasise outdoor learning. Their rivals are well-established, bigger operations, in big cities from London to Liverpool. Some are now chains, with their own slick branding. Emma and Hayley know it's a nice honour to be nominated but that they won't win.

The judge is high-powered, a retired magistrate: wise, grey-haired, and cool about Dandelion. I'm dropping Ted off on the day of her visit and join a line of parents keen to tell her about 'our' nursery. I can tell by her questioning that she's sceptical about its diversity. The pupils that day are all white, and the judge comments about all the nice middle-class parents and the absence of deprived families. One mother points out that she's a single mum; I mention the local children on government-funded places, and explain that though rural Norfolk is white, this does not make it affluent.

At the end of the month, one Saturday, Emma and Hayley

take their staff, including Julie, Tracey and Labone, to London for the awards ceremony. Lisa and I check Facebook on Saturday night and on Sunday. Nothing comes up; they haven't won. But they have! Belatedly, they post the news of their victory. The next day, their trophies are placed on a table by the gate and parents bring home-made cakes and flowers and booze to celebrate. Everyone feels so proud.

In the following weeks, a story in the local paper is followed up by Radio Norfolk and regional television. Then a news agency takes arresting photographs of cute Dandelions climbing trees and serious-looking boys sticking electric drills into bright orange pumpkins. This becomes a story in the tabloids, and then on national television. Cameras can't help but romanticise what they depict, and this scruffy patch of ground wreathed in woodsmoke looks bucolic in the autumn sunshine. But perhaps that just evens things up, for there is an awful lot of sensory goodness the cameras can't catch, from the smell of damp leaves to the somnolent chatter of the house sparrows.

My favourite time of the Dandelion day is after lunch, when a few children go home, and those who will be picked up later build a wall together or climb high into the sallows and gaze over their kingdom. It's a time for dreaming.

One afternoon, Ronnie decides he would like to plant some conkers and we proceed, on our hands and knees, scouring Dandelion for suitable ground for digging. We need bare earth but most is mazy little footpaths, too well trodden to ever produce a tree. Ronnie is indefatigable, though. He talks of a tree's need for sunshine and water and marks each planted conker with a stick. He does it at speed, as if on a deadline, or trying to plant the whole bucket-load. We plant twenty. Many will never branch forth but I'm sure we will have one or two successes. I feel sad that neither Ronnie nor I will be around Dandelion long enough to see them grow tall. But I wonder: will there be a tree standing here in two hundred years' time that was very deliberately planted by a four-year-old boy?

Another time I sit on the hard, damp earth beneath branches of young hazel with Ronnie and Yasin. Our spot is like a secret den, and we search for minibeasts around a log covered in fungi. The children don't want to touch the fungi but Logan, who reminds me of a benign older brother in an Enid Blyton series because he's so willing with the younger children, identifies it as edible chicken-in-the-woods. We scratch in the soil and discover a tiny spider and a minuscule shiny black springtail, which has a slender body and a pointed end. Yasin doesn't really like our best treasure – a millipede, coiled and sleepy in the cold – but he enjoys the woodlice. We hunt for some unusual-coloured specimens, yellow-orange, the same colour as the fungi. He gathers several in a grubby palm and holds them close; his finds, the riches of an autumn afternoon.

9

Collecting

*'If getting our kids out into nature is a search for perfection,
or is one more chore, then the belief in perfection and
the chore defeats the joy.'*

Richard Louv

Autumn brings a special currency raining down on the corner of our garden at home. It is hazardous to stand beneath the tall tree beside the entrance to the industrial estate. Thwack. Thud. Every minute or so, the tree slings a conker to the ground as if from the catapult of a tempestuous giant. Some spiny grenades open on impact. Others can be gently crushed under foot to reveal their gleaming treasure: cool to touch, encased in cream memory foam, and decorated with whorls that resemble a chestnut map of the world. Picked up, and put together, they clunk, not like money, and not like stones. They might be beautifully carved wooden pebbles but, as Robert Macfarlane's spell in *The Lost Words* says, no craftsperson could ever fashion these red-brown jewels.

It is a fine September afternoon, the calm after a storm, and Esme, always the first to race into the garden after her walk home from school, finds that the gales have liberated most of the horse chestnut's crop. I suggest we collect some conkers. First, Esme has her eye on something else.

'What's that bird in the tree?' she says. She has a child's genius for noticing when something is different in her immediate environment, and quivers with observations that intuit the emotion of a place and its inhabitants.

Now, she's homed in on this bird. 'It looks red,' she says. 'Is it a hawk?'

It perches on a portly green conifer in another garden two hundred yards away. It is probably a ubiquitous collared dove, caught by the late afternoon sun.

'We'll need our binoculars,' I say.

Esme runs upstairs and grabs them from my study window-sill. It isn't a collared dove. It has a speckled front like a mistle thrush but a big yellow cleaver of a beak, a head that tilts, and a beady eye that builds an ultra-high-definition Google Earth map of the patchwork gardens below, in one blink. She was right. It's a sparrowhawk, prospecting the neighbourhood. Now we've spotted this grand conductor on its dais, we realise how it is shaping the movement and sound around us. The usual garden orchestra is silent; blackbirds, robins and wrens are hunkered down in the shrubbery. Nothing to see here. The sparrowhawk pushes off with its strong legs and glides low. We run around outside the house to pick up its flight path. It changes direction and veers over our beech tree and then it is gone, heading to its next ambush. Wood pigeons scatter like a fistful of gravel.

Autumn is a time to make collections. It feels right to collect from the natural world at harvest time; we're gathering what has grown, ripened, fallen or is about to fall.

Esme takes a bucket and starts picking up conkers. There is no purpose and no goal. I know from previous autumns that children love the act of gathering. I point to the occasional 'big 'un' and ponder our tree. What I would've done for a gift like this in my garden as a child! It is one of the least handsome specimens of this naturally imperious species, a scraggy tree of early middle age with two trunks and a wobbly demeanour, having had the misfortune to grow up squeezed between a cherry and an overgrown evergreen hedge. It endures chestnut leaf miner, a moth that causes the leaves to mottle, wither and turn prematurely brown in July, but despite its unprepossessing appearance it produces elegant candelabras of flowers in the spring and a bumper crop of conkers in the autumn.

Conkers! Their cases are spiked medieval battle flails the colour of rust. Their creamy-white insides are a plumpen silk pad on which a precious jewel is displayed. This lining is smooth and often moist to the touch. After heavy rain, fallen conkers glisten with condensation inside their cases. Those that have been wet for a while are covered with a film of white mould that wipes away to reveal a still-gleaming orb. Each conker's face is smeared in a substance like the vernix of a newborn baby. Each face is almost babyishly soft. Esme presses one with her nail to create eyebrows, eyes, nose and mouth.

The horse chestnut is a relative newcomer to our tree family. It only arrived here, from Turkey, in the early seventeenth century and was popularised by Sir Christopher Wren, who planted a mile-long chestnut avenue in Bushy Park, the monumental approach to Hampton Court Palace. The name is derived from a horseshoe-shaped scar on the twigs, revealed when the leaves fall each autumn; tiny marks on it resemble nail holes.

Thanks to its conkers, the horse chestnut is a tree beloved of children. The game of conkers is not an ancient ritual – the first record is from 1848, on the Isle of Wight – but it has been a highlight of autumn for many generations.

When I was small, each September I twisted a skewer through

a freshly gathered conker, threaded a string through the hole and took it to school for contests. Twenty years before I was born, someone planted a short avenue of conker trees on the country lane on my way to school. There was a generous verge beneath it and on the way home we would stop and hunt along it. Plenty of other people collected conkers and it was never easy to find more than twenty, let alone a bucket-load. Each one was a prize. It was mostly boys who brought strung conkers to school and compared sizes, scars and fight histories. 'Mine's a thirty-niner,' one would boast, and we would debate methods for strengthening our conkers. Some would claim to bake them in the oven or pickle them in vinegar. The oven didn't work for me and a conker I covered in a suit of armour made from putty was an abject failure.

This sounds like a tale from a Victorian childhood, and I guess it was pretty much over for the game in my 1980s youth. Contests were half-hearted, fight histories fraudulent, and it was mostly an echo of a previous era when conker champions had real status. Even so, I remember being surprised when I moved to London in my twenties and noticed, for the first time, bountiful crops of conkers, unharvested and crushed on pavements as children walked by. Around the turn of the century, though, conker stories became a seasonal staple of the tabloids. A myth spread that the Health and Safety Executive had banned conker fights (the HSE described the story as 'an old chestnut'), while some schools said pupils could take part in contests only if they wore protective goggles. Lexicographers picked up the undeniable truth that the games were more legend than reality, and 'conker' was excised from the *Oxford Junior Dictionary* in 2011, part of a wider cull of 'natural' words that was lamented by artists and writers. In 2017, the conker became one of twenty species of neighbourhood nature revived in Robert Macfarlane and Jackie Morris's celebrated book, *The Lost Words*.

Milly, Esme and Ted do not yet know any of this history, and there are no conker contests at their rural primary school. But they know the gift that is a shower of conkers.

'What would you like it to rain?' is the question in Ted and Esme's philosophy session one autumn day when it's pouring down at Dandelion.

'Yurts, so that people without homes would have somewhere to shelter from the rain,' says Hayden, who is a gentle, kind boy.

'Motorbikes,' says Herbie.

Ted is thinking of his belly. 'Raisins,' he says.

Esme's eyes light up.

'Chocolate AND money,' she says.

Esme has a magpie's eye for trinkets. Her seventh birthday list does not reveal much of her passion for nature:

Mermaid stachue
Fake glasses
A Hachimal
A bungk bed with a desk
A upstairs cage for the guinea pigs
Ten Pikmi Pops
Hairdorables
Money
A squishy toy
A proper mermaid tail

Watch Strictly in the real stadium
A lemur costume

Milly's list is much the same, shaped by the adverts between children's programmes on Channel 5 and, increasingly, by their friends. I'm struck by how many of these plastic objects of desire are ersatz pets. A Hatchimal is a large plastic egg which eventually cracks and releases a fluffy toy that talks and can be 'reared' from baby to toddler to child. A year earlier, we caved in to Esme's desire for 'My Fairy Garden'. It was a miniature plastic garden with two real beans decorated with a pattern on their sides – a seed commodified into a toy. We planted them in the garden and they grew into a bean-like but beanless green plant.

Most modern toys are designed to be 'collectable'. Perhaps they speak to our innate desire to forage and gather stuff. Milly and Esme soon learn the toymakers' language of 'special edition', 'rare', and that pinnacle of desirability, 'ultra-rare'. Their drawers fill with those plastic toys that come stapled to the front of children's magazines.

Ted picks up another bucket and joins our conker hunt. Eyes down, engrossed, gleaning; the sun warms our backs as the first falling leaves slowly spiral down. The children collect with their eyes but also with their feet, feeling the lump of a conker through the soles of their boots. They spot other things too: pigeon feathers, and a baby frog, frantically dancing away from them in the long wet grass.

This mellow autumnal activity evolves into a competition, and a squabble.

'I'm the Queen of finding conkers,' announces Esme.

'I'm the King,' says Ted. He's an inveterate hoarder, stowing away pebbles, cereal boxes or milk cartons like an old craftsman, for the day they'll find a use. All the tool work he has done at Dandelion has made him an inventor, always busy with real tools.

'You've only found three conkers,' scoffs Esme. 'You haven't found as many as me. I'm the best at collecting.' She chunters on, as relentlessly provocative as an internet troll, rolling conkers into her bucket with a satisfying clunk that feels like the last word in an argument.

Ted is unfazed.

'I've got six,' he announces, and throws more in. 'I've got eleven . . . I've got eighteen now.' I see no sign that he's counting but whenever I check in his bucket he's got the number right.

'Look how much I've got now. I've got a squillion.' Well, almost.

Esme sighs, sounding the note of a deeply experienced, slightly jaded conker diva.

'I've got more than a squillion, babe. Look in my bucket and see.'

Ted is now preoccupied with the challenge of putting an uncracked case under his heel, and applying just the right amount of pressure to liberate the conker without crushing it.

Esme disappears to what she calls her 'secret spot'. This is outside our garden, on the verge of the rutted concrete road that ushers white vans, too fast, into the industrial estate. I've let her out of my sight, trusting that she will stick to the verge. Like every growing child, she strains to stray beyond the constant surveillance of modern parenting.

Milly wanders outside to show me her drawings of a made-up bird. When she realises we are collecting, she is keen to join in. Milly is our family's collector-in-chief. When we're on the beach, she's forever giving me stones to store for her. She's a tranquil person, and collecting is a tranquil pursuit; she quietly sings as she goes.

She and Esme collect in a harmonious fashion, bending and picking with the focus of seasonal workers on piecework rates.

'Look Mil-Mil,' says Esme. 'We've got twins.' She's found two conkers pressed together in a case, each with one flat side, like the simplest three-dimensional jigsaw. Then she finds triplets, a rarity.

After another twenty minutes, the buckets are almost too heavy to carry. We've gathered almost all the tree's fallen seeds and Milly, Esme and Ted have sated their desire for conkers. When I put my hand in their buckets these polished wooden stones possess a warmth that seems to promise incipient life.

I throw an old blanket on the grass and suggest that they count their bucket-loads.

In the late afternoon sunshine, Esme curls around her hoard like Smaug in *The Hobbit*. 'Ah, my precious conkers,' she says, turning a little Gollum.

We arrange them in lines of ten. I dash off on some household task and when I return Esme is still lying with her collection, in a post-conker-gathering reverie. Whatever she's thinking, she's relaxed, in the present moment, and not asking for anything.

We count two hundred and forty-four.

'Oh jeez,' says Esme. 'I'm going to tell Mum I'm breaking a record.'

For Milly, collecting is less about possession and more a kind of dream time. But she also collects to create. She fills a large sock with her conker collection and ties up the end, and then she and Esme make 'conker babies': Milly's stuffed sock wears glasses and a label that says 'Baby Conky'. Her greatest conker invention comes later: she pours warm water into her bucket of conkers to make a 'conker foot massage'. I can confirm it is genuinely restorative. Milly's appreciation of the sensory qualities of these fallen fruit reminds me how children are often more alive than adults to the physical pleasures found in the ordinary nature around us.

Milly begins a different collection – sweet chestnuts – one Saturday when we visit a wood. Unlike the sparse pins on a horse chestnut case, a sweet chestnut's green and yellow shells feature unbreakable clusters of fierce spikes. It's painful to pull these cases apart with bare fingers. Milly learns to gently stamp on the clusters to open them and pull the nuts out. She's collecting for collecting's sake but we tell her we can eat them. We choose the biggest eight, slit their shiny skins with a knife and rest them on a spade, which we hold over a campfire. They roast and Milly tastes her first chestnut. It's crumbly and so dry it sticks on the tongue, but she's surprised by its sweetness.

A few days later, our much-prized conker hoard is looking neglected – tarnishing, drying out and losing its new-minted magic. The buckets fill with September rains. One or two conkers burst forth in optimistic pink sprouts.

This is fine. The children do not love the conkers for ever, even though freshly fallen they exhibit all the beauty we require of jewelry. They love the hunt. Children collect for the pleasure of collecting. Later, they collect to make a collection. The makers of a million small plastic toys know this. It takes me a while to understand that the same process as conker-collecting unfolds when our children pursue a particular toy. They love taking their savings to the village toy shop (we must live in one of the last British villages to include a toy shop). Once their object of desire is bought, they will often play imaginative games with the Hatchimal, or whatever it may be, for several days. Then a new object of desire slides into view.

I belatedly realise that I assume a toy fulfils a need, whereas children are actually natural window-shoppers. It is the process they want; the possession is less important. At least the tarnished conkers will decompose; the plastic, not so much.

After Esme has completed one year of flexi-schooling, mixing her conventional education with Dandelion's outdoor schooling, I report to Becky Quinn with a sense of trepidation. Having seen how outdoor schooling has benefited Esme, we want to give Milly the opportunity as well.

I'm not sure I have an argument that will appeal to Mrs Quinn, who agreed to Esme's flexi-schooling because she recognised that the twins would benefit from some time apart. But I'm helped by Esme's end-of-year results. Despite being out of school for one or two days each week, the teacher's assessments show she has 'caught up' with Milly in every area of attainment and is one of the better readers in her class. But I'm still surprised when Mrs Quinn agrees that we can send all three children to Dandelion once a week during the next academic year, when Ted too will be old enough for school. It may be her simply being generous, but I hope there is a benefit for the school as well. By facilitating flexi-schooling, she can demonstrate to Ofsted inspectors that her school is providing personalised learning and is open to different options for pupils with different learning styles.

The head's blessing is a huge hurdle overcome; but there is another, more challenging issue. Milly loves school, and is decidedly lukewarm about going to 'forest school'. I don't believe that six-year-olds can make informed decisions about their education but nor do I believe in a child suffering because of their parents' ideology. We decide to take Milly to Dandelion for the first half of the autumn term, and then review it. We tell her it is a trial, to see how it goes, and we can decide together if she's to continue after half-term.

Dandelion's outdoor nursery mirrors how we have organised our lives for all but a century or two, since Neolithic times: the children live outdoors in an enclosure, with fire, security, elders. This term, some of the pupils take a leap further back in human evolution, and become hunter-gatherers. The older children, who are mostly home-schooled five- and six-year-olds and who come to Dandelion once a week for their taste of non-institutional learning, are now taken to the Heath, a common a mile beyond the village, part of a swathe of coniferous woodland and open heathland on the sandy acidic soils north of Norwich. Here, between gorse, heather and plantations of conifer and sweet chestnut coppice, the older children are schooled in the forest.

Esme adores this 'proper' Forest School iteration of Dandelion. 'I feel more kind of free,' she says after a few sessions. Although Dandelion's rules mean I cannot volunteer there alongside my own children, one day I run an errand to the Heath when Esme is there. She looks self-contained and self-assured and takes me through the wood, deftly weaving between the lower storey of spiky sweet chestnut saplings, to show me her den. It's a scrape in the forest floor under a small conifer, a circle of cosiness and warmth. It looks like a place where a deer might curl up for the night.

Milly and Ted are less enraptured with the Heath. Milly doesn't actively hate the first few sessions at Dandelion, but she is far from enthusiastic.

'Dad,' she says plaintively out of nowhere one day. 'Why do you make me go to forest school?' I worry she's earmarked me as the family's forest school ideologue, but she says the same to Lisa. When I pick them up after their third session, Milly is lying listlessly on the bank at the edge of the Heath.

What did you do today?

'Not much,' she says. 'We just walked and stopped for five minutes and then walked and stopped for five minutes and walked.'

Gradually, more stories seep out. They found a fly agaric, those white-spotted red fungi, which Ted adores. Jen, their teacher, discovered an antler discarded by a deer. And the three children were very taken with Jen's story from her weekend, about her cat somehow catching a mole in her garden. The mole died.

Despite all this interesting stuff, Ted gives the day a thumbs down too (thumbs up, thumbs in the middle and thumbs down comprise a rating system they seem to have acquired from Dandelion). What was your favourite thing from the day? 'Didn't have one,' he mutters.

Least favourite? 'When I fell over on some pine needles,' says Ted. 'The other one was I really wanted Milly to stay close but she kept running away.'

Poor Milly. Through Ted's depiction of the day, I realise why she is not enjoying forest school. All three Barkham siblings in one small group is no change from home. The Heath is new for Ted, he feels insecure, and so he leans, heavily, on Milly. She is forced into a mothering role. This is a drag for her. Another problem is more intractable: Milly and Esme don't have many peers. Last year at Dandelion, Esme regularly had the company of twelve girls and boys of a similar age. Unfortunately, most of that group have moved on and the newcomers on the Heath are five-year-olds like Ted. Girls of seven don't always want to play with what we used to call 'little 'uns'. There is only one girl in the forest school group who is Milly and Esme's age. As friendships become more important, this setup is not as attractive as a class with twenty-eight peers.

Emma and Hayley at Dandelion suggest we tweak our new arrangement by returning Ted to the main site in Marsham, thus liberating Milly to enjoy the Heath without the drag of a little brother. So we give this a go. It's a success, at first. Ted is happy to be back in the nest-like security of the main Dandelion site. He is more of a farmer than a hunter-gatherer. And Milly gives her first Heath day liberated from older-sister duties a thumbs up. She loved collecting and making things. Some time later, though, she's crying again.

'Dad, why do you want me to go to forest school? I just want to go to school.'

Again, I am troubled by the decision we've made. Are we putting dogma ahead of her happiness? Milly does not love the natural world in the overt way that her sister does but she is as comfortable as anyone in natural places, and the space and peace of outdoors spark her imagination. But also, Milly knows herself best, and it is undeniable that she enjoys school. She likes its rules and regulations, its predictability and its sociability. She loves stretching her hand high and calling out the answer. She adores 'work' and 'hard work'. Lisa is wavering. But I want Milly to give Dandelion a go until Christmas. I'm clinging to the hope that she'll grow to love it, not because I want my children to be obsessed with wildlife but because I believe the natural world provides an arena in which they grow well, and can be happy.

One fine autumn day, I collect them from Dandelion. On the drive home, they make plans, each one forming a clear picture of what they are going to do for the rest of the afternoon.

'Milly, when we get back can we play some Lego?' suggests Ted.

'I want to look at the school website and play some games,' says Milly. Their school website hosts some links to educational games. Any gamer-kid would find them boring but because Milly is deprived of computer games at home she is thrilled by a simple online counting test. And she knows that her case is boosted by the games' provenance, associated with the school.

It sounds melodramatic, but when a small child has dutifully obeyed the rules all day – even the subtler rules of a forest school

– and then finds they are denied any agency at home, they are devastated. So our decision to take them to the beach is greeted with great wails.

'I'm just so annoyed,' says Milly.

'By the old stupid beach,' finishes Esme.

Why don't you like the beach?

'It's just boring and sunny in summer. And now it's all wintery,' says Milly. 'I don't like getting sandy.'

I often meet with resistance when I take the children on modest nature adventures. Many glowing accounts of time spent in nature with children are written by enraptured fathers who belatedly discover the wonder of hanging out with a single child. It is easy to be a wildlife mentor to one child. There is a simple and intimate relationship between you, the child and nature. They are far more likely to relish the experience as well, because it is special time with one parent. It is very different taking two, three or more on a nature trip, especially if all three are having simultaneous meltdowns. The synchronised tantrums are quite comical, but I'm always relieved that they are too embarrassed to perform them beyond the privacy of our home or car.

Each time I press on with these outdoor plans, however, I feel vindicated by the fact that the children enjoy themselves. I'm sure this would also be the case if I dragged reluctant offspring to the shops; children can teach us a lesson in acceptance, and in making the best of a situation. But I'm not convinced there would be such a high level of contentment during and after a shopping trip.

The beach has a special place in our society, and a unique place in childhood. The strip of sand, mud, shingle or rock between land and sea is the last wild ecosystem where the child is still a thriving species, where children are granted almost as much freedom as they've ever had. While woodlands have been fenced off and commons enclosed, the beach remains the last public space. It is the biggest sand pit and the best water park. We bond with the beach during childhood holidays and our adult enthusiasm is so addling that we may cast aside rational fears of potentially lethal tides and currents and the less rational fears of strangers to allow our children to play half-naked among people we don't know. We let them roam further from us than we ever would in a city; sometimes a young child even strays beyond view. For children of five and above, the beach offers two things they value: a social space for meeting new children, and freedom. Parents may be better company on a beach too, but I know from once interviewing a class of ten-year-olds from Bloxham Primary in Oxfordshire about the beach that, when there, adults usually disappear from a child's consciousness. For children, this sandy Arcadia is all about liberation, an absence of rules, in the company of peers.

On this sunny autumnal afternoon, the children's resistance melts away as soon as we step out of the car behind the dunes at Sea Palling. A kestrel hovers against the westerly, eyes scanning the rabbit-shorn turf between the windblown marram. The salt in the cool air blasts us like a reviving potion. There is warm shelter in the dunes and a flash of bright orange, a late-summer small copper butterfly. Esme creeps in, trying to catch it with her hands. We walk, scuffing the sand, tracing patterns as we go. The surface is damp after recent rain and each footstep detonates the dry sand underneath, which fizzes like a firework. Because of the protests, I've brought a kite and also *Charlie and the Chocolate Factory*, which I've promised to read on the beach. Neither is requested. Shoes off, warm feet gingerly placed on chilly wet sand, and they're off, running away, imaginations ignited by the uneven lumps of Norwegian granite that form a sea defence.

They begin to squabble over the roles they will take in their imaginative game but it does not escalate into a major dispute, as it invariably would at home. On the beach there are no private possessions; conflict rolls away like seaweed hustled along the sand by the breeze. The enormity of the flat-calm sea is a peacemaker. There's an ever-present potential for serendipity and stimulation.

'Guys, look at this cool track,' calls out Esme, and the three crouch to inspect the treads of a tractor which has driven along the beach to retrieve a small boat from the water's edge. After I absent-mindedly trace a smiley face in the smooth wet sand left by the retreating tide, Esme draws her name in enormous letters. Milly follows her lead, and tirelessly makes patterns and words in stones and shells. The sea is serene and shimmies between silver, dark blue and brown. There is no noise apart from a distant dog barking at a swimmer it has mistaken for a seal. The soft light and soft air are a balm, a gift from the retreating sun, all the more precious for the knowledge that these days will not last and winter will soon be upon us.

The pavements around our home are papered with red leaves from cherries and ornamental acers, and one sunny half-term morning I take Milly, Esme and Ted on an organised 'fungus foray' at a country park, half an hour's drive away.

This is mainly an expedition for Ted. One morning he woke up and declared to me, apropos of nothing: 'I hate hunting for butterflies.' There had only been one day, back in the summer, when I took him to look for swallowtails at nearby How Hill. Another day he asked: 'Why do you like birds so much? They are just boring things that fly through the sky.' I guess this is his reaction against Esme, who has commandeered those passions for herself. 'I like things that move,' she says. She and Ted clash, and he needs to define himself against her, and perhaps against me too. Boys can't always follow their fathers; they must find a different path.

So Ted loves fungi.

When he began at Dandelion, I overheard him teaching Milly a song he'd learned:

Don't eat fungi
Even if you're hungry
It would be a mistake
You'll get a tummy ache

During the risk assessment at Dandelion, fungi are sought out, and identified if possible. The rule is 'don't touch', but I disagree. I think children should touch all fungi, as long as they wash their hands before eating; the chances of finding a seriously dangerous fungus such as a deathcap in Dandelion's half-acre are almost zero, but I understand why the teachers can't take that risk. (Esme is fascinated by zombies, ghost stories, fatal road traffic accidents and anything with 'death' in its name, from death's-head hawkmoths to deathcaps. She regularly coos over the deathcaps in my fungus field-guide, and craves gory tales of death by mushroom consumption since reading one guidebook that says untreated deathcap poisoning has a mortality rate of fifty to ninety per cent.)

For his fourth birthday Ted asks for a fly-agaric-themed party, an esoteric choice that is unexpectedly easy to deliver given that the internet is awash with fly agaric tat. I've not seen a fly agaric on my woodland walks for years, so I'm amazed when Ted returns home from the nursery at our local primary school with one he found in the small plantation of thirty-year-old trees at the bottom of the playing field. His teachers let him take it home too, which I was cheered by.

Ted is keen on the idea of the fungus foray, but Milly and Esme are opposed. My parents notice that my generation are much more likely to bow to our children's moods, but I think parents should pay attention when children are distressed. Whenever I listen to ours, I usually find that their reasons for being upset are flawlessly rational. Just like us, children rarely appreciate being hustled away from their own plans; equally, just like us, they don't always know what will make them happy and keep them well. And it's always tricky to convince young children to embrace an activity they don't understand in a place they've never been to before. Esme's opposition is the most adamant.

'I don't want to go on a fungus foray,' she says firmly over breakfast.

It's just like a play in the woods, I explain. You can run free.

'I WON'T go,' she announces, face buried behind a thick curtain of hair.

Volunteering at Dandelion has made me aware that most

conventional schools operate systems of reward and punishment. In my day it was stars – bronze, silver and gold – and now it's 'traffic lights' or smiley – and unsmiley – faces. I suppose life has to have carrots and sticks, but Emma and Hayley don't offer any rewards, or punishments, apart from precise words of praise or admonishment for positive and negative behaviour. They believe people aren't authentically moved or motivated by bribes. As parents, we know we probably shouldn't resort to sweets or money but most of us occasionally appeal to our children's baser natures.

If you come on the fungus foray, I say quietly to Esme, that's like a job, and I will pay you for doing a job.

The wailing stops. Hair is pulled aside as if the sun has risen. 'How much?'

It is probably a £2.50 job, I say, the most that Esme has ever earned, for washing the car. She is determinedly saving for a Kidizoom watch, a plastic 'smart' watch for kids that is a screen-on-a-wrist and contains various dubious games.

Esme's desire to save £50 for this watch is a powerful force. Resistance has been broken. Milly is reluctantly won round by the promise of £2.50 too, and starts day-dreaming about her birthday list. We pile into the car, the sun shines, the air is still, and hulking great crop-sprayers dispensing chemicals cast long shadows on the fields they are disinfecting of all life.

I prefer to discover nature for myself, but when we lack familiarity with certain wildlife, organised tours are an indispensable introduction. The people who volunteer to run pond dips and owl prowls, birdwatches and bioblitzes on their evenings and weekends are unsung heroes. And the fact that forty-seven people have turned up to look for fungi in Holt Country Park shows our hunger to spend time in nature and learn more about it. This free event isn't designed for children, but there are more than a dozen here, ranging in age from nought to eighteen. The nought is in her buggy, gazing up at autumn leaves that quake in the breeze as if fearing their imminent fall. 'She loves looking at the trees,' says her mum. The eighteen-year-old has green hair, a black Sea Shepherd beanie, and a black T-shirt that says: I HATE PEOPLE.

I've dragged my children on this trip for two reasons: first, I know nothing about fungi; and second, the leader is Tony Leech. Tony has white hair, a perpetual smile and a slight stoop as if he is forever about to pluck a mushroom from the ground. He is Norfolk's county recorder for fungi, tasked with authenticating sightings and logging new species, and his enthusiasm is undimmed by years at this Herculean task. He is a former biology teacher who is naturally learned but wonderfully open with his knowledge; a storyteller and teacher who also listens; a nature mentor who enjoys human company as well as the comfort of fungi.

He wears a hand lens on a red strap around his neck and holds a shallow woven basket that carries a knife. This has a fluorescent yellow handle so he can see it if he drops it on the forest floor. With an extremely clear voice that is never raised – a ninja skill of every gifted teacher – he explains the rules of the expedition.

Does it matter if we pick fungi? Fungi are blooms, or fruits; most live under ground as mycelium, a network of tiny threads called hyphae that we typically imagine as the slender subterranean branches of an enormous tree. Picking fungi is not dissimilar to picking blackberries, but Tony offers a couple of caveats. Commercial picking is a problem and in a dry season like this one, when there aren't many fungi, even our picking-to-identify could disadvantage fungal reproduction. The real conservation issue, he explains, is not the fungi but the creatures living within them. Picking and removing fungi will deny maggoty invertebrates the chance to turn into winged insects, bugs and beetles. Generally, though, we're permitted to pick on this trip.

Then there's safety. Take the deathcap, says Tony. Esme's eyes light up. 'Even if you rubbed a deathcap and then licked your hands you would not die,' says Tony. 'Although if you did it over and over again perhaps you would not be so lucky.'

After five minutes of chat, we're off into the woods. Sunlight spills through terracotta-coloured scenery. The autumn serenity is broken only by the dry scrabble of grey squirrel claws as they twist around tree trunks. Children zigzag through brambles and bounce on a carpet of freshly fallen leaves. An eight-year-old girl is first to spy a cluster of pale-brown caps rising from a low black tree stump: honey fungus.

Taxonomists have identified around 120,000 species of fungi, but we know only a fragment of their true diversity: there may be anything between 2.2 and 3.8 million species. We lack a language to talk about this astonishing kingdom, and often use inappropriate analogies from the world of plants. Tony makes this complex universe pleasingly simple as we find various specimens and take them to him. He quickly names a false chanterelle and an orange bonnet, a tiny very beautiful fungus with a slender stem and an orange cap ('very common but overlooked – you just think it's a berry').

Most wildlife identification looks like witchcraft, but it is simply a question of practice and paying attention to detail. It comes naturally to children. Fungus identification demands more of our senses than, say, identifying butterflies, which we assess using our eyes only. We identify birds by sound as well as sight; with plants we may use touch as well as sight, and the occasional peer through a microscope. But fungi can require touch, smell, taste and dissection.

Our next find is a butter cap. Tony holds it high as we cluster around. 'Even on a dry day it's quite greasy,' he explains. 'Who found this one? Do you want to stroke it?' He pauses. 'It's always got a soggy bottom.' He pinches the base of its stem.

Smell is a neglected skill. 'We have a very good memory for smells,' he says. 'What we don't have is a vocabulary for them.'

He holds up a pretty little fungus called the lilac bonnet which smells 'a bit like either raw potatoes or radish'. Then there's a small cream button of a fungus called the chemical knight. The knights are a group of fungi and this one is named after its 'rather odd' bleachy smell. Next, Tony passes around an earthball, which looks like a small beige puffball. What does it smell like? Tony asks the group. Trust your instincts, he urges us. People close their eyes, and pass it around.

'Rubber boots!' exclaims one woman.

'Hot rubber,' says another.

'Brakes,' says someone else.

There is another fungus, recalls Tony, which old guidebooks describe as smelling 'like a fresh nurse's blouse'. Like much fungal nomenclature, there is a whiff of innuendo about it. But we can understand where the old mycologists were coming from when we learn its scientific name, *Tricholoma saponaceum*: *saponaceum*, derived from the Latin, means 'pertaining to soap'. Its French common name is *tricholome à odeur de savon*; in Britain it's known as the soap-scented toadstool, or the soapy knight. Until recently, most fungi were identified in Britain using their scientific names. Few had common names, which are, in effect, folk names, and an important clue to a species' place in our culture. The absence of most species from folklore shows the scant attention we have historically paid this vast group of organisms.

A few years back, mycologists formed a committee to devise folk names. It sounds terribly dull, says Tony, but he thinks they did their job with panache, inventing a plethora of evocative names, from the hairy curtain crust to the scurfy twiglet.

After a while, Tony has to use his taste buds to identify a bracket fungus attached to a mossy log. He pops a piece into his mouth and masticates in a bovine sort of way before spitting it out again. 'This is not the bitter bracket,' he decides. 'It's the grayling bracket.' Fungi, Tony reveals, defy our binary notions of edible and poisonous. Some people react violently to eating species that leave others untroubled. Tony thinks the brown rollrim – it has a roll to the edge of its cap – is edible but unappetising. Then he checks himself. During the Second World War, people suffering food shortages in rural France ate them. Unfortunately, repeated brown rollrim meals killed them. This fungus sensitises the body and causes red blood cells to burst. Guidebooks say its toxin is cumulative. This is not like, say, lead, where the poison slowly builds up. The human body appears to become more sensitive to the brown rollrim the more it is eaten, until a final serving becomes fatal.

Tony turns now to field dissection, to identify one. 'What I'm looking for is red juice. It's either a bleeding bonnet or it's a burgundy bonnet.' The fungus is dripping with a deep-crimson substance. Burgundy bonnet, like the wine, he decides. The 'egg' of the dog's stinkhorn is even more alluring. 'This is the "egg" from which the stinkhorn hatches,' he announces, holding up a small cream package. 'It smells of dog muck. I don't think that's the only reason it's called a dog's stinkhorn but I'll leave that to your imagination.' He prises the egg open with his knife to reveal an orange-yellow 'yolk'.

Finally we find a fly agaric, and this celebrity fungus draws excited 'Ohs' from Tony's audience as he holds it up and describes its features. The white spots on its bright scarlet-fading-to-orange cap are not part of its skin but the remains of a membrane that completely encloses the fungus when it's young, and then mostly disappears except for the fragments on top. This fungus, at least, does play a starring role in folklore and fairy-stories. On cue, an elderly member of our group tells the children: 'When you go to bed at night all the elves, pixies and fairies come out to work in the woods,' he says. (The woods as a place of work are almost a foreign concept to us now.) 'They sit on the toadstools and have their lunch and the white specky bits are where they've left their crumbs.' I can see the children drawing a picture of this in their minds; it's lovely how older and younger generations can share stories during these group events.

The sunny day is becoming somniferous and the foragers are chatting, distracted, as we wander along a leaf-strewn, yellow-lit track. The children in the group are still searching keenly, except for my own epitome of eagerness. Esme is drooping. This surprises me because we are enjoying a hands-on experience, and many of these ornaments of autumn must appeal to her appreciation of jeopardy and morbidity. It's clear that the edibility of fungi is an attraction for many foragers but this sensory pleasure is not open to Esme: she hates eating mushrooms. She has a superb sense of smell but she doesn't appreciate the deliciously earthy, mushroomy scents we meet today.

Here on the heath, I belatedly realise that our use of the term 'nature lover' is too vague and generalised a label, and a symptom of our wildlife-bereft lives. There are as many types of nature lover as there are music lovers. As we move between gorse thickets, Esme spies a movement on the ground and is instantly animated. A small copper flicks its wings and dashes off, and she does her utmost to catch it in her discarded coat. Esme is a hunter and a tracker; she likes the thrill of the chase. She's got less time for inanimate objects: for plants, rainbows or sunsets. She wants chicks and lemurs, owls and death's-head hawkmoths. She's less keen on structured activity. Above all else, she wants to run free, and follow the serendipitous happenings that catch the air, flare the nostrils and quicken the blood; the constant shifting constellation of stimuli offered by any outdoor green space.

By contrast, Milly is enjoying pottering about. She possesses the patience to keep looking, and takes pleasure in assembling her collection. She also likes showing things to Tony, receiving praise and information about her finds. Ted loves fungi but would be happier as his own chief fungus identifier, inventing his own names for them and 'teaching' them to me and Tony. His favourite find of the day is a shard of smashed glass, translucent pale green and unusually thick. 'This is definitely a car window screen,' he says with grave authority.

Each child brings away different things from the day. But wild time does not always deliver instant gratification for parents in terms of visibly transformed children. As mine grow older, they are becoming less uncritically accepting of my choices for their attention. I'm sure they will turn away from nature in their teens. But if we've spent enough time in green places in our younger years, I believe we are bequeathed a sensitivity and a basic wild literacy that can serve us well if we seek to return at a later point in our lives. Perhaps a snapshot memory of one marvellous fungus will stay with my children; perhaps this day is another tiny dose of a positive essence, a joy for the natural world that is slowly accreting inside them; perhaps it will be swiftly forgotten; perhaps it is enough that we have bathed in the forest for an afternoon.

At least I am calm enough afterwards to cope with the irony of the children gleefully spending their £2.50 fungus-foray earnings on the cheap thrills, the blare and the lights of our local amusement arcade.

10

Growing Up

'What is the extinction of a condor to a child who has never seen a wren?'

Robert Pyle

The woods are along a lane past the old engine house in the former pit village. They are a dry, heathy place, all unexpected ups and downs, cloaked in mustard and gold. The wind runs through the canopy in waves, worrying the leaves, but it is calm and snug in the green brambly understorey. The slender trunks of silver birches shine in the low November sunlight.

I sit in Bestwood Country Park at the top of a hill on the edge of Nottingham. Waiting alongside me is Kate Milman. Kate is a youthful early forties, and looks just the sort of person who works with children: kind, fit and slightly weary, cheeks flushed from working outside. We are both layered in the warm, shapeless garb of the Forest School practitioner. From somewhere above us comes the anxious 'cheeeept-cheeept' of a great spotted woodpecker. Then another call, carried on the wind.

'Kooooo-eeeeeeeeee!'

Kate replies, with a completely unexpected volume:

'Kooooo-eeeeeeeeee!'

Out of our sight at the bottom of the hill, the children's anticipation rises. They are allowed to run free, to seek out Kate.

I hear the heaving of a small pair of lungs before I see the boy, Mohammad, a slim child bent double with effort, legs flying out sideways like a skittish calf, eager to win his own personal race. Next up the hill is a tiny beaming ten-year-old from Syria. 'I'm Amira but you can call me Lion,' she grins.

All nine children are effervescent. I can't banish the image of a group of puppies, bouncing around outdoors for the first time. Kate and I walk to the Wild Things base camp. The children scamper ahead, shimmying around brambles, poking around the site with the sharp-eyed curiosity of chickens, investigating branches, tree stumps, and some interesting-looking clippers laid out on a tarpaulin.

These ten-year-olds are members of an 'English as a second language' group from Forest Fields Primary and Nursery School. The school's bucolic name belies its position in central Nottingham. Its 620 children speak fifty-two languages. All of today's group arrived in Britain within the last two years. Several started school only two months ago. They are from Pakistan, Afghanistan, Romania and Syria. Some have arrived via refugee camps. 'You don't know what they've seen,' says their teaching assistant, Yasmin Khaliq, who speaks five languages and has been bringing groups to Wild Things for nine years. 'It's a godsend,' she says. 'It's all outdoors, they are seeing things with their own eyes, there's no language barrier.'

When I talk to people about forest schooling, everyone agrees that it's very important to help children 'connect' with the natural world. But, they often say, it's terribly middle-class and white, isn't it? How is it relevant to the life experience of an impoverished Asian girl living in a big city?

I don't like the idea that nature is a luxury. I believe good-quality green space in every neighbourhood should be a modern-day human right. And nature is even more important for disadvantaged children, who cannot buy green experiences like middle-class ones can. During my year at Dandelion, I've seen how simple time outdoors benefits very young children but, over two decades, the project Kate Milman is part of has demonstrated how it has enhanced the lives of older children as well as those with little opportunity to run wild in their everyday existence.

Twenty-one years ago, when she was barely out of her teens, she and some friends set up a workers' cooperative called Wild Things. Ever since, they've been providing six-week woodland experiences for inner-city schoolchildren.

When I first speak to her on the phone, the brief story she tells me feels like a ray of sunlight through the trees. The daughter of teachers, she grew up in comfortable, leafy Sevenoaks in Kent. When she was fourteen and attending the local girls' grammar school, her best friend was at an all-boys school. He invited her on night walks with his friends. They would throw a dart at a map, and just hike there. Having reached the spot, they would make a fire and sit around it, then stroll back at dawn. Kate joined them and found respite from the travails of being a teenage girl. In the dark, in the woods, she did not worry what she looked like. She found herself thinking, 'I like myself out here. As a young woman, that's what saved my self-esteem – the ability to be outside,' she says.

When she was twenty-one and studying at university, the woods called her again. She paused her degree in 1996 to join protests against the Newbury bypass, which was being carved out through idyllic wooded countryside in Berkshire. She took up residence in a treehouse, in the path of the bulldozers, and lived there for months. It was a revelation. 'I had a massively privileged upbringing in Sevenoaks but I'd never felt at home in myself,' she says. 'This wood felt like home.'

She lived intimately with the catkins, the calling birds, the slow-slow-fast change in the seasons. Despite being in a precarious position of protest, she felt completely safe and her brain was calmed. 'You know when you go camping and you go back to your house and everything just feels wrong? The lighting is harsh and everything seems complicated indoors. It just got under my skin, this feeling – this [living in the woods] is like being at home.'

Finally, however, she was evicted from her forest heartland. The men and their machines arrived beneath her tree. Kate was arrested under a newly created 'aggravated trespass' law and barred from joining the protests again. The wood was ripped apart.

'That level of grief – it felt like losing somebody.' It was a highly complex woodland and she had come to know it intimately. 'I knew how beautiful it was at dawn and at full moon, and then it was bulldozed. What are we capable of? How can we destroy such diversity and then just move on? When you watch that amount of stupidity, when you have that much grief and impotence, what can you do with it?'

The idea for Wild Things was born.

For three days each week, she and her fellow co-op members, Kath, Kat and Nick (her partner), provide half-day sessions for groups of nine pupils from various city schools. The other two days they 'scrat around' for charitable funding because, mostly, the only way to get pupils from cash-strapped state schools into the woods is to offer their sessions for free. So they survive on a minuscule co-op 'share' wage and she lives with Nick and their eight-year-old son in a small rural housing co-op. They drive a battered high-top Transit stashed with bow saws, loppers, clippers, ropes, tarpaulins, plastic mugs, hot chocolate and other essentials such as children's wellies and woollen gloves – their pupils rarely bring clothes suitable for outdoors.

The children sit around the fire circle while Kate, Kath and Kat ('the three Ks') show them how to use loppers and saws and explain today's activities. The pupils choose their own adventure. This child-led approach is intended to offer an alternative to the standard didactic, adult-led education which misses 'that whole chunk of experience where children are just getting to be a wild animal', thinks Kate. Ten-year-olds 'are at that stage of development where they need to feel liberated and free'.

Today the children can learn to use bows and arrows; build a fire and cook on it; or lay a trail, hide, and have another group track them down. The activities, says Kate when we break for lunch, are really giving them an excuse to mooch and dream in the forest. No two children respond to the wood and its 'loose parts' in the same way. Kate and her colleagues are constantly surprised by the infinite span of children's creative thought and their willingness to express it in the woods: one boy decides to build a gym, another a mask; one girl says she spies a frog and a turtle crossing their path.

I join Kat and a trio of girls – keen little Amira; Homa, a gracious Pakistani girl; and Cristina, a Roma Gypsy from

Romania with a long plait, who wears a purple jumpsuit and a shiny purple puffer jacket. Cristina has very little English but understands more than she says.

Our mission is to lay a trail of arrows made from sticks through the wood to where we will hide from the other members of the group.

'Like da?' says Cristina, fashioning an arrow from three large branches.

'Make it smaller?' suggests Kat.

'No. Big!' says Cristina.

Cristina gasps exclamations as we twist along a narrow path, passing a tree stump decorated with a gleaming bracket fungus as improbable as a white Cadillac in the dark woods. Beech leaves shine luminous orange on the forest floor. 'Come on guys!' says Cristina. Last week she didn't talk at all, says Kat.

I struggle to break a large stick into arrow pieces. Homa laughs: 'Cristina is stronger than you,' she says.

They shape another arrow.

'Gorgeous!' exclaims Homa, twice, proud of this shiny new word.

We lay arrows at every turn and eventually reach an old quarry, where there are good hiding bushes. Three wood pigeons crash through the trees.

'I think someone is coming,' giggles Homa. 'Perhaps a wolf.'

We hide together behind some gorse. Kat calls the others on her walkie-talkie and invites the girls to say something.

'Come, come,' whispers Cristina, delightedly, into the walkie-talkie.

After ten minutes, we hear shouts and crashings. The other

group run into the quarry. We huddle and giggle and Sanaya, a ten-year-old who loves to run, hurtles into the clearing and finally spots us. 'She might not be able to stretch her legs and run at home,' says Yasmin of Sanaya. 'She's expressing her character.'

I assumed that most refugees come from big cities in their homeland, but Wild Things have worked with many migrant children who have grown up in rural areas. British-born city children belong to a country called Indoors – they ask Kate, 'What's mud?' or 'Why are there so many trees here?' It is often only now, in Britain, that children from rural places overseas are confined to city-centre flats. Their questions – 'Are there elephants?' 'Are there deadly snakes here?' – are rooted in real experiences in their country of origin. For many, says Kate, the woods awaken lost memories, and a yearning for home. 'As soon as we light a fire they say, "Ahhhhh, I know this", or they point to a plant and get really animated. They are in their element.'

Last spring, one group included a partially sighted girl. 'Walking up into the woods, she stopped and said, "Listen to that sound!"' remembers Kate. 'It was the buzzing of the insects.' It reminded the girl of life in her former country. At the end of her six weeks, she said, 'I feel like I've come home.' The Wild Things staff frequently hear similar declarations. 'Often children can feel at home in the woods in a way they find more difficult in the community they have been landed in, where technology is everything, money is everything, they are at the bottom of the pecking order, and there are massive tensions in the area. In the woods they are on a level playing field. They can just be kids again.'

We return to the fire circle and the children discuss their plans for next week.

'Make a wood house,' says Sanaya. 'I made a house with sticks in Pakistan. My grandma makes a fire like this.'

It reminds you of home? 'Yes.'

I ask them what's the best thing about the wood.

'Everything,' says Homa. 'Hide-and-seek, the fire, and the bread, because that makes us all hot.'

This prompts Adnan to reminisce about his life in Syria. 'I used to like playing with my cousins. It was just like this but with less trees.'

Cristina is the most reluctant to leave.

'Next time, again?' she asks Kate, looking worried. Kate counts on her fingers to show Cristina seven days.

Cristina's face lengthens at the prospect of such a long wait, but she joins the rest of the group hurtling back down the hill to their minibus heading for the city, and their new homes.

Kate and her fellow Wild Things often feel the weight of the children's longing to stay in the woods. 'They constantly say things like I feel so free out here,' she says. Already today, on her second of six sessions, Sanaya was saying, 'I know I won't come back because my family haven't got a car.' At the end of the six weeks, Wild Things give every child a leaflet with bus routes, showing how they can reach Bestwood Country Park from Nottingham. But the bus drops them in the nearest village and there's no cafe in the woods. It will be a very strong-willed ten-year-old who makes her own way here, and an act of faith for her parents to follow her.

'We help a child fall in love with nature and we don't know if they'll ever be able to access it again.' Kate thinks for a moment. At least the children now know there's a place called the woods, she says. It may call to them at any point in the future. 'It's better to know there's a bit missing. It might be something you can use in your later life,' she says. 'To know that the woods can make you feel better.'

Wild Things know that their work enhances the lives of these children but, as Kate points out, 'It's very hard to measure improvements in confidence, self-esteem, friendships, behaviour. Sometimes you do see something tangible; other times you don't. That's not to say it's not happening.'

Practitioners repeatedly record similar benefits from outdoor schooling – children developing greater confidence, independence, social skills and physical aptitude – and there is a small but growing body of evidence revealing those benefits. Forest School is still relatively new, educational research is poorly funded, and outcomes are shaped by such a myriad of circumstances that it is difficult for academics to control for every confounding factor. Some educationalists also worry that an obsession with measuring 'outcomes' is a kind of reductionism, a 'coarsening of our imaginings of childhood'.

For better or for worse, however, arguments about resources and schooling in our modern era are won and lost on assessments of outcomes. The physical benefits of outdoor schooling are easiest to measure. A group of Scottish nine- to eleven-year-olds were fitted with accelerometers to measure their physical activity during a typical school day and a day at Forest School. These revealed that activity levels were 2.2 times greater during Forest

School days than on state school days that included PE lessons, and 2.7 times greater than on 'inactive' state school days.

Perhaps the clearest beneficial impact on mental development and learning is the enhanced attentiveness and concentration that appear to come from green spaces and outdoor schooling – which won't surprise anyone who accepts the classic theory of 'soft fascination' first proposed by the psychologists Rachel and Stephen Kaplan in the 1980s. A study of more than 2,500 seven- to ten-year-olds across thirty-six primary schools in Barcelona found that better progress in memory and reduced inattentiveness were associated with the level of greenness within and surrounding the school, and the greenness of their neighbourhoods. Researchers said the way green space reduced air traffic pollution explained up to sixty-five per cent of these findings. Other positive influences on cognitive development may include reduced noise, increased physical exercise and an enriched microbial environment derived from green space.

Studies of outdoor schools in Scandinavia have also found they improve children's attentiveness. In 1997, Swedish researchers revealed that children attending outdoor day care surrounded by orchards and woodland possessed better motor coordination and a better attention span than children attending an urban day-care centre surrounded by tall buildings. A four-year study from Norway twenty years later found a positive relationship between hours spent in an outdoor preschool and children's attention spans, with more inattention and hyperactivity symptoms the less time they spent at such a preschool.

There is also accumulating evidence that outdoor schooling can produce better attainment within mainstream curricula. In

Britain, the impact of weekly Forest School sessions for a group of five- to seven-year-olds who were 'struggling to thrive' at primary school was measured over three years. A high degree of wellbeing, involvement and engagement (according to a widely used measurement in childhood studies) was sustained throughout the project and, unsurprisingly, the sessions enhanced these children's knowledge and appreciation of the natural world. When given a sixteen-point questionnaire measuring a child's enjoyment of nature, empathy for other species and a sense of 'oneness' with nature and responsibility for it, children who took part in the Forest School session scored 4.5 out of 5 on this 'connection to nature' index compared with 3.9 out of 5 among their peers who remained at conventional school all week.

Most interesting for those seeking hard academic outcomes is that the children who received weekly Forest School sessions achieved better overall attendance than their primary-school-only peers, and markedly better attainment. The Forest School pupils' writing improved by 18 per cent compared with 7 per cent among comparable pupils from disadvantaged backgrounds (for whom the state school received a 'pupil premium' – additional funds – to support their education); reading improved by 27 per cent, compared with 22 per cent among pupil-premium children. Maths attainment rose by 27 per cent compared with 11 per cent among pupil-premium peers.

The researchers said they could not attribute these improvements solely to Forest School, because attainment rose across the whole primary school during the three-year study period, but those undertaking the sessions recorded better than expected progress. Their Forest School sessions saw them grow in 'visibility' when back in primary school. These children found status and pride in becoming 'wild experts', both in the classroom and at home.

I travelled to Northumberland to learn about another 'outcome-focused' approach to outdoor learning.

Toby Quibell, a lean, ginger-haired and extremely fit-looking middle-aged teacher picks me up from Newcastle station to visit a group being taught not in some wilderness but in the grounds of Seaton Delaval, a grand hilltop hall built in the 1720s by a wealthy admiral. Toby runs Wilderness Schooling, which provides outdoor schooling devoted to helping children succeed in Britain's test-based educational system. He is convinced that children learn more effectively outdoors, and not just about wildlife but the core curriculum too – English, maths and science. And he is gathering the data to prove this.

Toby became a militant 'lefty' during his time as a student at Newcastle in the 1980s. He protested against the Poll Tax and later, rather self-consciously, chose to live among the labourers of Wallsend, a working town of coalmines, shipyards and now, after the industrial age juddered to a halt in north-east England, of warehouses. After qualifying as a teacher he stayed in Wallsend, working at a school on a rough estate. 'I found I had a real knack with naughty kids, which is a bit surprising because I'm posh and skinny,' he says. He began to wonder how best to help underprivileged, under-motivated children achieve good grades. He studied for a doctorate, gathered data, and carried on teaching. What worked, he concluded, was simple: put them in small groups, be nice to them, and take them outside.

In this data-driven era, though, Toby wanted proof. Since setting up Wilderness Schooling he has collaborated with Jenna Charlton, a researcher at Newcastle University, to undertake quantitative as well as qualitative assessments of 223 pupils he has taken on his six-week courses, comparing them with 217 who remained in class. They were surprised by the results. Those taught outdoors saw their attainment in reading jump by 19 per cent, compared with 6 per cent in class. The outdoor-schooled children's writing improved by 12 per cent, versus 6 per cent in class. Their mathematical attainment increased by 16 per cent against 10 per cent in class. These effects were measured some weeks after the assessments, and teachers reported improved behaviour as well.

We reach the grand entrance to the baroque former residence and it is only here that I realise that this handsome yellow-stoned National Trust property is a ruin. The interior of the central hall was gutted by fire in 1822 and has never been fully repaired. In one open-skyed room, a group of seventeen children sit cross-legged in a circle on little plastic mats set upon the cold stone floor.

They are eleven-year-olds, on the third of six Wednesdays when they have been taken out of conventional lessons at a local middle school, for Toby's special brand of schooling. It's that awkward in-between age when some pupils are de facto teenagers while others seem much younger. The boys wear Nike trainers and Adidas hoodies; the girls wear Superdry jackets. Some girls are far taller than the boys; one boy has a moustache, another is as small as a seven-year-old.

This group are here because they have been marked down as under-achievers, performing worse than expected in their SATs. When these children were extracted from class and put together, the teachers could see them trying to work out why they were here. Once they realise, grimaces Toby, 'normally they will start behaving like children who are underperforming'. Despite this presupposed incipient rebellion, the children are not harangued or corralled. They are given relative freedom, and three simple rules – look after yourself, look after each other, look after the site. They must assess their own risks too. It reminds me of Dandelion. What works for toddlers also works for pre-teens, and probably any age.

Inside this eerie shell of a building, Anita Foster, their main teacher today, is reading the children a spooky poem. Her words fly like bats around the high stone walls. I realise the poem has been chosen because it is amplified, given solid form, by the setting. 'They don't like poetry,' whispers Lynn Johnston, a retired head teacher who is Toby's operations manager. When they were first told they were going to hear a poem, there were groans, so Anita, a woman who exudes calm and never raises her voice, asked them for their favourite song. The cold air crackled with suggestions. It's the same thing, she explained: songs and poetry both connect feelings with words.

After listening for a second time, the children, who are holding red clipboards and green notebooks, are asked to pick out words or phrases they like. Rooks tweak their nests and call to each other overhead.

'The first word, it echoed in here. That's what I liked about it,' says Ben, a small, lively boy. They are experiencing the poem physically, as well as simply hearing it.

The group move outside, taking the stone steps leading down into a formal garden. Here we read a second poem, about the wind. It is breezy and cold and the children shake; most aren't dressed for the outdoors. But hands shoot up to volunteer observations. One boy talks about the line 'sending shivers to the tips of my toes' as he shivers. 'That's called experiential learning,' says Anita.

After ten more minutes sitting – we never sit for longer – Anita announces we're going to do a treasure hunt. The children are delighted, although less so when Anita tells them they need to look for slips of laminated paper hidden in the ornamental garden. One girl, Monika, who seems a loner and wears a cap backwards, suddenly comes alive, springing across the turf, racing the boys. The boys relish competitive hunting, and team up against each other.

The pink slips turn out to be metaphors and the white ones are similes. The class discuss the different phrases.

'A heart of ice?'

'You don't want a boyfriend,' suggests one girl.

'As hard as nails?'

'They think they are tough,' explains one boy.

The group sit beneath an ash tree, not yet in leaf, to read a third poem, about a tree. Not everyone is impressed.

'That one was a bit boring because it was literally just explaining the tree,' says one boy. But we can see the poem: a real ash, there in front of us, reaches 'for the sky with bony fingers', like in the poem. It has a cleft and a tear in its trunk, just like the 'rough brown bark folds and crevices'. There's a nice phrase about gold and copper leaves, but one girl doesn't understand it.

'What colour do they turn in the autumn?' Anita asks.

'Like this,' says Ben. He picks up a fallen beech leaf and shows everyone.

I watch the children, and they beautifully illustrate that state of 'soft fascination': a quality of being focused and yet relaxed, which is created by natural environments. One boy picks at a grass stem while he listens; another fingers the floppy leaf of a dying daffodil. A third rocks, distractedly, on a log, but when Anita asks him a question he answers immediately. He *is* listening. But his rocking would have been frowned upon in the classroom.

Ben notices the contrast with school. 'In the classrooms people are storming out and shouting, but here it's a lot different,' he says. 'It's quite a calm, good atmosphere.'

After a break of juice and biscuits, during which the teachers keep on chatting to the children, subtly continuing their education, the children read a haiku by the ornamental pond. After discussing it, they have to hunt down slips of paper with onomatopoeic words written on them. Monika is running again; there's something visceral about her need to run, and the way it delivers a much-needed moment of freedom. This active, physical learning reminds me of 'spaced learning', another innovative teaching method practised in the north-east, which has been successfully deployed to coach children for GCSEs. It typically intersperses intensive twenty-minute PowerPoints with ten-minute breaks during which the children do physical activities. Ten years ago I tested it out myself by going to Monkseaton High School, in Whitley Bay, and juggling some coloured balls between GCSE biology presentations. It seemed to work: I took the exam and got an A.

But Wilderness Schooling is a bit more subtle. As the hunt for onomatopoeic words winds down, the children are distracted by beetles and skaters on the pond.

'I've got newts in my pond,' says Lee, conversationally.

'Newts, what are they?' asks Ben.

Then another boy spots a frog.

'It's dead,' he declares.

Even a girl with a designer bag who has been squirming at the sight of the pond-skaters crowds in to look. The frog is hanging in the water, grey and bloated, tangled in dark weed. I pick it out and lay it on a lily pad. The children are fascinated, and repulsed.

'We should be back writing poems by now,' whispers Anita, 'but we don't want to stop them doing this. It's awe and wonder when you see something you haven't seen before.'

The class decides when it's lunchtime. 'A group of children taken out of school like to know if the same boundaries are going to apply as at school,' says Lynne. 'There's no point being outside if they are so straitjacketed they don't gain anything from it.'

While the pupils eat their packed lunches, I warm up in Seaton Delaval's cafe with some soup. Toby explains our three learning styles: visual, auditory and kinesthetic. In other words: looking, listening and doing. Most young children prefer to learn by doing, but classroom teaching focuses almost exclusively, he believes, on visual and auditory. A child underperforms, says Toby, because their learning style is out of kilter with the method in their classroom, because they are unhappy, or because they are poorly socialised. Address all three, and their learning is transformed. A child who fidgets and can't concentrate is sucked into a vicious circle. As Toby puts it, 'Jumpy kids don't achieve at

SATs.' The school's response is usually to keep them in at break and make them do more of the same lessons. Or worse, attend extra classes during the holidays when kids should be running along a beach.

'If you take children seriously and listen to them and provide them with an alternative means of achieving that doesn't depend on them being "good, quiet children", then you're away,' he says.

What does being outside bring to learning?

'Perhaps there's a general sense of being chosen, which pupils really respond to,' says Toby. 'But it's awe and wonder. Being with an interesting person in a beautiful place – that makes a huge difference. You're already on good territory. When they step off the bus, they look at the venue, which is carefully selected, they look at the practitioner, and think: This stands a good chance of being interesting.'

Then there's the data. Toby believes his approach is unique because he is seeking statistical evidence to show schools that his methods have 'hard outcomes'. Schools are 'driven by data', he explains, because their Ofsted inspectors are driven by data. And yet while plenty of test results are harvested from the children, there is far less evidence about the relative efficacy of the teaching methods. This is because collecting such data from schools is 'crushingly hard', he thinks. Schools are too pressed for time and money. And yet, as he puts it, 'Without the kick of the data you just end up being another *Guardian*-reading lefty who wants kids to be outdoors.'

After lunch, Anita reads the children one of Roald Dahl's 'Revolting Rhymes'. The moment when Red Riding Hood draws a pistol from her knickers receives a delighted gasp. Then the children are divided into small groups and asked to write a poem together, each contributing a line. Or they can write their own. Everyone can choose where to find inspiration and where to sit and write. They wander off to seek a niche in these grand ruins. I'm reminded of Kate Milman's observation that ten-year-olds need some autonomy and a chance to shape their own space. Indoor spaces are adult spaces, governed by our rules. Children can find a room of their own more easily outdoors.

One group takes inspiration from a sleepy bumblebee they find in a stone turret. One girl, Ashley, savours finding her own spot on the stone steps above a paddock and a pair of cold-looking horses. She looks, listens, and writes lines about their 'soft and gentle' chewing of the grass, about 'branches like witches' fingers' and sticks that 'snap and click like human fingers as they keep the beat'.

Her grandma used to read poetry to her when she was little, she says, and she has always liked words. I ask her how these sessions compare with school. 'It's like a day off school but it's not, because it *is* school,' she says. 'You're still learning new things – poetry, maps and coordinates and scientific words. You can learn more when you're outside because you're getting fresh air. When you're inside you're a bit trapped. You can't get as much air as you can outside. It helps you create when you've got some nice nature around you and you've got a peaceful, quiet place and you can listen to the teacher.'

Ashley visibly glows when Anita reads over her work. Anita is very specific with her praise. There are no insincere throwaways such as 'great work'. She also insists that each child tries to improve their first effort.

I join in, and write my first poem since I was sixteen:

Speckled legs, feet like lily pads – a frog we said
It should be tense when I touch it
It should leap when I look at it
But it turns its blue eye towards us – dead.

As the gloomy day turns chillier, we head into a wooded area where the teachers have lit a fire. Here, in a big circle, each group must perform a collective poem. I rehearse alongside Ashley and Ben. Then we step forward, in turn, saying one line each. I find this an unexpectedly buoyant collective experience and I can tell that the pupils have been moved by it too.

Before we leave for the day, I talk to some of them and to Anita. 'The children don't know that they are learning but they've done amazingly well,' she says. 'What we've done today is pure "National Curriculum". We've just done it in a different background. There is more to outdoor learning than Forest School and there's lots of possibilities. Schools just need the confidence and the tools and the permission to do it.'

Ashley is still beaming about her poetic achievements.

Would working outside still help someone who didn't like the outdoors?

'Definitely,' she thinks. 'If they are given the chance, they'd like it. If we had more lessons outside in the summer that would be nice.'

I ask Ben how he found learning outdoors: he thinks it

helps him remember more. 'When you're actually experiencing something you can remember it,' he says.

Anita gives us one last task. We must complete the following two sentences: 'I am a great learner because . . .' and 'I'm proud of myself for . . .'

Ashley writes: 'For working in my group and putting my confidence out there. And I'm proud of myself for writing my poem.'

11

Dandelions in Winter

'A true conservationist is a man who knows that the world is not given by his fathers, but borrowed from his children.'

John James Audubon

Dandelion is a place of leaves, in autumn. In winter it is defined by its mud. Green slips from the hedges and trees, doors are opened on dens and the once secluded glade of the forest school area is laid bare. The evergreen laurel hedge still offers hiding holes; the straggly conifers are unchangingly loyal but they cannot stop the north wind that rakes our faces. A low sun brings no appreciable heat and barely rises above the pantile roof of the cottage beyond the site. Its shadows shift the contours of the place.

The mud shapes the nursery and its play. All year, gambolling on the dusty dirt, I've marvelled at Dandelion's fortune in being established beside a sandy heath in one of the driest parts of Britain. Now the whole site is a mud kitchen. In an attempt to create some solid ground in the meadows, old bales are broken up and straw is churned into the quagmire. By the entrance, sticks are laid on the ground like a Neolithic causeway across a marsh. The mud still wins.

We've forgotten how the lives of our recent ancestors were dominated by it for six months or more of every year. The heavy clays of the Weald in Sussex gave rise to more than thirty dialect words for mud: 'clodgy', a muddy field path after heavy rain; 'gubber', the black mud of rotting organic matter; 'slub', thick mud. You cannot fight mud, you must tolerate it, roll with it. Or roll in it. As a substance it is supremely accommodating; forgiving, creative, a sensory pleasure, a flexible friend. The children are naturally tactile, and either unbothered or actively enthusiastic about mud. Mostly.

'A lot of them don't ever see mud,' says Emma. 'Parents say, "My child doesn't like getting dirty hands." That's really common.' Ted doesn't like the feel of mud when it dries on his hands. Me neither. But Ted and I adapt and, after a term or so, muddy hands are the norm. 'It's an incredible material,' says Emma. 'It's cold, it's warm, it's hot, it's dry, it's dusty.'

For centuries, mud meant toil, and it still does. When Milly, Esme and Ted return from a Dandelion day, it's a time-consuming chore, washing down their waterproofs and cleaning and drying their boots. There's extra labour for parents who send their children to an outdoor school, but at least we are forced to relax about them wearing muddy clothes. My clothes are as filthy as the children's. I wear four bottom layers and seven tops now. Hats are essential, and so are gloves. Most children wear two pairs. I soon realise I need a scarf.

On the first Dandelion day of the longest, hardest winter I can remember, the world is cold, still and silent. The only sound that drifts over the site is the creaking of the oil-starved wheel of a barrow, pushed by Wilf, who with his white hair, crinkly eyes and steady demeanour reminds me of the elderly man who lived next door to me when I was a boy. Working with the young often brings to mind the old; and working outdoors intensifies this exposure to the cycle of life, the ebb and flow of seasons, plants, animals and people.

Today is novel because there is a pebble-dashing of ice on every surface: old hail, set like concrete. The children are delighted with this new substance. It's the closest most have got to snow because there hasn't been a proper snowfall in this part of eastern England for five winters. A few Dandelions gather the ice into snowballs and begin a fight. I'm not sure what is permitted but Tracey suggests it's fine if they are thrown below the waist. Unfortunately small children are random-throw generators, and a deadly ice-ball is as likely to hurtle backwards at eye level as it is to trundle obediently into its below-the-waist target. Fortunately, the game doesn't catch on. Instead, we harvest great sheets of hail-ice from the corrugated plastic roof of the reading pod (made from reeds). The children hold each piece up and drop it, and it shatters satisfyingly, like glass. Then Hayley and I whack the tarpaulin that stretches over the dinner table to create hail-ice showers. The children queue to feel ice shower over their heads and shoulders.

I lose count of the number of Dandelions I see eating ice. It reminds me of that scene in *Dumb and Dumber* where Harry, played by Jeff Daniels, spots the ice-covered rail of a chairlift. 'Oh look, frost!' he exclaims, licks it, and his tongue sticks fast. This classic silliness is a timeless sensory urge. Esme, Ted and even indoor identifier Milly all stuff ice into their mouths and crunch it whenever they find it on the water butt at home. At Dandelion, Rory sits contentedly on a straw bale munching ice for half an hour. Another teacher tells him it's not a great idea because the ice might have germs in it. I relay the same caution but don't want to stop the ice-crunchers.

I sit with Violet at the big outdoor table and we use a microscope to enter a miraculous miniature world. Under magnification, the ice droplets on leaves become gigantic hexagonals. Their edges are sharp and angular; their middles are opaque and shine with a mysterious light. Violet is a kind, sensitive girl who has the most pronounced form of autism among Dandelion's children. She spends most of her time on a rope swing, her home base and comfort, and any change or disruption is very disturbing for her. She struggles to play with or trust others, and she becomes hurt and furious when people don't behave in the way that she expects. But she is content to admire the ice.

'The veins in the leaf look like blood vessels,' she says, an observation both beautiful and true. So many children possess what appears to be an innate gift for poetry as well as an aptitude for precise, comparative observation. (Over lunch, one child describes his cashew nut as looking like a croissant.)

Sitting at the microscope is chilling, and special measures are required to keep warm. Today our fireside snack is jammy porridge, which spreads its warmth deliciously. Lunch is eaten around the fire circle. Afterwards, Hayley and Emma introduce active games. Toilet tag is like the conventional 'it', but if you get tagged you have to squat as if sitting on the toilet, holding out your arm as if it's the old flushing toilet handle. To release you, an untagged person must flush your arm. This is good fun. Next is shark tag, where I'm a shark and the children are little fish, and they're safe in the 'coral reef' – the reading pod. The children must dash across the rough meadow to another 'coral reef', the mud kitchen, without being caught. Then Hayley instructs us in turtle tag. In this game, if you're in danger of being caught, you fall on your back and put your arms and legs in the air like a beached turtle. You can stay like this for ten seconds and not be tagged but then you must get up and run. Usually the catcher hovers by you and grabs you as soon as you roll onto your side.

Hayley uses these games to assess which children can adapt to new rules and which struggle. The children's favourite is pick-pocket tag. Hayley and Emma tell them the briefest version of *Oliver Twist*. Then they hand out coloured silk hankies that the children take and run with. If the chaser grabs a hankie, the child must stand still until another child can free them with a touch. Grubby, pink-cheeked and covered in mud, the children make picturesque Dickensian urchins.

Every young child, even Violet, adores being chased, but they need the security of a sanctuary too. They constantly bend the rules to help themselves, inventing new 'safety zones' where I can't reach them. Childhood is a continuous run to test every kind of boundary; not just our complicated human arrangements but the boundaries of physics, chemistry and biology.

I love how speeding children can turn so quickly, dart round corners and dodge the logs and pallets and spindly fruit trees and chickens and bricks and everything else on site. I'm so big and sluggish; I don't have to pretend very hard to fail to catch them. Boundaries are more fixed for me now. I can no longer enter childhood as a child; nor can I quite catch my old childhood, but I just about feel it in the cold air, warm cheeks, tingling hands, wet grass, muddy ground and running around. For a moment, I'm transported back to being twelve again, and playing a version of football we called the Fouling Game – headlong dives, sliding tackles, outrageously creative fouls, shouting and laughing and shirt-tugging and feigning injury until we were jelly-legged with exhaustion.

For most of this first icy day at Dandelion, the only non-human I see is a blackbird, who hops hopefully near our lunch. The world's living things are huddled, dormant, hibernating, hunkered down, tucked away, except for the Dandelions. On another numbingly cold day when the murk is almost eerie, Hayley offers the children a walk. She isn't afraid to use the W word. I hated walks when I was little, so at home I tend to deploy 'adventure', or 'expedition'. Children see through my crude Orwellian newspeak.

The walk is to what Hayley calls Mermaid's Bridge and Craggy Oak. It is optional, but all thirteen older children and a couple of five- and four-year-olds are keen. We line up by the gate and I'm reminded of my primary school nature walks down a local lane, with no risk assessments and almost no cars. This walk has been meticulously scrutinised for risk. Hayley brings out a long blue rope with loops tied in it. The children each put their right hand in a loop and we trot along in a train like a family of shrews. If we had tails, we would hold each other's.

There is no need to take a road to our destination because there's a public footpath from Dandelion's gate across the fields. We trudge in train northwards over a bleak field of winter wheat. This is not my idea of free-range children, but Hayley doesn't want them scattering from the trodden path onto the newly sown crop. Traffic hums on the main road beyond a line of low grey sheds containing caged chickens.

Then, a sonorous, spirit-soaring cronking high in the sky. A straggling skein of fifty Brent geese, a child's wobbly V, approach. Hayley asks the children why they fly in such a pattern. Several home-schooled six-year-olds know all about aerodynamics. The geese are followed by a more marvellous sky-passing: twenty lapwing, casting their eyes over the village that celebrates them in its signs, flying with a distinctive bounce of their wings.

The field curves into a small valley and the path joins a dead-end lane by a few old cottages. We turn left up a track and, thankfully, Hayley casts off the shackling blue rope. The children can run free, although we must make sure there's always an adult at front and rear. Beyond Marsham village are numerous smallholdings, tiny farms with tatty fences and a horse or two. These are not wealthy horses, but wear shabby coats and stand stiffly on patches of overgrazed pasture demarcated by electric fences. There are asbestos barns and farmyards commandeered by car mechanics or filled with rusting machinery. Everything is brown and muddy.

Bare hedges reveal last year's bird's nests and the silhouette of each tree that has been hedged. The track heads uphill, overseen by an ash that has shed bone-pale branches in recent storms. The children gather Pooh-sticks for Mermaid's Bridge. Lily insists on dragging an enormous multi-pronged branch. We cross a freshly ploughed field with a surprisingly steep descent. They hurtle down the ruts made by tractor tyres, legs almost buckling beneath them. At the bottom is a valley of abandoned water meadows, tatty alders and two little streams.

One is actually called the Mermaid, and it is crossed by a wooden footbridge.

We stop, and in a hushed voice Hayley tells a story. Years ago, when the children's grandparents were their age, they were told not to play by the river. But they did, and one day they saw the flash of a fin in the water, and long hair, and heard singing. Ever since, the bridge has been called Mermaid's Bridge.

The children are enthralled. Even world-weary Lily buys into the tale. We enter a small thicket of alder and birch in the valley bottom and reach a less picturesque concrete bridge. This is better for Pooh-sticks. The tiny stream tinkles with promise. While we sit down, eat ginger-snaps and drink water, Hayley organises the children into threes in preparation for the game.

Many sticks stick – in the bank, in tangles of weed, in other sticks. But a few pop through to the far side of the bridge like victorious kayakers. Some are short and heavy; others are slender and tiny; there is no logic to each finisher. The children are only moderately fussed about winning or losing, and soon drift away from the game to climb trees, sit in the mud, or throw stones; children love messing about by water, midwinter or not. A family of siskins is doing the avian equivalent high in the alder: flitting, shifting, chatting.

The return journey to Dandelion is much slower. James has tired legs and keeps stopping. Rex throws clods of ploughed field around; they detonate with great satisfaction, showering soil shrapnel everywhere. Herbie and even peaceable Hayden fire stick guns at each other until Hayley stages a gentle intervention.

We take a different turn to find Craggy Oak, an old tree set high on the bank of a sunken lane, trailing its roots over the bare earth below. The mud banks around it make an excellent slide. Everyone clambers up and takes two turns sliding down, bumping over the roots and finishing with a sideways roll down the final ascent. The air feels refreshingly cold on our cheeks. The children discuss trolls and dinosaur footprints, building their own picture of the world and its boundaries. A couple of dog-walkers look perplexed to see children messing about in the countryside.

When I first work with Emma and Hayley on the Heath, the nearby common where they begin Forest School lessons for their older pupils, it's another cold, blustery, unsettling winter's day. A distant farm vehicle beeps as it reverses, a crow caws, and the conifer tops sound like traffic on a motorway. I'm late, and must find where they have set up camp. I park in the muddy entrance, where stands a metal barrier to prevent vehicles driving onto the Heath – and step into glutinous mud. The umber stems of last year's bracken are bent and snapped into submission by the season, skeletal leaves stooped low. A packet that once held similarly orange Wotsits scuds beneath them.

A track of grey mud heads diagonally across the gently undulating heathland of gorse and heather. Every now and again, I find a small boot-print in the mud. It must be them. Clumps of heather still carry last year's blooms, now fading to beige. Small dark reeds grow from permanent puddles by the track. A common gull blows over. After five hundred yards, the track reaches an oblong plantation of sweet chestnuts in the middle of the Heath. There's a narrow opening between hollies, a shimmy of a path and a cry on the wind. Not a gull: a child.

Inside the wood, the first thing I see is a crime scene: red-and-white plastic tape hugging trunks, sectioning off an area. Emma and Hayley have staked out a plot in the wood for the children to play in, the size of a couple of football pitches. This seems a dismal compromise, reining in the potential of woodland roaming. But Emma and Hayley explain: the taped boundary is not imposed on the children but is being unfurled by them. The children assess each tree, choosing which ones they want to include in their play area. They are setting the boundary. And within a few weeks, the tape will be removed; the children will have learned their limits. They won't need to be taped in. True to their word, this happens and, week by week, the children discover and name for themselves the most interesting corners of this wild place.

Emma and Hayley are unpacking equipment from a sturdy metal trolley of the kind that is popular at music festivals. The children have dispersed to all corners. The wood is bright in winter. Slanted sunshine reaches into the stands of chestnut. These are slender and tall, fifty years old, with four or five trunks sprouting from much older, broader, mossy bases. Between these coppiced trees are spindly saplings, struggling to get going beneath the shade of what is left of the summer canopy. The trunks of each chestnut are pale and shine like well-worn chinos.

The wood reminds me of a church. My mind loosens in both places; they are sanctuaries from materialism, from being sold stuff. I can't decide if this plantation's most splendid thing is the trees, which shelter us from the wind, or the forest floor. Totally forgiving, fragrant and of imponderable depth, it scuffles with sound but muffles all noise; it can be read, listened to, smelt and probably tasted too. It is delicious. Leaf litter, leaf mould – common phrases insult this most miraculous of life forms, a soft quilted pouffe of damp sweet-chestnut leaves, brown and beige with serrated edges. Best of all, it isn't mud. I'm tiring of mud.

Our play flows over the forest floor, and springs from it too. For the first time in my life I consider the importance of the ground. For how much of our lives do our neglected feet tramp carpet and concrete? We all need something less predictable beneath our feet. Barefoot used to denote poverty; now it's a concept that sells luxury holidays. Hippies, disciples, holy people, tech billionaires: they all go barefoot for a reason.

The fire circle becomes more important in the woods. It is a symbol of sufficiency, competence and our ability to survive. I'm impressed that Emma and Hayley are prepared to light one; lighting fires in public spaces isn't the done thing any more, closed down by regulations, most of which are necessary in an era of climate crisis, drought and raging wildfires. Emma tells the children how to determine if a twig is dry – if it makes a snapping sound – and they enthusiastically collect a plethora of damp offerings for our fire. I'm pessimistic about our prospects. I lit a fire in my garden for my birthday last week. Even after creating the crucial hot core thanks to conventional firelighters that stink of paraffin, my attempt smouldered and hissed all evening. On wintery days, a woodland floor is damp to the touch. So are the trees. The air is full of droplets, damply sinking. Nothing will catch alight. 'Broadleaved woodland,' wrote Oliver Rackham, the great chronicler of our English forests, 'burns like wet asbestos.'

My matches don't strike. Head after head breaks off. The cardboard matchbox softens, soggy, in my hand, losing its shape like a retired bodybuilder. Even with a lighter, the newspaper I bought this morning is already too sodden to flame up. It would be simpler with paraffin-soaked firelighters, but Emma and Hayley are purists and have brought a pocket of environmentally friendly wood-shaving twizzles.

The only thing that burns with any conviction is from the forest: a few precious strips of bark which we peel from the trunk of a silver birch. I tear it into strips and stuff them into a wigwam of the driest sticks. This propels into fiery life, natural oils burning with a green flame.

Emma lies down and applies yogic breathing to the flame. I join in from the other side, mimicking a pair of bellows. The children toss on more sticks. Emma and I blow the orange embers of paper. Then, only smoke. The fire struggles, as do we. Flames twitch and shift into different parts of the wigwam, teasing, raising hopes, then dying back.

We start again. More twizzles, and a firmer wigwam of the tiniest of sticks. Emma and Hayley dig out a few pieces of dry carpenter's offcuts from their trolley and Emma begins chopping one piece expertly with an axe. I take a small saw to another piece, resting it on the soft forest floor. The wood and the saw slip and I cut myself. I ignore it but Lily spots the blood and is horrified. Hayley insists I apply a plaster. Emma tells me that virtually every accident in Forest School involves an adult only. Children don't tend to injure themselves.

With birch bark, four slivers of dry wood, and forty minutes of bellowing, blowing and coaxing, two flames emerge from either side of the wood wigwam and touch, like a reluctant hug. Fire. Finally.

I love fire, I declare to Emma and Hayley.

We can tell, they reply drily. Everyone gathers round the

flames, holding hands out to feel the heat, and we eat our sandwiches, starving, even though it isn't yet twelve.

The wood fires our imaginations. The children spread in all directions to play. The mossy bases of the sweet chestnut coppice stools are easy to climb into, natural safe havens and fortresses.

Herbie invites me to play 'natural disasters'.

'Arrrrgggh, acid!' he cries. The forest floor is acid, and it's devouring his leg. We must jump onto a coppice stool for safety. A moment later, the forest floor turns into shark-infested waters. One Dandelion has wedged a foot-long stick between a chestnut trunk and an accompanying tendril of ivy. Held horizontal in the tree's embrace, the stick becomes motorbike handles. 'I'm on my motorbike,' says Seb, steering the tree this way and that. James and Hayden use sticks to excavate the moss from around the base of one coppice. They plough the sandy soil with their sticks. 'This used to be sea and it was right up to here,' says James, pointing to the tree-tops. They are fossil-hunters, treasure-seekers, den-builders. Angel and Willow devote several hours of focused attention to constructing a serious den, with a little help from Emma who ties a long stick as a horizontal beam between two trunks so the children can tie on diagonals to create a tent-shaped hideout.

The first day in the forest isn't all rapture, though. The spindly saplings cause Little Silver Riding Hood some problems.

'I think nature is trying to blind me,' says Lily.

I'm increasingly appreciative of her morbid wit but my appreciation is the ironic sensibility of an adult. Lily is actually struggling. She's not being caustic; she's distressed. Our relocation from Dandelion's homely garden to the wild wood is troubling her and she's searching for an upside.

'Luckily, if I'm blind, I don't have to come here,' she says, in her heartfelt misery.

I kneel in the soft leaves and listen properly. I haven't heard many complaints from her about boredom in recent weeks but in this new forest environment she reverts to her old self. I suggest various games we can play, then coax her to join the other children's.

'I don't like play,' she says. 'I like playing video games.'

Without prompting, she explains herself further. 'They are serious business. Some people make a living from them. They are called YouTubers.'

Tears streak down her chilled pink face. Her hands are cold but she's Dandelion's only glove-refusenik; she retracts her hands into her silver sleeves. She misses her mum. She doesn't want to be here.

After failing to cheer her up, I tell Hayley she's not happy. She tells Lily that if she is upset then she will call her mum and dad. It sounds like a threat; Lily says, no no, she doesn't want that. But actually, she does. Tears continue. She can't be distracted into any sort of game. Or into woodland 'jobs', such as collecting the grand surplus of chestnuts that can still be found amongst the fallen leaves.

Eventually, Hayley calls Lily's parents and her mum arranges to collect her in an hour. Time passes slowly. Every five minutes, Lily asks how much longer. She worries she will be cross. Last time she was angry, she wasn't allowed to play Xbox. After an hour, Lily's convinced she's had a car accident. Could we call the police? I cannot divert her attention. She is fixated upon her hatred of this wood. And Dandelion. She's going to tell her mum she wants to go to school. I gently offer some things she likes about Dandelion: the chickens, for instance. She resists. She doesn't like large groups of children, she says. There are only twelve children today and three adults – there would be far more children in a school. But Lily won't be won round by reason, or by the forest, today. Finally, Hayley takes her to the entrance of the Heath to meet her mum.

The snow, when it begins, is a source of wonder for the Dandelions. Snow is such a scarce resource for children in southern England in the twenty-first century that two Dandelion boys collect it in buckets. Feather the chicken wears a dusting of snow on her back. Rory catches a flake with his tongue, which steams like a hot pink ham. When we reach the Heath for another Forest School session, big flakes are falling slowly, like parachutes. They are not crystalline but sprawling birds' nests in miniature. They attach themselves like cuckoo spit to the bare red branches of silver birch and turn small conifers into Christmas trees. Cold radiates from the ground, like a freezer. The Beast from the East is coming.

Only five children make it out today. There's only a dusting of snow so far but it's still the best in a lifetime for a whole generation of six-year-olds. Willow tells her mum she's found 'a horn made of ice': a precise observation of an icicle. She had seen icicles in books and on telly but they don't have the same impact as the real thing. When we don't directly experience something, we lose its name, and a wider vocabulary associated with it.

Extinction – of things and their words – reduces the richness and complexity of our world.

The Heath is cold and quiet. Even a modest sprinkling of snow draws the world closer. There are a few sprigs of flowering gorse but no signs of spring. The snow changes to small flakes and lies dry and powdery in the cold. It creaks under foot like a leather sofa. Each shiny serrated holly leaf holds its own snow rug. The cracked mud track is frozen and the icy ruts flex and bend when you step on them. Occasionally a deep rut gives way and a boot enters the mud below.

Today the woods are even more nurturing than usual. We are tucked away in the chestnut coppice, the plastic tape has been taken down, and these tall, slender, pale-trunked trees feel like our guardians, as they rise over us and give us shelter. Their bark is gently textured, and light pours between their empty canopies. I touch the more rugged-barked silver birch affectionately now, knowing it anew as a provider of good oils for the fire. The leaf litter, crusty and dusted with snow, absorbs all sound. Old sweet chestnut cases resemble sea urchins in a frozen lake. The wood is both enclosing and open; welcoming, giving and free; a place of peace, a place of stimulation and a place of play. The best school in the world.

The silence is broken by two jays, screeching and quarrelling, then the creaking of a tree.

'It sounds like a door,' thinks Willow. 'It might be a fairy, opening a door.'

We check the fairy house, a miniature home at the base of a tree built from twigs and leaves by the children several weeks earlier. Willow is convinced she's found the print of a butterfly in the snow. A very cold butterfly. She loves turning wild things into pets. She starts with a tiny thumb curl of snow and rolls and rolls, and slowly it becomes a square of snow the size of a melon. She calls it Snowbie and for its short life it travels with her everywhere.

The snow stops and the sun comes out and shines through the branches, trunks hatching us in diagonal shadows. Green sheaths belonging to a small patch of daffodils are rising at the base of an ivy-clad tree. The ivy has cast a snow shadow, and no snow has fallen on the budding daffodils. It looks like magic.

The only creature who ventures near us is a robin, a watchful woodland cousin of our tamer garden friends. It tilts its head minutely when we scuff the forest floor. Robins once followed wild boar through the forest, seizing invertebrates exposed by their rootling. Now these birds shadow our gardening. Emma decides we should help. We scuff the top layer of our leaf carpet and trowel into the deeper layers. The compressed leaves are a nut loaf in cross-section. We draw back from our diggings and crouch beneath a conifer's low boughs to wait. Two minutes pass. The robin flits in, cautiously, bouncing from one sweet chestnut sprig to another and then down onto our diggings. I haven't seen a single worm during our excavations but the robin finds one within two seconds and slugs it down as if slaking a deep thirst. It pecks over other slabs of leaf litter, prospecting for more tiny invertebrates to sustain itself. Thereafter it dances around our encampment.

Lily, who is content today, goes off alone to watch the robin. 'It's adorable, it has little brown eyes,' she says. Later, she directs a horror movie in the woods, instructing me to fall over as if dead. I tumble into the leaf litter; it smells damp, fruity, woody; alive, not dead.

Beneath the ivy-clad tree, we gather to hear Emma read *The Lost Words'* spell for ivy. Robert Macfarlane's words are crafted to be read aloud, but I'm struck by the additional power of reading it outside. Emma's voice carries through the woods; the trees carry the words to the ivy above, a prayer, an incantation, an appreciation of this smart species. We eat our lunches and, motionless, we become chilled and so after sandwiches we play 'farmer, sheep and wolves'. The wolf is the chaser, the farmer is a guard, and if the wolf catches a sheep he turns it into another member of the pack. Lily discovers a bouncy low branch which becomes a broomstick. She shares it with other girls, playing with them for the first time.

At the end, we each volunteer what we liked best about our day. Willow likes Snowbie. Lily, the broomstick.

'I made a broomstick song,' she says:

Down the street
On my broomstick
All day long
Down through the street
Down through the forest
All day long
Then we go to the beach and get ice cream
And then we go over the sea to the other countries like Greece and Spain

12

The Spinney at the Bottom of the Field

'Nature is not a place to visit. It is home.'

Gary Snyder

After twelve months of volunteering at Dandelion, I retire for a variety of reasons. I had only ever planned to do a year; also, I realise I want to work on the Heath, feeling the magic embrace of the woods, but Emma and Hayley run only one day a week there, which my children attend, so that means I can't be there too. When the next school year starts, I'm surprised to learn that St John's, our local primary school, has started regular Forest School sessions in the little spinney at the bottom of its big grassy playing field. I'm sure it's an addition that the head teacher Becky Quinn has been considering for a while, but perhaps our determination to send Milly, Esme and Ted to Dandelion added a small persuasive spark.

St John's Forest School leader is Cathy Howes, a teaching assistant who is fully trained in Forest School. She also has an encyclopedic knowledge of campfire songs from years of working with the Beavers, Cubs and Scouts. I want to help my local school, which has done so much for us, and so I start volunteering for one afternoon session each week.

The spinney is a patch of native trees – birch, field maple, oak, hawthorn and wild cherry – that were planted at one bottom corner of St John's playing field thirty-five years ago. The trees are middle-aged now, and as soon as we become inhabitants of the wood we are shielded from the school and wrapped within its own quiet world, sharp sounds softened by the carpet of last year's leaves. Ms Howes is an industrious woman who loves the outdoors, and she has acquired a secondhand bell-tent and a small shed, as well as hammocks, saws and a plethora of den-building tools. She has built a fire circle and devised dozens of other bright ideas for activities. But she's also alive to the concept that children require free play in nature, and does not seek to be too prescriptive.

It should not surprise me, but it still does: every primary-age child I see taken to the woods responds to it with energy, excitement and often something that in an adult could be labelled unconfined joy. The chatter of voices rises as classes are led by their teacher and teaching assistant from their classroom across the tightly mown playing field to the woods. The children have changed out of their uniforms into scruffy clothes including coats, which they've been asked to bring for Forest School. For most of them, the woods are a new experience. Unlike Dandelion, these are not the children of parents who have specifically sought out an outdoor experience for their offspring. They are a typical sample of working families from a large suburban commuter village. There are one or two country types, but most are children whose days inside are dominated by screens and whose days out most often comprise adult-led activities. And yet in my first term of helping out, I don't meet a single child who doesn't want to be in the woods or isn't having fun there. In the whole school of 200 pupils, Ms Howes has had just one resistant child so far. This girl hadn't brought any warm clothes that day, didn't want to wear any, and sat miserably by the fire circle for one session.

There may be an unquenchable hope in all our encounters with the natural world, but I have experienced the same sensation in almost all my dealings with schoolchildren. I have repeatedly been struck by how inspiring it is to work alongside children of all ages. They are the most open, fair-minded and adaptable work colleagues I have ever had, and they remind me how to make the most of each moment and how to seize the miracle of another day on Earth.

In the little spinney, I put the lesson I've learned from my belated exposure to early-years education into practice: I follow the children's interests. During my first Forest School session with Year 4s, I become an assistant to an eight-year-old who has an unstoppable vision of fashioning a home-made zip line from a rope and a stout stick. During the second session, I help a group of boys dig 'a man-trap'. A trio of nine-year-olds devote enormous commitment to this task. The boys are very confiding when engaged in practical work. One, who is incredibly adept with tools, tells me this is a welcome break from lessons, where he struggles. Another tells me how he recently dug a grave for his mum's boyfriend's snake. A third slowly reveals a story about his separated parents, and how he is currently staying with his granny, which is great because she lets him play as much Xbox as he wants.

One winter week, I bring five fruit trees for us to plant around the perimeter of the wood. Although the boys usually show more enthusiasm for digging in the normal course of play, our tree-planting reminds me how gender differences dissolve in the woods. The girls are just as keen to plant a tree as the boys, and stick at the task for longer. Other disparities recede as well, from pocket-money status to academic achievement. We are here as equals; what a balm for the children.

In my eighteen months of part-time work at forest schools, I come to learn that working outside in the winter requires stamina and stoicism. Some days in early January barely seem to lighten at all. There's no sign of even a snowdrop. My instinct is to hibernate.

As the January weeks tick over, however, I notice the tug-of-war between winter and spring. Even on the coldest midwinter day, there's a sign of life, or two. A sallow shows purple-brown buds, shiny like an armadillo, and the children and I break them open to find furry silver inside. I'm not sure that the sparrows ever stop chirruping, but their conversations become busier. By late January, a wood pigeon stations itself in the sallow and begins a tentative woo-wooing. Three notes, not the usual five. The blackbird isn't singing yet but he's hunting for scraps.

The season is turning. Each week, another note is added to the spring symphony. The sunlight becomes more tender. A dunnock begins its sharp little song, as intricate as a piece of needlework. Catkins turn a brighter yellow. A pair of sparrows shine like conkers in the sunny willow hedge. A hundred rooks fly over, twirling in the sky, a community of darkest indigo on the move. One wood pigeon becomes two. One sidles up to the other. They are less shy now and sing all five notes: wu wooo woo wu-woo.

In February the shadows shorten, the sun is appreciably higher in the sky, and the lane-side pheasants are triumphal survivors of the shooting season. From a high bough, a great tit begins its see-saw song, the ultimate sign of spring. Then, suddenly, spring stops again. The see-sawing stops. The cold returns – not that it was ever warm. Six top layers aren't enough to keep me snug. The mud is beginning to get to me. I kneel in it and resent the sludge. I'm impatient for it to draw back, for the ground to harden and dry, as it usually does in March. I'm weary of cold hands and demand more warmth from the sun.

We are more susceptible to the seasons if we spend more time outside. Our mood is shadowed or brightened by the weather. I've also been softened by a decade of mostly mild winters; I've come to expect February and March to be mild and dry in my part of the world. Connoisseurs of the present, children are far more accepting of the long winter than I am. Snow flurries continue until Easter. As spring struggles forth, the children play in the mud and robins haul moss and leaves into their nests. The circle of life turns again.

'Dad, you know Little Miss Red Riding Hood in Roald Dahl's *Revolting Rhymes*?' says Esme when she comes home from school one day. 'You know she has a wolfskin coat and a pigskin carrying case?' I nod, delighted to be clueless about what's coming. 'I've seen the video. And the wolfskin coat looks so comfy. Could I get a wolfskin coat?' She pauses before one final, grave question. 'Can we go out and shoot a wolf, Dad?'

As I've discovered, there are many different wild children, as many as there are personalities, and at this moment in their lives Esme is a hunter, just as Milly is a collector and Ted is a carpenter-inventor. All three still attend Dandelion one day each week, and I still notice how calm they are and how more likely they are to undertake excursions in their imagination after a day in the woods.

For a small animal as sensitive and adaptable as a child, being in the woods or on the beach or in a field is a release from so many roles and strictures that already weigh heavily on their malleable minds. Here, they are freed from being a passive consumer, or a dutiful learner; they are let loose from the requirement to compete, and they can escape – for a second or half an hour or a day – the overbearing scrutiny of an adult world that never ceases to watch over them. It is not just children, of course: we are all blessed when we choose to be out here, cocooned by the woods, given life by the air, peace by the trees, and constant slow-burning stimulation and exhilaration from the movement of the wild world around us.

I have made in this book what might appear to be an individualistic appeal to rewild the lives of our children. I've sought to show that, however imperfect our lives and our homes, we can add doses of daily nature in a way that enriches us all. But any aspiration to do this dies a small death each day at the hands of broader forces and bigger institutions. Without radical changes to urban neighbourhoods, without a revolution against the primacy of the car on our public highways, without a transformation in how we obtain our food and without major reform of our stultifying National Curriculum and test-based schooling, it's difficult to see how the next generation can grow up any more cognisant of nature than my own did.

I've wanted to show, not tell, and so I write this quietly. While I have made the kind of human-centred appeal for nature that is in keeping with our times, I hope it is self-evident that there is also an inescapable moral case for taking care of the planet and its non-human inhabitants too. Every other species has as much right to be here as we do. I believe that if we become a bit wilder ourselves, we bring a benefit to our community and to wider society too: people with nature in their lives are more likely to be good citizens and behave more kindly towards each other and to our fellow species.

Not so long ago, in a modest but revealing experiment, a social psychologist showed a group of students an awe-inspiring image of mighty Tasmanian eucalyptus trees. He gave another group a rather less inspiring view of a cluster of office blocks, with not a natural feature in sight. Then he staged an accident: he dropped a box of pens. The students who had been studying the trees proved more helpful, and picked up more pens.

We behave better when we enter the world beyond ourselves, and when we look to places and life forms beyond our own homes, workplaces and families. Whether in countries where most of us have forsaken religion or in places still governed by it, I cannot think of anything more worthwhile than opening our eyes to the wonder of the planet and seeking to help its plants and animals to thrive. We can express this respect and devotion in many ways – from what we eat to how we travel – but there are two essentials that we cannot do much without. One is to spend time in nature ourselves, and the other is to grant our children that gift.

The revelations in these pages are modest, the wildlife humble, the settings unglamorous, but the moments of wonderment keep coming, each one accreting like another micro-organism drifting to the bottom of the ocean. And something forms inside me that is just as life-giving as are today's chalk grasslands – created by those tiny organisms millions of years ago – to the thyme and scabious that bloom upon them and the chalkhill blue butterflies that fly over them.

Even in midwinter, the tiny spinney between St John's playing field and suburbia beyond is a ceaseless giver of serendipity. Stuff happens outdoors. One dark winter's afternoon, a class draws around the fire circle as Ms Howes explains what they can do today. Suddenly, her eye is caught by a scuttling – ten yards beyond, a hedgehog is making its way through the dead leaves.

'Look, everyone!' She points.

We all turn, and gasp with pleasure. An eight-year-old in our group has been raising money for hedgehogs at a local wildlife rescue centre and the children have been told in class how hedgehogs are declining, and that we must help them. The group are also tutored in not touching.

'Stand back,' cautions their teacher, as they rush over to look. 'Don't touch – you'll hurt it.'

A tug-of-war is sparked between these words and the children's instincts. They so much want to touch, but waver, and pull back.

I grab my gardening gloves and walk over to the hedgehog. I think we can admire it for a moment, I say, and I kneel down, pick it up, and invite the children for a close inspection.

'Wow!'

'Look at its little nose.'

'So cute!'

A few reach out to touch its prickles. The boundary between us and this other animal dissolves for a second. I can sense the children placing themselves in its tiny grey paws and thinking about its life, its daily struggles. We talk about the hedgehog, what it's doing out and about on a winter's day, how it has curled up to defend itself. Perhaps the children worry a bit too much about it: we are often made to see wild nature as a fragile and threatened thing. We're taught to stay away, to leave other species in peace, at the moment in our lives when we need to be touching, embracing and learning to love them with all our senses.

Nevertheless, we must take care not to disturb this should-be-hibernating creature, and so we set it down in the leaves close to the edge of the wood, where there are good 'hedgehog holes' in the fence through to some gardens. We plump the leaves around it in case it wants to hibernate there and then, and give it some space. When we check again at the end of the session, it has vacated the home we cobbled together, and slipped away. We are disappointed, but relieved that it has made its way in the world. Somewhere in the spinney, its feet are pattering alongside ours.

Appendix

Sixty-One Things to Do and Ways of Being with Children Outdoors

'The best place to begin is wherever you happen to be.'

Scott Sampson

I dislike being told what I should do. Quite a lot of parenting advice is patronising or banal or the equivalent of a ludicrously over-complicated recipe. We have so little time, and so much pressure to be a 'perfect' parent. Adding 'providing wildlife good times' to the list can feel like just another obligation. Another thing we are failing to provide. So I hesitate to offer any ideas to you, dear reader, as if I am some paragon of parenting. I certainly am not.

But, in the spirit of sharing ideas, here are some outdoor activities that work for me, or that I've heard about from other people and think are good. I'm writing from the perspective of a parent, but hopefully these suggestions will be as useful for aunties, uncles, godparents, grandparents, guardians, teachers and friends.

Please feel free to share your ideas with me too. My email address is patrick.barkham@theguardian.com, you can find me on Twitter at patrick_barkham, or by good old-fashioned mail c/o Granta Publications, 12 Addison Avenue, London W11 4QR.

1. Add the outdoors – and nature – to your daily/weekly routine
For wildlife to thrive, and to work its magic on us, it needs to be part of our daily life – not a special treat. If you currently have no wildlife in your life with your children, could you slip some into your usual routine? Can you walk to school once a week? Or to football/Brownies/swimming or whatever other activities you do after school? Or go for a walk every weekend? Then, when you're out there, what can you see? As the urban birder David Lindo says, if you're in a city, look up. If you are anywhere, look up. You will be amazed at the natural dramas being played out in our city skies – peregrines swooping on pigeons, sparrowhawks flashing through suburban gardens. How much wildlife can you find, identify, and enjoy looking at close up in your home? Spiders, woodlice, ladybirds, interesting beetles. Wildlife is all around us.

2. Become a nature mentor – or not
You don't need expertise. In fact, I think it's better to have none. My father appeared to have wildlife superpowers to me as a small boy. I am very fortunate: I owe him most of my wildlife knowledge today. But I fell in love with butterflies as a boy not because Dad was an expert but because it was a subject about which he knew nothing. Going looking for butterflies was something that we did together, and learned about together. So he wasn't a great authority figure informing little know-nothing me – even as an eight-year-old, I could contribute.

Many parents feel intimidated by wild places because they can't name and explain everything around them. But the fact is, your child will have a much more memorable experience if learning how to distinguish a wood pigeon from a feral pigeon, for instance, is something you do together. You can easily find help with identification – on social media, on apps, on wildlife charity websites or in field-guides. The RSPB has a superb free guide to birds online. Butterfly Conservation, similarly, offers a guide to butterflies, as does the excellent UK Butterflies website. Field-guides have never been more accessible or more affordable. You can also find cheap ones in charity shops or free ones in libraries. An increasing number of people use the iNaturalist website.

The American author Scott Sampson talks of 'nature mentors'. It's useful for a child to have a mentor – someone who is willing to learn or simply to appreciate the natural world alongside them. Sampson argues, 'raising a wild child is much more about seeding love than knowledge'. As Antoine de Saint-Exupéry put it: 'If you want to build a ship, don't drum up people to collect wood and don't assign them tasks and work, but rather teach them to long for the endless immensity of the sea.'

For all the benefits of nature-mentoring, plenty of people have formed deep and intimate bonds with nature in childhood with no adult standing over them. More important than any didactic approach is to simply provide your child with time and space in nature. They will wild themselves.

3. Cultivate a local patch

Find an outdoor space as close to your home as possible, within walking distance or a short drive, where you can hang out with your child or children. The sort of place you can pop to after school. This could be a park, cemetery, common, waste ground, garden, allotment, wood, or nature reserve, Go there as often as you can. Start when they are still in their buggy, if you can.

Children love familiarity and routine. They will soon develop bonds with the place; even, later, nostalgia for it. Try and let them lead what you do, so they make it their space.

You might play imaginary games, climb trees, race, play ball, watch birds, take photographs, collect stuff, keep lists of what you see, do some gardening, make friends, build dens, sing, dream. You'll see the seasons change. What your child does there will change over time. And the place will change you, too. You can have more than one local patch, of course, but don't feel that you have to constantly take him or her to 'new' or 'more exciting' places. They are usually very happy with their old favourites. And it's amazing how many new experiences you can have in a familiar spot. Be bold too: if you know of some derelict ground near you, or an under-used garden, why not find the owner and ask if you and your child can use it, quietly, to enjoy nature?

4. Find a 'sit spot'

This is an idea I particularly like, from Scott Sampson. It works best with one child, and when they are a bit older. Identify a place in some green space where you can sit together. Perhaps a secret spot where no one can see you. Or a spot with a view. Go there regularly. Sit quietly, and just chat, look at what goes by. Don't feel you have to bring 'equipment' (except perhaps binoculars). It's amazing what you'll see, sitting quietly amid nature. If your child is especially boisterous you might think this is unachievable, but they may surprise you: children love spending one-to-one time with a parent or other favourite adult. It's special time for you both.

5. Go camping

If you have your own garden, you can start there. Everywhere, even your local patch, looks very different by night, with a different – hopefully star-studded – canopy for the sky and a whole new range of creatures on the earth below.

6. Climb trees

This is five-year-old Ted's top tip for children. Esme, seven, agrees. 'Climbing up to the top of trees and listening to the trees swish, and learning what kind of trees they are', is the best thing to do outdoors, she says.

7. Be child-led, or try some 'modelling'

While volunteering in Forest School I've seen the power of the child-led approach. Children have the most amazing ideas, and are far more likely to enthuse about being outdoors if they are given the freedom to pursue those ideas. We don't need to provide organised games all the time. But when he or she is introduced to a new place, a few suggestions can sometimes help break the ice – or maybe more subtle parental modelling will work. For example, I've just got back from an evening at the beach. The children didn't want to go. After fifteen minutes during which they hung out restlessly, I found some nice smooth wet sand and started writing the ages of our family in it. Ted saw me enjoying myself and started drawing an alien. My daughters copied Ted. So did I. Soon we were all drawing aliens in the sand. Then Esme designed her own 'sand graffiti' tag. Which brings me to . . .

8. Beach art

'Sand graffiti' is an easier sell for children of a certain age than drawing in the sand. Why not invent your own tags? Or you could collect pebbles and shape names on the beach with them, or write out messages in huge letters for passing planes, or instructions for aliens or greetings to other beach-goers. The artistic possibilities on beaches are infinite. You could do sums in the sand, or noughts and crosses, or draw a word-search game, or play beach chess. You can draw lines on the beach to measure the tide coming in or going out, or play at guessing which line it will reach by a certain time. Take photographs of your art, or your play, for posterity.

9. Sticks

What is your stick going to be today? (See page 144.)

10. Go pond-dipping or stream-skimming

You need a basic fishing net (you can buy nets for 99p) and an old ice-cream tub or Tupperware box – to put your finds in and to observe them more closely – which you fill with water from your pond or stream. The appeal is timeless and the ethics are simple: if you're transferring live creatures, make sure they have enough water in the tub, and put everything you catch back where you caught it after a few minutes.

11. Start a species list

Find a beautiful hardback notebook, one that will stand the test of time and that your children will value. Use it to record all the species you see in your home, from your window, or in your garden if you have an outdoor space. You can divide it into sections – birds, insects, plants, mammals, reptiles and amphibians, for example; or list species separately – fungi, beetles, spiders, moths, etc. You can note things down and identify things together. People on Twitter and other social media will always help ID things if you post photographs of what you've seen. See how long it takes you to get to fifty items. A hundred. You will be amazed how long your list gets over time. Focus on different things at different times of year. Autumn is great for spiders, so try to identify all the different kinds of spider you find in your flat or house. Let your child define how the notebook works – let them write down the species and devise the categories. They could give each item a star rating – how much they like it – or a rarity rating. It will become their own personalised 'I Spy' book.

12. Things to take

When you head out to the woods or beach or park or wild space, always make sure you have these two things: (1) a collecting bag (or 'treasure bag' if you want to hype it up) and (2) food and drink. I'm amazed how famished my children get outdoors. And hungry or thirsty children won't have fun. Mine have devoured their lunchtime sandwiches by 11 a.m., and I don't feel so guilty handing out crisps and chocolate if they are sitting under a tree. Hot chocolate is a massive winner.

13. Forage

Go on an adventure to find something for supper. In spring and summer it could be dandelions or wild garlic or stinging nettles. Later, it might be elderflowers for cordial, sea-beet, or samphire (my children love this – it's full of salty badness!). In late summer and autumn it might be wild plums, damsons, blackberries, sweet chestnuts or rosehips. Richard Mabey's classic book *Food for Free* will give you many more ideas. It always surprises me that children will often enjoy the act of collecting a food they have no intention of eating. It's the search that's fun.

14. Play in the mud

The possibilities are endless: mud pies, mud slides, mud kitchens, stuck-in-the-mud, mud sinkholes, mud baths, muddy puddles, painting with mud. Playing in mud is endorsed by Peppa Pig, so it's not even mildly controversial in the eyes of wider society.

15. Pooh-sticks

As played by the 'bear of little brain' and every generation since. If you've missed A. A. Milne, the rules are: find a stream with a bridge, throw one stick each from one side of the bridge, and see whose floats under and out the other side first. As also seen in Julia Donaldson and Axel Scheffler's *Stick Man*. If you're on a beach with one of those rivulets flowing across it, try having a seaweed race.

16. Turn things over

Young children are naturally fascinated by minibeasts. Get into the habit of looking with your children under logs in the woods or beneath stones, especially when it's a bit damp. There are always surprises. And almost always woodlice. Carl Cornish, a naturalist who recommended this to me via Twitter, says the trophy his daughter always remembers is the Scilly shrew they found on St Agnes (a lesser white-toothed shrew, and an island rarity). If you know a sunny spot where you can put down a sheet of corrugated iron and leave it for a while, you can lift this and – hopefully – find slow-worms or lizards underneath.

17. Beach art at home

If you collect beach treasures to bring home, there are masses of things you can make with pebbles and shells. Three-D shell pictures, shell signs for a bedroom door, shell picture frames. You can polish stones, or build a tower (stone-balancing is almost a sport, but frowned upon at picturesque wild places where the sea won't wash these mini-monuments away). I've seen friends make amazing mobiles from razor shells and starfish (a rare beach find), and stones with holes in (another rare and valuable beach treasure). Collect small amounts of seaweed to mount on card to make seaweed pictures, or to make cyanotypes – a photographic printing process that produces a vivid blue print (to find out how to do this, Google it).

18. Start a nature table, a nature drawer, or a collection

Some children are inveterate hoarders and collectors. See what yours enjoy collecting from the natural world and facilitate their collection by providing space for it at home – a drawer, a window-sill, a special box. Treat the collection (and the collector) with respect! It might be feathers, pebbles, shells, leaves, bark, sticks, conkers, snail shells, seeds and berries, fungi or flowers (yes, you can pick flowers – just not on nature reserves – and do check before you pick it that what you have your eye on isn't a rarity). I have a small collection of skulls found in the outdoors. Esme enjoys collecting (old) bird's nests (do this in autumn, once you are sure they are no longer being used). You can encourage children to draw their collections or make lists of them. Best of all, when the clutter becomes too much and you want to get rid of it, it's all biodegradable.

19. Make a bird table

Put up a bird feeder or make a bird table. A bird feeder should attract them, even on a balcony. Your child can create their own seed mixes or bird food from leftovers (check online for suitable food). Don't offer birds mouldy food. Good leftovers include fruit such as bananas, cooked rice and mild cheddar. You can feed birds all year round, but winter (when it's very cold, and when food in the wild is in short supply) and spring (during the breeding season) are particularly crucial. You will need to keep your tables and feeders clean to prevent rats and the transmission of bird-to-bird diseases. It's fun to record what species visit. In the last week of January, take part in the RSPB's Big Garden Birdwatch and record the birds you see over an hour.

20. Wildlife gardening

Make your garden, allotment or local park more wildlife-friendly. Children can help build or put up bird boxes, bug hotels, hedgehog hibernacula, bat boxes or bird baths. Instructions on how to make these animal shelters are all over the internet. Don't forget to cut hedgehog holes in your fence; and avoid using slug pellets and other chemicals.

21. Build a wildlife pond

A pond, no matter how small, is the single best way you can increase the biodiversity in your backyard. Use an old washing-up bowl, or buy a small piece of pond liner. Dig a hole (see page 123). Provide stones or other ways for small creatures to enter and exit the pond. Fill with rainwater and pond weeds, which are best collected in a small handful from any nearby pond.

22. Go cloud-watching

Lie on your backs and see what you can see in the clouds – wolves, dragons, buses, islands, seas, funny faces, people, maps. Your child will see more wonderful things than you will. You may seek to identify the types of cloud, but first, let your imaginations run.

23. Build a secret den

I've found dens to be successful only when the children play a part in their construction. Even if your child is very young, give them a chance to identify possible locations, or to design the den. Follow their instructions as far as you can. Plant one with fast-growing willow or sallow. Or make one out of pallets (free, if salvaged from skips or industrial parks or garden centres). Or if it's not on your land, make a den from sticks and branches that you've found. Let your child have lunch in their den, or drink hot chocolate there, or be alone there for 'privacy'.

24. Go skimming

Find some good flat stones. See if you can skim them, in any body of water you can find. See what sort of plop and splash they create. See what happens next.

25. Fruits of the forest

One of the best things I learned to make at Forest School was a crown from leaves. Ideally, you'll need quite large fallen leaves such as sweet chestnut or plane. Thread the stalk of one leaf through the leaf of another and continue, with the leaves facing the same way, until they begin to form a natural circle. Join up – but not before you've measured it around your or your child's head – carefully turn it inside out, and you have a crown. Another nice piece of forest craft is making a stick person. Cut pieces of elder (a soft-centred wood) about 1 centimetre long and the thickness of your finger. Hollow out each piece. Thread green garden wire through, to make a little wooden person with joints. Or make a bow and arrow. 'Making things from wood' is seven-year-old Milly's recommended outdoor activity.

26. Swing on a rope – or make your own rope swing

It's amazing how many country parks and woodlands have rope swings, either official or unofficial. If you have a large enough garden, and a tree, you can create your own. Swings can be exhilarating, but they're also places for swaying and dreaming.

27. Gadgets

Gadgets aren't good or bad, it's just how we use them. Generally, you don't need anything extra to enjoy the natural world. All the same, cameras (especially with macro lenses for close-up photography) and binoculars can deepen our experience of wildlife. Walks can be turned into photographic challenges. Geo-caching with GPS is fun for older children. Bat detectors and camera traps can be great (if pricey) wildlife toys. You can buy bat detectors (also expensive) that plug into your phone. The one thing I'd definitely recommend for younger children is a good microscope. And the one thing I'd definitely recommend for older children and adults is to go phone-free, at least for a bit, on trips into nature.

28. Create a wildlife calendar

Make a calendar from treasures collected during each month of the year. Or from photographs you've taken of wildlife in your garden or with your children. Or from photographs of your children in wild places. I stumbled upon the fact that mine love calendars containing photos of themselves. I now make each of them an individually tailored one every year (they cost about £10 via photographic websites). If they also feature your wild adventures, they'll provide a lovely seasonal touchstone for all of you. 'Look, last January we were in the woods on that really frosty day.' If you value your trips out together, so will they.

29. Pebble poems

Find a large pebble and write a poem on it, or draw a picture on a pebble. Leave for someone to find.

30. Count butterflies – and other 'citizen science'

I'm a big butterfly fan so forgive such an obvious one. There are fifty-nine species of butterfly in Britain. You can get a free butterfly ID app from Butterfly Conservation, or print off an ID sheet. From late July all through August is their Big Butterfly Count – spend fifteen minutes, whenever suits, in a green space in the sunshine and record all the butterflies you see. Each year, a hundred thousand people join in – it's the biggest insect citizen-science count in the world. But you don't have to wait until the summer holidays: you can submit butterfly-sighting records at any time to Butterfly Conservation. There's loads more citizen-science surveying you can do to help academics and charities monitor species – from the UK Shark Trust's Great Eggcase Hunt to counting moths, ladybirds or beetles or spiders. Look at surveys undertaken by the British Trust for Ornithology, the Bumblebee Conservation Trust, the Mammal Society, Project Splatter . . . the list is (almost) endless.

A small PS: you are allowed to catch the common butterfly species with a proper butterfly or entomological net (available over the internet), so you can examine them and then release them unharmed. I was amazed when I visited my old high school and found that fourteen-year-old boys relished an afternoon of competitive butterfly hunting with nets.

31. Track down the source of a stream
Or put on paddling shoes and follow it for as far as you can.

32. Breed butterflies
The internet kits with painted-lady caterpillars are an unsatisfyingly hands-off experience (apart from the release of the butterfly). You can rear your own native caterpillars. Best to start with something easy and common – small and large whites. Even if you only have a window box, plant some kale and wait for the caterpillars to arrive. Or visit a local allotment in July or August and ask the gardeners if you can help by removing some of their pest caterpillars. When the caterpillars grow larger, rear

them indoors, in a large ventilated tub. Provide a stick or brick for them to fix their chrysalis onto. Wait for them to emerge. If you seek out caterpillars in the wild – such as peacocks or small tortoiseshells from nettle patches – only take a few, and not from nature reserves.

33. Run a moth trap

You can make your own trap with an outdoor light and a white sheet, or buy one over the internet (a small basic light-based trap costs £50; more sophisticated ones cost £150 and upwards).

Your home at night is a very different place. There are 2,500 moth species in Britain. and you will almost certainly have scores, if not hundreds, flying about in your area during the dark hours, even in urban areas. Moth traps are harmless: the creatures are lured by a bright light positioned above a plastic box. They are held in the box overnight, and in the morning you can carefully pick out each live moth and put it in a small transparent tub to identify it (there's a good online guide to moth species and some excellent field-guides). After you have identified it, release it – placing it carefully on the underside of a leaf or in some cover. Sometimes sparrows or other birds learn to hover around traps and snaffle all the moths as they are released, so beware of predators!

34. Go on an excavation

This can be fantasy, archaeology or natural history. Real fossils or imaginary. Jane Lovell on Twitter says: 'I once made a metre-long dinosaur skeleton out of salt dough and buried it in the ground in a far spot of the woods to be discovered, bone by bone, by little archaeologists.' I've learned at Forest School that children love digging for treasure, real or imagined – stones, pottery, bones, junk. If you find a dead animal, why not bury it, mark its grave and excavate it in six months' time? I've done this with mice and hedgehogs in our garden.

35. Animal forensics
This won't appeal to everyone, but many great naturalists spent their childhood messing around with dead animals. Rather than anything too gory, I'd recommend the burial treatment and then you can further clean the bones by boiling them or carefully treating them with bleach.

36. Build a dam
Dam-building in streams is great fun as long as you don't actually aim to *really* block the stream. Leave that to the beavers. As a child, I loved building sand dams across the saltwater streams that wash over big Norfolk beaches when the tide goes out. You can redesign their flow, and take them through obstacle courses and around sandcastles. I still love building dams. I was ecstatic when I discovered that Ted loves building them too.

37. Potions and perfumes
My children (the boy as well as the girls) have loved making 'perfume' from scented and unscented petals – all kinds of rose petals, especially – and magnolia leaves. Potions are pretty exciting too: rosehips, mushrooms, mud – you can add anything to the mix. Just don't let them drink it.

38. Build an outdoor fire, and sit and sing and cook around it

Fire. The fundamental building block of Forest Schools. The fundamental building block of *Homo sapiens*. Our most important discovery. Life-saving, nourishing, safe *and* dangerous – we are programmed to adore real fires. With care, you can have a fire in more places than you might imagine. But always have enough cold water handy to extinguish your fire if necessary; don't light fires in dry weather, or on dry heaths or dunes or in woods. And always, always leave no trace (I say this as someone who regularly cleans up lumps of wood, wire, nails, bricks and old molten plastic from fires on our local beach). Get your children to help. Even very young ones can be taught to use matches safely. They can collect firewood and build the fire. And who doesn't like marshmallows? A fire is lovely to huddle around in the evening, but don't rule out a dawn fire – and cooking breakfast on it.

39. Channel the spirit of Andy Goldsworthy

Outdoor artists such as Andy Goldsworthy like to channel the spirit of childhood. We can take lessons from them. There is so much (unobtrusive) art we and our children can do, using natural substances. Bark rubbings. Leaf rubbings – instant results with wax crayons. Or make Green Men out of clay and stick them to the trees.

40. Keep a nature diary

This could be a secret diary or a communal, family diary, kept in the living room, where you can all enter interesting observations, happenings or thoughts.

41. Animal tracking

Go out into the countryside on a muddy day and see what prints you can find and identify – dogs', humans' (man or woman?), common gulls', deer's? There are ID guides online. Or look for hair – badger hair, for instance, may be snagged on barbed-wire fences – and poo too.

42. Go rolling

We still boil eggs, paint them, and have an egg-rolling contest each Easter (to see whose egg lasts longest). If you can't find a hill, do egg-bowling instead (aiming them for a container). Or find a nice grassy hill and roll down it yourself.

43. Take a night walk

The world is a different place at night. And children love staying up past their bedtime. Go for a walk in the woods after dark. See if you can hear a tawny owl, or identify one or two constellations. If you're short on knowledge (and most of us are pretty clueless about nocturnal nature), a guided walk is a good place to start. Many of the regional Wildlife Trusts, the National Trust and local bat groups offer night walks, 'owl prowls' and bat walks, and usually provide equipment such as bat detectors as well as expertise. Various Wildlife Trusts, camping sites and farm-stays offer the supreme pleasure of any dusk – badger-watching. (Read my book *Badgerlands* or contact me if you want badger-watching tips.) Even walking down your own street – perhaps to the local playground – will be a different experience from doing it in the daylight hours.

44. Build a secret den for a cuddly toy

Outside, obviously. Making a fairy door from natural materials at the base of a tree is another nice den-creating activity.

45. Hapa-zome, or leaf bashing

The Japanese name for the art of pounding plant parts onto cloth to make images. Collect leaves, flowers or fronds to extract colour from – they will need to hold some moisture, but autumn leaves often still have enough. Place the leaves behind fabric or paper on a firm surface. Gently but firmly tap the area with the head of a hammer (the flat part), and the colour and pattern of the leaf will transfer onto the fabric.

46. Go on a sensory walk

Create a barefoot or blindfold trail for your child. Record what they feel, hear and smell.

47. Rise for a dawn chorus

Late April or early May is the best time of year to hear a glorious orchestra. Rise at dawn, head out to your local woodland or park, and listen. Apps can help you identify birdsong. Many Wildlife Trusts run dawn chorus walks at this time of year. Guides such as Nick Acheson, who leads walks for the Norfolk Wildlife Trust, are geniuses at explaining birdsong so you can improve your identification skills.

48. *Make a colour wheel*

Collect objects from outdoors – the woods, the beach, a park – and arrange them in colours in a circular pattern. Then take a photograph of your creation.

49. *Play 'knock the rock' in a stream*

Knock the little rock off the big rock in the stream by throwing pebbles at it.

50. *Dig a hole*

In your garden, in a wood, on the beach – and fill it up with water.

51. *Make a trail*

If you can round up enough people in your family or from among your friends, one group can lay a trail with stick arrows in a wood and then hide, and the other group can hunt them down by following it. Or you can lay a trail to treasure . . . See Chapter 10 for how it works at Forest School.

52. *Build a nature kebab*

Pick up a stick at the start of a walk and add things to it (with string, and ingenuity) as you go. I tried this at Forest School but we called them 'journey sticks' (see page 67) – I think 'nature kebab' is much better.

53. *Collect seeds and sow them*

Stripping seeds off grass-heads is surprisingly and satisfyingly tactile. Poppy seeds are great for rattling and scattering. Also, collecting wild-flower seeds and dispersing them is a great public service. Sticking burdock seeds on Mum and Dad's backs, less so.

54. A beach-glass hunt

My children adore collecting little fragments of smoothed glass that wash up on beaches. They look like little jewels. Some beaches, particularly shingly ones, seem to have more than others.

55. Join a club

All this stuff can be discovered by yourselves or in a community of like-minded people. The regional Wildlife Trusts run loads of events for children, so do the RSPB and the National Trust. Local branches of Butterfly Conservation run butterfly-spotting walks and moth-trapping. There are many more local natural history societies, both ancient and modern, that would be only too delighted to share their events with children. One or two people may have had the occasional bad experience, but most wildlife groups are hugely welcoming to children and new members. It's worth remembering that the quickest way to learn is from other people.

56. Clean a beach

I find this bizarre, but my children love picking up litter on beaches. Numerous parents say their children are just as keen. There are loads of organised schemes, or you can start your own. I hope the next generation of eco-warriors will make Greta Thunberg look timid.

57. *Use your umbrella*

Slide an open umbrella beneath a bush, then give the bush a good shake. See what insects and other invertebrates you catch, and how many you can identify.

58. *Ditch the don'ts*

There don't need to be lots of 'Don'ts' outdoors. I liked the rulebook at one of the outdoor schools I visited. It had three: treat each other with respect, treat the place and its wildlife with respect, treat yourself with respect.

59. *Enjoy yourself*

Do the things that appeal to you. If, say, you hate fishing, don't take your child fishing! If you, the adult, are enjoying yourself outdoors, the child alongside you almost certainly will too.

60. *Follow that child!*

Over and above all these suggestions, your child, or the wild world itself, will invent their own, more wonderful, ideas if you spend time out there. Don't feel you have to provide a buffet of entertainment; allow serendipity, surprise and serenity to take hold.

61. *For more ideas, you could ask your friends online, or read:*

the National Trust's *50 things to do before you're 11¾*

https://www.nationaltrust.org.uk/50-things-to-do

Richard Louv, *Vitamin N: The Essential Guide to a Nature-Rich Life*, Atlantic Books, 2016

Kate Blincoe, *The No-Nonsense Guide to Green Parenting: How to Raise Your Child, Help Save the Planet and Not Go Mad*, Green Books, 2016

Scott D. Sampson, *How to Raise a Wild Child: The Art and Science of Falling in Love with Nature*, Mariner Books, 2016

Richard Mabey, *Food for Free*, Collins Gem, 2012

Thanks for some brilliant ideas shared on Twitter by Ann Lingard, Carl Cornish, Mike Collins, Clare Connolly, Jane Lovell, Anna (@tozagurl), Abigail Pedlow, Concepta Cassar, Lucy Ward, Anna Iltnere (@BeachBooksBlog), Jimthepoet (@BaitTheLines), Sam (@BlackLabrador10), Hilary McKay, Lauren Baker, Susan Jones, Emma Wrighty, Elaine Ground, Patrick Limb, Rachel Murray, Anna Blewett, Berni W (@BerniW7), Cassie Waters, Pippa Hill, Ieuan Evans, Kevin (@Kevla7270), and everyone else who took part in our conversation. Thanks also to Lisa Walpole, my mum Suzanne Barkham, and the staff at Wild Things and Dandelion Education.

References

Chapter 1

p. 4   *there are now thirty-two countries even more urban than us*: CIA World Factbook 2018, https://www.cia.gov/library/publications/the-world-factbook/

p. 7   *Hope, writes the naturalist Mark Cocker . . . the natural world*: Mark Cocker, *Our Place: Can We Save Britain's Wildlife before It Is Too Late?*, Jonathan Cape, 2018, p. 286.

Chapter 2

p. 17   *I interviewed the filmmaker David Bond*: https://www.theguardian.com/lifeandstyle/2013/jul/13/no-freedom-play-outside-children

p. 17   *Project Wild Thing* can be watched online via https://www.thewildnetwork.com/inspiration/project-wild-thing

p. 17   *An academic study of three generations of families . . . Sheffield*: H.E. Woolley and E. Griffin, 'Decreasing experiences of home range, outdoor spaces, activities and companions: changes across three generations in Sheffield in north England', *Children's Geographies*, 13(6) (2015), pp. 677–91. doi.org/10.1080/14733285. 2014.952186

p. 18   *Failure to supervise has become . . . declared the American writer Hanna Rosin*: Hanna Rosin, 'The Overprotected Kid', *Atlantic Magazine*, April 2014. https://www. theatlantic.com/magazine/archive/2014/04/hey-parents-leave-those-kids-alone/358631/

p. 18   *In Britain in 1970, eighty per cent of seven- and eight-year-olds . . . just nine per cent did so*: Mayer Hillman, John Adams and John Whiteleg (1990), *One False Move*, Policy Studies Institute. https://mayerhillman. files.wordpress.com/2014/10/one-false-move.pdf These findings are backed up by other more recent studies in the West such as M. Kyttä, 'The last free-range children? Finland in the 1990s and 2010s', *Journal of Transport Geography*, 47 (2015), pp. 1–12.

p. 19   *Four children in Britain . . . in the year to March 2018*: Office for National Statistics (2018), 'Homicide in England and Wales: year ending March 2018'. https:// www.ons.gov.uk/peoplepopulationandcommunity/ crimeandjustice/articles/homicideinenglandandwales/ yearendingmarch2018

p. 19   *In the year to June 2018 . . . seriously injured in Britain*: Department for Transport (2018), 'Reported road casualties in Great Britain'. https://assets.publishing.service.gov.uk/ government/uploads/system/uploads/attachment_data/ file/754685/quarterly-estimates-april-to-june-2018.pdf

p. 19   *Mayer Hillman . . . we have removed children from danger*:
Mayer Hillman, 'Children's Rights and Adults' Wrongs',
Children's Geographies, vol. 4, no. 1 (2006), pp. 61–7.

p. 21   *Susanne Nordbakke found . . . from fifty-one per cent
in 2005 to thirty-nine per cent in 2013/14*: Susanne
Nordbakke, 'Children's out-of-home leisure activities:
changes during the last decade in Norway', *Children's
Geographies*, vol. 17, no. 3 (2019), pp. 347–60. doi.org/
10.1080/14733285.2018.1510114

p. 21   *In her brilliant book* Kith, *Jay Griffiths*: Jay Griffiths
(2013), *Kith: The Riddle of the Childscape*, Hamish
Hamilton.

p. 28   *the Environmental Protection Agency . . . 200–800
milligrams of dirt per day*: Gerald N. Callahan, 'Eating
Dirt', *Emerging Infectious Diseases*, 9(8) (Aug. 2003),
pp. 1016–21. doi.org/10.3201/eid0908.030033

p. 30   *A survey of Australian three- to five-year-olds . . . well
before they can read*: Anna R. McAlister and T. Bettina
Cornwell, 'Children's brand symbolism understanding:
Links to theory of mind and executive functioning',
Psychology & Marketing (Feb. 2010). doi.org/10.1002/
mar.20328

p. 30   *one of many similar British surveys found . . . couldn't
identify an oak leaf*: PCP (market research) survey
of 1,000 adults and 1,000 children aged 5–16, June
2019. Press release issued by family activity app, Hoop.
Survey results reported by news organisations including:
https://news.sky.com/story/british-kids-cant-identify-a-
conker-or-a-bumblebee-11784960

p. 32   *biophilia . . . theory by the American biologist E.O. Wilson*: E.O. Wilson (1984), *Biophilia*, Harvard University Press.

p. 32   *Society seems to consider it almost as bestial as otter hunting*: Matthew Oates (2017), *Beyond Spring*, Fair Acre Press, p. 36.

Chapter 3

p. 43   *draws the gaze of television news and the tabloids*: *Sun*, 'Nursery that Swaps Tots' Plastic Toys for Power Tools Crowned Best in Britain', 17 Oct. 2017. https://www.thesun.co.uk/news/4717132/nursery-that-swaps-tots-plastic-toys-for-power-tools-crowned-best-in-britain/ *Daily Mail*, 'Outdoor pre-school where children kept outside in all weathers and can only play with toys they've made themselves is named Britain's best nursery', 17 Oct. 2017. https://www.dailymail.co.uk/news/article-4992200/Pre-school-children-kept-outside-weathers.html

p. 44   *In England, one in five pupils . . . aged ten or eleven, is obese*: NHS Digital (2019), Statistics on Obesity, Physical Activity and Diet 2019, government publication. https://digital.nhs.uk/data-and-information/publications/statistical/statistics-on-obesity-physical-activity-and-diet/statistics-on-obesity-physical-activity-and-diet-england-2019

p. 44   *Unicef's assessment of childhood wellbeing . . . British children bottom*: UNICEF Office of Research (2013), 'Child Well-being in Rich Countries: A comparative overview', Innocenti Report Card 11, UNICEF Office of Research, Florence. https://www.unicef-irc.org/publications/pdf/rc11_eng.pdf

p. 44   *the Children's Society's annual survey . . . a steady decrease in happiness since 2010*: Children's Society (2018), *Good Childhood Report 2018*. https://www.childrenssociety.org.uk/sites/default/files/the_good_childhood_summary_2018.pdf

p. 44   *One in eight people under nineteen . . . government statistics published in 2018*: NHS Digital (November 2018), Mental Health of Children and Young People in England, 2017, government publication. https://digital.nhs.uk/data-and-information/publications/statistical/mental-health-of-children-and-young-people-in-england/2017/2017

p. 45   *Another unsettling trend, detected . . . decline in creativity since 1990*: Kyung Hee Kim, 'The Creativity Crisis: The Decrease in Creative Thinking Scores on the Torrance Tests of Creative Thinking,' *Creativity Research Journal*, 23:4 (2011), pp. 285–95. http://dx.doi.org/10.1080/10400419.2011.627805

p. 46   *In the 1980s, the American psychologists . . . of natural environments*: Rachel Kaplan and Stephen Kaplan (1989), *The Experience of Nature: A Psychological Perspective*, Cambridge University Press.

p. 46   *There is a library-load . . . benefits of high-quality green space*: I don't want to retread well-trodden ground – more on this evidence can be found in Richard Louv's seminal work, *Last Child in the Woods* (2005) and *Kith* (2013) by Jay Griffiths.

p. 46   *A study of twenty thousand people in England in 2019*: Matthew P. White et al., 'Spending at least 120 minutes a week in nature is associated with good health and wellbeing', *Scientific Reports* 9, article no. 7730 (2019). https://www.nature.com/articles/s41598-019-44097-3

p. 47   *A famous study in the 1980s . . . more quickly from their operation*: R.S. Ulrich, 'View through a window may influence recovery from surgery', *Science* 224(4647) (27 Apr. 1984), pp. 420–21. https://science.sciencemag.org/content/224/4647/420

p. 47   *Researchers studying Shinrin-Yoku . . . in Japan – found that exposure . . . pulse rate and blood pressure*: Qing Li, 'Effect of forest bathing trips on human immune function', *Environmental Health Preventative Medicine*, 15(1) (Jan. 2010), pp. 9–17. doi.org/10.1007/s12199-008-0068-3

p. 47   *Further studies have found . . . higher percentage of natural killer cells*: Tsung-Ming Tsao et al., 'Health effects of a forest environment on natural killer cells in humans: an observational pilot study', *Oncotarget*, 27: 9(23) (2018), pp. 16501–11. https://www.ncbi.nlm.nih.gov/pmc/articles/PMC5893257/

p. 47   *Scientists sent text messages to Dundee . . . to sample their saliva*: Catherine Ward Thompson, Jenny Roe, et al., 'More green space is linked to less stress in deprived communities: Evidence from salivary cortisol patterns', *Landscape and Urban Planning*, vol. 105, no. 3 (2012), pp. 221–9. doi: 10.1016/j.landurbplan.2011.12.015

p. 48   *Other studies have stuck walkers in . . . mobile electro-*

encephalographs: Peter Aspinall, Panagiotis Mavros, Richard Coyne, Jenny Roe, 'The urban brain: analysing outdoor physical activity with mobile EEG', *British Journal of Sports Medicine*, 49(4) (2015), pp. 272–6. doi.org/10.1136/bjsports-2012-091877. https://bjsm. bmj.com/content/49/4/272.info

p. 48   *In 2009, researchers examined . . . green space around each household*: J. Maas et al., 'Morbidity is related to a green living environment', *Journal of Epidemiology and Community Health*, 63(12) (2009), pp. 967–73. https:// jech.bmj.com/content/63/12/967

p. 49   *In 2019, scientists analysed . . . Danes between 1985 and 2013*: Kristine Engemann, Carsten Bøcker Pedersen, Lars Arge, Constantinos Tsirogiannis, Preben Bo Mortensen and Jens-Christian Svenning, 'Residential green space in childhood is associated with lower risk of psychiatric disorders from adolescence into adulthood', *Proceedings of the National Academy of Sciences of the United States of America*, 116(11) (12 Mar. 2019), pp. 5188–93. doi.org/10.1073/pnas.1807504116

p. 50   *Graham Rook, emeritus professor . . . studies are not specific enough*: Graham Rook, 'Regulation of the immune system by biodiversity from the natural environment: An ecosystem service essential to health', *Proceedings of the National Academy of Sciences of the United States of America*, 110(46) (12 Nov. 2013), pp. 18360–67. doi. org/10.1073/pnas.1313731110 See also: Graham Rook, interviewed on A Dose of Nature podcast, Jake Robinson, 2019.   https://soundcloud.com/adoseofnaturepodcast/

a-dose-of-nature-podcast-episode-5-prof-graham-rook-and-the-old-friends-hypothesis

p. 52   *In this century, Finnish studies of skin microbiota*: I. Hanski et al., 'Environmental biodiversity, human microbiota, and allergy are interrelated', *Proceedings of the National Academy of Sciences of the United States of America*, 109(21) (2012), pp. 8334–9.

p. 52   *In Finnish Karelia . . . fourfold higher, than in Russian Karelia*: A. Kondrashova et al., 'A six-fold gradient in the incidence of type 1 diabetes at the eastern border of Finland', *Annals of Medicine*, 37(1) (2005), pp. 67–72. J. Pakarinen et al., 'Predominance of Gram-positive bacteria in house dust in the low-allergy risk Russian Karelia', *Environmental Microbiology*, 10(12) (2008), pp. 3317–25.

p. 53   *Another pertinent set of studies revealing . . . Hutterite people of the United States*: Michelle M. Stein et al., 'Innate Immunity and Asthma Risk in Amish and Hutterite Farm Children', *New England Journal of Medicine*, 375 (2016), pp. 411–21. doi.org/10.1056/NEJMoa1508749. https://www.nejm.org/doi/full/

p. 58   *Ancient Greek children made balls . . . played with toy soldiers*: Joan Santer and Carol Griffiths with Deborah Goodall, 'Free Play in Early Childhood: A literature review,' *Play England*, Children's Play Council (2007).

p. 58   *British schools that emerged . . . as dour as their Victorian architecture*: For an accessible history of formal government schooling in England see: Derek Gillard, 'Short and Fraught: the history of primary education

in England', *FORUM*, vol. 51 (2009), no. 2. http://
www.wwwords.co.uk/pdf/validate.asp?j=forum&
vol=51&issue=2&year=2009&article=5_Gillard_
FORUM_51_2_web See also: Derek Gillard (2018),
Education in England: a history, online publication.
http://www.educationengland.org.uk/history/
chapter20.html#04

p. 59   *The heroes of the children's books . . . Edith Nesbit . . .*
encounter talking animals: Humphrey Carpenter (1985),
Secret Gardens: The Golden Age of Children's Literature,
Allen & Unwin.

p. 60   *Margaret McMillan, who with her sister . . . the welfare*
of slum children: Margaret McMillan (1904), *Education*
Through the Imagination, republished online by the
University of Michigan. https://archive.org/details/
educationthroug01mcmigoog/page/n14

p. 61   *Almost half a century later . . . the outdoor schooling*
movement in Britain: What is Forest School?, Forest
Schools Association website, accessed online May 2019.
https://www.forestschoolassociation.org/what-is-forest-
school/

p. 61   *Since then, in Britain, a blueprint . . . Forest School*
Association: What is Forest School?, Forest Schools
Association website, accessed online May 2019. https://
www.forestschoolassociation.org/what-is-forest-school/

Chapter 4

p. 90   *Chris Packham once declared that children . . . slithered*
on and scratched': https://www.express.co.uk/news/uk/

488405/Parents-must-let-children-be-stung-slithered-on-and-scratched-BBC-presenter

p. 101 *they have seen only in a picturebook by Julia Donaldson and Axel Scheffler*: Julia Donaldson and Axel Scheffler (2017), *The Ugly Five*, Alison Green Books.

p. 102 *A nest is a circle of infinite intimacy*: Jay Griffiths (2013), *Kith*, Hamish Hamilton, pp. 1, 2.

p. 104 *ditch vision*: Diana Wallace, 'Review: *Ditch Vision: Essays on Poetry, Nature and Place* by Jeremy Hooker and *Under the Quarry Woods* by Jeremy Hooker', *Planet* magazine, 232 (no date). https://www.planetmagazine.org.uk/planet-online/232/review/diana-wallace

p. 104 *those wonderful lines from the Irish writer Patrick Kavanagh*: In Robert Macfarlane, 'Where the Wild Things Were', *Guardian*, 30 July 2005. https://www.theguardian.com/books/2005/jul/30/featuresreviews.guardianreview22

Chapter 5

p. 117 *The nature writer Richard Kerridge admires toads' portly dignity*: Richard Kerridge (2014), *Cold Blood*, Chatto & Windus.

p. 128 *Her garden, beside a wood . . . red squirrels to roe deer*: She wrote about it in Jane Ratcliffe (1986), *Wildlife in My Garden*, Cicerone Press.

p. 130 *Mohawk mothers commonly take their crying babies . . . something in the distance*: Scott D. Sampson (2016), *How to Raise a Wild Child: The Art and Science of Falling in Love with Nature*, Mariner Books, p. 151.

Chapter 6

p. 144   *The technological magazine* Wired . . . *best toy in the world as the stick*: *Wired* magazine, 'The Five Best Toys of All Time'(2011). https://www.wired.com/2011/01/the-5-best-toys-of-all-time/

p. 151   *We know from a 2018 government survey . . . a diagnosed mental disorder*: NHS Digital (November 2018), Mental Health of Children and Young People in England, 2017, government publications. https://digital.nhs.uk/data-and-information/publications/statistical/mental-health-of-children-and-young-people-in-england/2017/2017

Chapter 7

p. 162   the *Victorian butterfly enthusiast . . . hideous their bearing, ugly their figure*: Edward Newman (1871), *An Illustrated Natural History of British Butterflies*, William Tweedie.

p. 166   *She also loves the swallowtail that entranced Vladimir Nabokov as a boy*: Vladimir Nabokov (1967), *Speak, Memory*, Penguin Books, p. 64.

p. 168   *A recent review of seventeen academic papers*: Helen Louise Brooks, Kelly Rushton et al., 'The power of support from companion animals for people living with mental health problems: a systematic review and narrative synthesis of the evidence', *BMC Psychiatry*, 18:31 (2018). doi.org/10.1186/s12888-018-1613-2

p. 168   *One recent US study . . . their mood, behaviour . . . and other confounding factors*: Jeremy N.V. Miles, Layla Parast, Susan H. Babey, Beth Ann Griffin and Jessica M. Saunders, 'A Propensity-Score-Weighted Population-

Based Study of the Health Benefits of Dogs and Cats for Children,' *Anthrozoös*, 30:3 (2017), pp. 429–40. doi.or g/10.1080/08927936.2017.1335103

p. 168   *An American study found . . . for primary and secondary school girls*: Karen E. Martin, Lisa Wood, Hayley Christian, 'Not Just "A Walking the Dog": Dog Walking and Pet Play and Their Association with Recommended Physical Activity among Adolescents', *American Journal of Health Promotion*, vol. 29, no. 6 (2015). doi. org/10.4278/ajhp.130522-ARB-262

p. 169   *Children in dog-owning families . . . active than non-dog-owning families*: Rebecca A. Johnson, Alan M. Beck, and Sandra McCune (2011), *The Health Benefits of Dog Walking for People and Pets*, Purdue University Press. Online at: https://www.researchgate.net/profile/ Sandra_Mccune/publication/290438903_The_health_ benefits_of_dog_walking_for_pets_and_people/ links/5698af2808aec79ee32c1471/The-health-benefits-of-dog-walking-for-pets-and-people.pdf

p. 173   *ragwort's potential to be poisonous . . . an unscientific panic*: Isabella Tree (2018), *Wilding*, Picador, p.114.

Chapter 8

p. 189   *As the Oxford don Charles Foster discovered*: Charles Foster (2016), *Being A Beast*, Profile.

p. 199   *prolonged use in the evening disrupts human sleep patterns*: Nadeem Badshah, 'Limiting screen use for one week may improve teenagers' sleep', *Guardian*, 20 May 2019. https://www.theguardian.com/society/2019/may/20/

limiting-screen-use-may-improve-teenagers-sleep-blue-light Amy Fleming, 'The truth about blue light: does it really cause insomnia and increased risk of cancer?', *Guardian*, 28 May 2018. https://www.theguardian.com/lifeandstyle/2018/may/28/blue-light-led-screens-cancer-insomnia-health-issues

p. 199   *I could quote a critic such as Sarah Trimmer*: Humphrey Carpenter (1985), *Secret Gardens: The Golden Age of Children's Literature*, Allen & Unwin, p. 3.

Chapter 9

p. 212   *'conker' was excised from the* Oxford . . . *lamented by artists and writers*: Alison Flood, 'Oxford Junior Dictionary's replacement of "natural" words with 21st-century terms sparks outcry', *Guardian*, 13 Jan. 2015. https://www.theguardian.com/books/2015/jan/13/oxford-junior-dictionary-replacement-natural-words

p. 213   *In 2017, the conker became . . . celebrated book,* The Lost Words: Robert Macfarlane and Jackie Morris (2017), *The Lost Words*, Hamish Hamilton.

Chapter 10

p. 247   *Some educationalists also . . . coarsening of our imaginings of childhood*: H. Butcher and J. Andrews, 'How well am I doing on my outcomes?' in R. Eke, H. Butcher and M. Lee (eds.), 'Whose childhood is it? The roles of children, adults and policy makers', *Continuum* (2009), p. 36.

p. 247   *Scottish nine- to eleven-year-olds . . . a typical school day and a day at Forest School*: Rebecca Lovell (2014), 'Physical activity at Forest School', Forestry Commission and Central Scotland Forest Trust. https://www.owlscotland. org/images/uploads/resources/files/Physical_Activity_ at_Forest_School_Research.pdf See also: Janine K. Coates and Helena Pimlott-Wilson, 'Learning while playing: Children's Forest School experiences in the UK', *British Educational Research Journal*, vol. 41, no. 1 (2019). doi.org/10.1002/berj.3491

p. 248 *A study of more than 2,500 seven- to ten-year-olds ... better progress in memory*: Payam Dadvand et al., 'Green spaces and cognitive development in primary schoolchildren', *Proceedings of the National Academy of Sciences of the United States of America*, 112(26) (2015), pp. 7937–42. doi.org/10.1073/pnas.1503402112

p. 248 *In 1997, Swedish researchers ... by orchards and woodland ... better attention span*: Patrik Grahn et al. (1997), in N.M. Wells, G.W. Evans, 'Nearby nature: A buffer of life stress among rural children', *Environment and Behavior*, vol. 35, no. 3 (May 2003), pp. 311–30. doi. org/10.1177/0013916503251445

p. 248 *A four-year study from Norway twenty years later*: V. Ulset, F. Vitaro, M. Brendgen, M. Bekkus and A.I.H. Borge, 'Time spent outdoors during preschool: Links with children's cognitive and behavioral development', *Journal of Environmental Psychology*, 52 (2017), pp. 69– 80. doi.org/10.1016/j.jenvp.2017.05.007

p. 248 *In Britain, the impact ... seven-year-olds ... measured over three years*: Mel McCree, Roger Cutting, Dean Sherwin,

'The Hare and the Tortoise go to Forest School: taking the scenic route to academic attainment via emotional wellbeing outdoors', *Early Child Development and Care*, vol. 188, no. 7 (2018). doi.org/10.1080/03004430.2018.1446430

p. 251 *Those taught outdoors . . . compared with 6 per cent in class*: T. Quibell, J. Charlton and J. Law, 'Wilderness Schooling: A controlled trial of the impact of an outdoor education programme on attainment outcomes in primary school pupils' *British Educational Research Journal*, 43(3) (2017), pp. 572–87.

Chapter 11

p. 263 *The heavy clays of the Weald in Sussex . . . thirty dialect words for mud*: Isabella Tree (2018), *Wilding*, p. 28.

p. 273 *Broadleaved woodland, wrote Oliver Rackham . . . burns like wet asbestos*: In Isabella Tree (2018), *Wilding*, p. 66.

Select Bibliography

Peter Aspinall, Panagiotis Mavros, Richard Coyne, Jenny Roe, 'The urban brain: analysing outdoor physical activity with mobile EEG', *British Journal of Sports Medicine*, 2015, 49(4), pp. 272–6

David Attenborough, *Life on Air*, BBC Books (2002)

Kate Blincoe, *The No-Nonsense Guide to Green Parenting*, Green Books (2016)

Helen Louise Brooks, Kelly Rushton et al., 'The power of support from companion animals for people living with mental health problems: a systematic review and narrative synthesis of the evidence', *BMC Psychiatry*, 2018, vol. 18, no. 31

Gerald N. Callahan, 'Eating Dirt', *Emerging Infectious Diseases*, Aug. 2003, 9(8), pp. 1016–21

Humphrey Carpenter, *Secret Gardens: The Golden Age of Children's Literature*, Allen & Unwin (1985)

Janine K. Coates and Helena Pimlott-Wilson, 'Learning while playing: Children's Forest School experiences in the UK', *British Educational Research Journal*, 2019, vol. 41, no. 1

Mark Cocker, *Our Place: Can We Save Britain's Wildlife before It Is Too Late?*, Jonathan Cape (2018)

P. Dadvand, J. Pujol, D. Macià, G. Martínez-Vilavella et al. 'The Association between Lifelong Greenspace Exposure and 3-Dimensional Brain Magnetic Resonance Imaging in Barcelona Schoolchildren', *Environmental Health Perspectives*, 23 February 2018, 126(2)

Gerald Durrell, *My Family and Other Animals*, Rupert Hart-Davis (1956)

Kristine Engemann, Carsten Bøcker Pedersen, Lars Arge, Constantinos Tsirogiannis, Preben Bo Mortensen and Jens-Christian Svenning, 'Residential green space in childhood is associated with lower risk of psychiatric disorders from adolescence into adulthood', *Proceedings of the National Academy of Sciences of the United States of America*, 12 March 2019, 116(11), pp. 5188–93

Charles Foster, *Being A Beast*, Profile Books (2016)

Edmund Garnweidner, *Mushrooms and Toadstools of Britain & Europe*, Collins (2014)

Tim Gill, 'Let Our Children Roam Free', *Ecologist*, 23 September 2005

Jay Griffiths, *Kith: The Riddle of the Childscape*, Hamish Hamilton (2013)

Mayer Hillman, John Adams and John Whiteleg, *One False Move*, Policy Studies Institute (1990)

Mayer Hillman, 'Children's Rights and Adults' Wrongs', *Children's Geographies*,
2006, vol. 4, no. 1, pp. 61–7

Rebecca A. Johnson, Alan M. Beck and Sandra McCune, *The*

Health Benefits of Dog Walking for People and Pets, Purdue University Press (2011)

Rachel Kaplan and Stephen Kaplan, *The Experience of Nature: A Psychological Perspective*, Cambridge University Press (1989)

Richard Kerridge, *Cold Blood*, Chatto & Windus (2014)

Kyung Hee Kim, 'The Creativity Crisis: The Decrease in Creative Thinking Scores on the Torrance Tests of Creative Thinking', *Creativity Research Journal*, 2011, 23:4, pp. 285–95

A. Kondrashova et al., 'A sixfold gradient in the incidence of type 1 diabetes at the eastern border of Finland', *Annals of Medicine*, 2005, 37(1), pp. 67–72

Mark Leather, 'A Critique of Forest School: Something Lost in Translation', *Journal of Outdoor and Environmental Education*, 2016, 21(1), pp. 5–18.

Qing Li, 'Effect of forest bathing trips on human immune function', *Environmental Health Preventative Medicine*, January 2010, 15(1), pp. 9–17

John Lister-Kaye, *Nature's Child*, Canongate (2004)

John Lister-Kaye, *The Dun Cow Rib: A Very Natural Childhood*, Canongate (2017)

Richard Louv, *Last Child in the Woods*, Algonquin Books (2005)

Richard Louv, *Vitamin N: The Essential Guide to a Nature-Rich Life*, Atlantic Books (2016)

Rebecca Lovell, 'Physical Activity at Forest School', Forestry Commission and Central Scotland Forest Trust (2014)

J. Maas et al., 'Morbidity is related to a green living environment', *Journal of Epidemiology and Community Health*, 2009, 63(12), pp. 967–73

Anna R. McAlister and T. Bettina Cornwell, 'Children's brand symbolism understanding: Links to theory of mind and executive functioning', *Psychology & Marketing*, February 2010, vol. 23, no. 3, pp. 203–28

Mel McCree, Roger Cutting and Dean Sherwin, 'The Hare and the Tortoise go to Forest School: taking the scenic route to academic attainment via emotional wellbeing outdoors', *Early Child Development and Care*, 2018, vol. 188, no. 7

Robert Macfarlane and Jackie Morris, *The Lost Words*, Hamish Hamilton (2017)

Margaret McMillan, *Education Through the Imagination* (1904), republished online by the University of Michigan

Karen E. Martin, Lisa Wood, Hayley Christian, 'Not Just "A Walking the Dog": Dog Walking and Pet Play and Their Association with Recommended Physical Activity among Adolescents', *American Journal of Health Promotion*, 2015, vol. 29, no. 6

Jeremy N.V. Miles, Layla Parast, Susan H. Babey, Beth Ann Griffin and Jessica M. Saunders, 'A Propensity-Score-Weighted Population-Based Study of the Health Benefits of Dogs and Cats for Children', *Anthrozoös*, 2017, 30:3, pp. 429–40

Vladimir Nabokov, *Speak, Memory*, Penguin Books (1967)

Edward Newman, *An Illustrated Natural History of British Butterflies*, William Tweedie (1871)

Susanne Nordbakke, 'Children's out-of-home leisure activities: changes during the last decade in Norway', *Children's Geographies*, 2019, vol. 17, no. 3, pp. 347–60

Matthew Oates, *Beyond Spring*, Fair Acre (2017)

Liz O'Brien and Richard Murray), 'A marvellous opportunity for children: A participatory evaluation of Forest School in England and Wales', Forest Research and Forestry Commission (2016)

Chris Packham, *Fingers in the Sparkle Jar*, Ebury (2016)

J. Pakarinen et al., 'Predominance of Gram-positive bacteria in house dust in the low-allergy-risk Russian Karelia', *Environmental Microbiology*, 2008, 10(12), pp. 3317–25

T. Quibell, J. Charlton and J. Law, 'Wilderness Schooling: A controlled trial of the impact of an outdoor education programme on attainment outcomes in primary school pupils', *British Educational Research Journal*, 2017, 43(3), pp. 572–87

Graham Rook, 'Regulation of the immune system by biodiversity from the natural environment: An ecosystem service essential to health', *Proceedings of the National Academy of Sciences of the United States of America*, 12 November 2013, 110(46), pp. 18360–67

Scott D. Sampson, *How to Raise a Wild Child: The Art and Science of Falling in Love with Nature*, Mariner Books (2016)

Joan Santer and Carol Griffiths with Deborah Goodall, 'Free Play in Early Childhood: A literature review', *Play England*, 2007, Children's Play Council

Michelle M. Stein et al., 'Innate Immunity and Asthma Risk in Amish and Hutterite Farm Children', *New England Journal of Medicine* (2016), 375, pp. 411–21.

Isabella Tree, *Wilding*, Picador (2018)

Tsung-Ming Tsao et al., 'Health effects of a forest environment on natural killer cells in humans: an observational pilot study', *Oncotarget*, 27 March 2018, 9(23), pp. 16501–11

R.S. Ulrich, 'View through a window may influence recovery from surgery', *Science*, 27 April 1984, 224(4647), pp. 420–21

V. Ulset, F. Vitaro, M. Brendgen, M. Bekkus and A.I.H. Borge, 'Time spent outdoors during preschool: Links with children's cognitive and behavioral development', *Journal of Environmental Psychology*, 2017, 52, pp. 69–80

Catherine Ward Thompson, Jenny Roe et al., 'More green space is linked to less stress in deprived communities: Evidence from salivary cortisol patterns', *Landscape and Urban Planning*, 2012, vol. 105, no. 3, pp. 221–9

N.M. Wells and G.W. Evans, 'Nearby nature: A buffer of life stress among rural children', *Environment and Behavior*, May 2003, vol. 35, no. 3, pp. 311–30

Alex White, *Get Your Boots On*, Dived Up Publications (2019)

Matthew P. White et al., 'Spending at least 120 minutes a week in nature is associated with good health and wellbeing', *Scientific Reports*, 2019, vol. 9, article no. 7730

E.O. Wilson, *Biophilia*, Harvard University Press (1984)

H.E. Woolley and E. Griffin, 'Decreasing experiences of home range, outdoor spaces, activities and companions: changes across three generations in Sheffield in north England', *Children's Geographies*, 2015, vol. 13, no. 6, pp. 677–91

John Wright, *The River Cottage Mushroom Handbook*, Bloomsbury (2007)

Acknowledgements

Thank you to the children at Dandelion, St John's, other schools and forest schools who are so interesting, open and honest, and have allowed me to join in or witness their outdoor play.

Thank you to the teachers and practitioners, many of them mentioned in the book but some not – Emma Harwood, Hayley Room, Julie Proudfoot, Labone Choudhury, Tracey Marrison, Jen Armstrong, Tony Brunt, Kate Milman and her fellow Wild Things, Toby Quibell, Anita Foster, Becky Quinn, Cath Howes, Clare Joy, Tehseen Jaafri and Caroline Watts.

Thank you for specific ideas and inspiration – John Snape, Annabel Hill, Isabelle Mudge and Nick Morritt at Norfolk Wildlife Trust; Damian Carrington at the *Guardian*; Robert Macfarlane, Paul Blezard, Tina Milman and many other friends, colleagues and acquaintances whose thoughts I have unwittingly absorbed over the last five years.

Thank you to both Karolina Sutton at Curtis Brown and my editor at Granta, Laura Barber, for your wisdom and clear-headed professional help over what has been the most challenging book

I've so far written. Thank you to Sue Phillpott once again for her superb copy-editing.

Thank you to everyone at Granta who has helped bring this book into being, including Sigrid Rausing, Lamorna Elmer, Christine Lo, Sarah Wasley, Katie Hayward, Simon Heafield and Ka Bradley. I've been so fortunate to work with many of you for five books now.

Thank you to my family for their enduring love and support: Suzanne Barkham, John Barkham, Henrietta Barkham, Jan and Rob Palmer and especially Lisa Walpole. Writing a book is a selfish, self-important enterprise and Lisa both listens to me and laughs at me, which helps a lot.

I can't really find the words to thank Milly, Esme and Ted except to say to them: this is your book, in that it is brimming with your ideas, creativity, and life. (The flaws in it are of course mine.) I hope it does not cause you any anguish in the future. It is a fleeting portrait of one corner of your lives at a particular age; this is not who you are or what you do. Esme appears more in this book than Milly and Ted simply because at this stage of her life she has yearned to spend time with wildlife. Milly and Ted occupy just as much of my time and reside in just as deep a place in my heart. I love you all immensely, and equally. Thank you for being who you are; and thank you for giving me and Lisa and those around us such joy and laughter.